PEOPLE OF THE JANGAL

People of the Jangal

Reformulating Identities and Adaptations in Crisis

Edited by

MARINE CARRIN
HARALD TAMBS-LYCHE

MANOHAR
2008

First published 2008

ISBN: 81-7304-582-8

Published by
Ajay Kumar Jain *for*
Manohar Publishers & Distributors
4753/23 Ansari Road, Daryaganj
Delhi 110 002

Typeset by
FineCurve Computers
Meerut City 250 002

Printed at
Lordson Publishers Pvt. Ltd.
Delhi 110 007

Contents

Contributors

PETER B. ANDERSEN, sociologist of religion, is senior lecturer at the Department of the History of Religions, University of Copenhagen, Denmark.

DEEPAK KUMAR BEHERA is professor of Anthropology at Sambalpur University, Orissa, India.

MARINE CARRIN is an anthropologist, and director of research with the CNRS at the Centre d'Anthropologie, Toulouse, France.

GUNNEL CEDERLÖF is senior lecturer at the Department of Ethnology and Social Anthropology, Uppsala University, Sweden.

HANS HADDERS is a doctoral student and teaching assistant at the Department of Social Anthropology, University of Trondheim, Norway.

SRIKANT PATEL is lecturer of Anthropology at Sambalpur University, Orissa, India.

GEORG PFEFFER is professor of Social Anthropology at the Freie Universität Berlin.

TINA OTTEN is a doctoral student and research assistant in Social Anthropology at the Freie Universität Berlin.

HARALD TAMBS-LYCHE is professor of Ethnology at the Université de Picardie-Jules Verne, Amiens, France.

YASUSHI UCHIYAMADA is professor of Anthropology at the University of Tsukuba, Japan

Introduction

MARINE CARRIN AND HARALD TAMBS-LYCHE

ENVIRONMENT AS A PRODUCT OF CULTURE AND HISTORY

While globalization today, may well be linking the various centres of power and culture, these are still surrounded by peripheries, whose integration, surely, is not the result of the inevitable or automatic process that a naïve version of the globalization paradigm might lead us to believe. Similarly, the global nature of environmental crisis must not make us forget how differently the crisis appears, say, to the ecologist statesman and to the herdsman looking for pasture. What tends to get lost, in the global debate on environment, is the perspective and the agency of people of the periphery. As Kottak puts it, 'People must come first . . . Anthropology's contribution is to place people ahead of plants, animals, and soil' (1999: 33).

In this volume,[1] the authors all try, in different ways, to document the agency and environmental perspectives of people of the periphery, without denying the importance of natural constraints or power relations. The contributors deal with various kinds of peripheries to the main Indian civilization, faced with intrusion by more powerful groups, as well as by environmental crisis, making traditional produce uneconomic or access to productive resources difficult. No tribal or peripheral community is untouched by these forces, which compel subaltern groups to adapt to new relations of production or dominance.

Ecological anthropology must be concerned with the mutual constitution of persons and their environment, says Ingold, while 'orthodox theory creates a barrier between the "interior world" of human subjects and their exterior conditions of existence' (Ingold 1992: 40, see also Descola and Pàlsson 1996). There is a dialectical relationship between man and environment: 'in the course of reshaping nature, society gradually reshapes itself' (Biersack 1999: 9). Nature itself is not independent of culture but 'the embodiment of past activity' (Ingold 1992: 50). Our approach, then, includes symbolic, historical and political 'ecologies' (Biersack 1999: 8-11). Environment, here, refers to the object of a discursive construction of nature by human actors.

Certainly, we do not wish to ignore current threats to global survival, by putting all symbolic constructions of nature on the same level (Benton 1994). Clearly, the biological sciences may produce kinds of knowledge not available to local actors. But our purpose here is to render the perspectives and motives of the latter audible and intelligible. To them, 'the meanings of forests are not determined by their physical characteristics' (Jeffery 1998: 2-3). The symbolic pertinence of the landscape is forged in and through the interaction of people with their environment, which, beyond the landscape, also includes neighbouring groups. Thus the meaning with which natural as well as social surroundings is invested, tends to produce an identification as against others, expressed in terms of ethnicity. Similarly, changes at the symbolic level imply a danger of losing identity. Traditional knowledge may become blurred, with dominant discourses silencing local voices.

ENVIRONMENTALIST VISIONS OF SOUTH ASIAN SOCIETY

Such constructions clearly take their place in a larger cultural framework, and so we need to look at the meaning of the *jangal*—the periphery—in the traditional Indian context. In the South Asian wilderness—*jangal*—we find societies whose adaptations are closely tied to the environment but peripheral to systems of power and stratification.

But *jangal* did not always connote the wilderness. For the pastoralist settlers of Vedic times, *jangal* meant dry land, savanna: the kind of landscape where herds could graze. In post-Vedic times, the ritual installation of the king stresses the 'conundrum' of the king's authority: he must belong to the village, but must base his authority in the 'alien sphere' of the forest (Heesterman 1978: 9-10).[2] Important here is\ the complementary relationship: the forest is the 'other' of the village (Malamoud 1996: 86). In classical Sanskrit, the *jangal* is where a king decides to establish himself, abundant with grain and free from disorders (Zimmermann 1987: 39). By the eighteenth century, however, the Hindi term *jangal* had come to mean a dense growth of bushes and creepers (1987: vii). In today's Pakistan, Urdu speakers use the term *jangal* to describe clearings. The inversion of meaning is due to changing relations between man and nature: 'The culturally desirable jangala 'savanna' became transformed into the culturally undesirable jangal 'forest waste' (Dove 1992: 231).

In spite of their rich ambiguity, classical Hindu texts represent the views of the dominant. Adivasi[3] myth and legend provide a different perspective. The multiplicity of cultures makes us reluctant to identify Indian tradition with a particular ecological wisdom. Gadgil and Guha (1995) hold that Indians have encoded and transmitted an ecological wisdom: The caste system, by sharing resources, aids a sustainable relation to the environment (Gadgil and Malhotra 1989, 1994). Idealizing an indigenous tradition of biodiversity management, they blame colonialism and capitalism for the degrading environment (Gadgil and Guha 1992). We doubt, with Madsen, whether 'the caste system—which allows some segments to monopolize strategic knowledge to an extraordinary degree—has been capable of prudently adapting to changing natural circumstances over the centuries' (1995: 5). Gadgil and Guha, here, stay close to an orientalist view (Said 1978; Inden 1990) of India as an essentially passive civilization, unchanged for centuries. With Uchiyamada (this volume), we see such constructions as part of a nationalist assertion, appropriating ecological phraseology to an idealized image of the past, and this past to a modern project which uses religious and traditional views to produce a political agenda for the future. We hold, rather, that the subcontinent has always been a theatre of opposition and conflict: to construct a pre-colonial harmony is to deprive India of historical reality.

Indeed, the conservationist traditions early Europeans found in India—such as planting of hedges to prevent erosion from sun and wind—were probably the practice of very specific populations.

Typically, the pioneer herbalist van Reede turned, for botanical information, to the Izhava toddy-tappers of Malabar, subalterns struggling with the particular ecology of saline coastlands, rather than to the general lore of brahmin *vaids* (Grove 1995: 84-90).[4] Such local traditions may well incarnate knowledge that aids sustainable resource management. Behera and Patel (this volume) hold that the ritual cycle of the Pengs, a tribal community in Orissa, provided for regulation of resource use during the year, and thus contributed to an equitable distribution of food and other necessities.[5] But such local knowledge cannot be identified with a complex civilization, where even in ancient times, many dynamics worked at the translocal or transregional level.

Sacred groves, found all over India, have been seen as an example of ritual regulation of ecosystems. Gadgil and Vartak (1976, 1981) explain their preservation in Maharashtra by their ritual use in a hunting and gathering economy. Kalam (1996: 8, 1998), Freeman (1994, 1998), and Uchiyamada (this volume) criticize the ecological romanticism implied here. Uchiyamada shows how the disappearance of the forest may leave a single tree still sacred, while the symbolic meaning of the intact groves of Kurava untouchables is adulterated by high-caste Hinduism as the groves themselves are encroached upon by more powerful groups. In Jharkhand, the sacred grove retains its symbolism even when lost among giant industrial installations—while those who gather there grieve the destruction of a forest degraded out of all recognition (Carrin, this volume).

Environmental categories are construed from known landscapes, which then serve as tableaux of memory, allowing subaltern people to evoke their own past and history even in a degraded environment. Hills, rocks or rivers evoke mythical and past events, and oral narratives are re-enacted in their setting to reinvent traditions as tropes of resistance (Carrin, this volume).

CENTRE AND PERIPHERY IN INDIAN HISTORY

In dealing with centre-periphery relations we join a long tradition in anthropology, starting from Lattimore's ideas on the influence of nomads on surrounding civilizations (1962), through Fried's criticism of the notion of tribe (1975), to the view pioneered by Leach (1954) and developed by Barth (1956, 1964, 1969), in which ethnic divisions in the regional context are seen as products of a history of frontier construction and maintenance.

The opposition between centre and periphery, though changing, remains fundamental to Indian history. From the Mauryas onwards, we may envisage classical India as a network of trade routes controlled by the centre (Kosambi 1975). As Njammasch (1992a, 1992b, 1993) has shown for the Vallabhi kingdom of Gujarat, we would then find a zone of villages where part of the land was held by the urban elite. This pattern, characterized by Kosambi as 'feudalism from above', implies that this zone was controlled by the state. But between the trade routes and the state-controlled villages, there must have been large areas where state control was superficial and probably indirect, constituting in effect a tribal periphery.

The middle ages introduced a fundamental change. There is evidence of considerable immigration to the periphery, leading to a new balance of power (Tambs-Lyche 1997). The cities declined, and what Kosambi calls 'feudalism from below' meant that control of agriculture, rather than trade, became essential: the base of power was in the periphery. From about the eleventh century, however, new developments in agriculture, such as the Persian wheels of northern India or the step-wells of Gujarat, mark a new kind of centre, based in the plains (Habib 1974). Rulers established domains where settled peasants produced a surplus for the urban population, with the financial links between city and countryside provided by grain merchants who also acted as moneylenders (Hardiman 1999, Tambs-Lyche 2003). Such rulers could field real armies. Outside these domains, minor lords based their power on local populations, producing what we may term a tribe-king alliance (Kulke 1993; Tambs-Lyche 1997: 39-41). 'Pushing back the jungle and subduing *jangli* (indigenous forest peoples) were central elements in the kingly role' says S. Guha (1999: 154), but he stresses that the same *jangli* people became the fighters on whom the king depended for his defence. Beyond these kingdoms, peripheral populations—tribal chiefdoms or 'republics' ruled by lineage elders—resisted royal authority. This pattern persisted till British times, while there was a constant ebb and flow of central authority.

Guha stresses that different populations were constantly fighting for access to ressources and that subsistence often implied predation[6]:

> Forests . . . co-existed alongside, and among, the cleared lands of peasant settlement, and forest peoples existed as specialists in the optimal use of this niche . . . Woodland—especially the thorny secondary growth that came after human interference—was also a political and military resource. It was both a base and a refuge. Dispossessed elites and aspirant rulers both needed to use it as such, and to secure the support of its denizens. Control over and knowledge of this strategic domain was thus a tradeable resource in the regional political arena. (1999: 199)

Forest kingdoms were different from those in the plains: peripheral populations posed themselves in opposition to the centre. Skaria stresses the 'raids and similar activities' typical of the periphery, which founded 'a particular kind of political order, one that put wildness at the centre' (1999: x). Such wildness was not a tribal prerogative, however, but a central feature of the Rajput political order that spread over large parts of northern India—but away from the main centres—from the twelfth to the eighteenth centuries (Tambs-Lyche 2002).

Pre-British rulers claimed ownership of forests and used them for hunting and defence.[7] Yet expansion of the centre implied clearing the forest, already intensive in pre-colonial times, and particularly in periods of military expansion by aspiring state builders (Grove 1995: 386). Deforestation increased as the Mughal empire gave way to successor states from the late seventeenth century onwards. They, and their commercial elites 'caused dramatic crisis in timber demand' long before the East India Company took over (ibid.: 387).

Grove (1995) and Rangarajan stress that the British, like their predecessors, wanted to push back the forest and extend the cultivated area, but also to check 'mobile groups which were seen as threats to law and order' (Rangarajan 1996: 44-5; also Sivaramakrishnan 1999). Clearly, forests were seen as hindering central control over the periphery. Yet till the mid-nineteenth century the East India Company, as a relatively weak state, was still trying to minimalize its involvement in the periphery. This rendered it possible, for peripheral groups, to defend themselves by political and legal means, as Cederlöf (this volume) shows for the Toda.

After a period of state control of forests—legitimized by alleged indigenous practice—a free-market policy was enforced from 1823 in Madras Presidency.[8] By the 1840s it was realized that this policy led to rapid deforestation, and from 1847-8 measures were taken which led to the later system of state conservancy, marked by Dalhousie's 'memorandum' of 1855 and the first Indian Forest Act in 1865 (Grove 1995: 387-473). From the 1860s onward, there was a new interest in scientific forestry—a regime including maximization of timber and other forest revenues, as well as conservation of the environment (Sivaramakrishnan 1999: 21). While earlier ideas on conservation built on Indian practice, the British now turned to modern forestry as developed in Germany (Grove 1995). This led to replacement of diverse forests by monospecies, depriving local communities of minor forest produce, an important element in their adaptation.

The British had come to possess an essential superiority in arms and technology by the second half of the nineteenth century. Their transportation network, with railways as the most striking example, allowed them to control the periphery far more closely than earlier empires had done. Wildness, as a political resource of rulers and people in the periphery, was no longer useful to the centre, and no longer tolerated. Withdrawal, as an alternative to subjection, was possible only for small groups in isolated pockets, such as the Bondo (Pfeffer, this volume). With independence, the princely states disappeared, and the centre's presence is now felt everywhere.

The centralized structures established during colonial rule still dominate Indian forest management, legitimized by the need to protect the forest. The colonial rules and categories are still there, as are the limitations for locals to access water, grazing lands, and forest produce. Blamed for encroaching on the forest or illegally harvesting forest products, they, in their turn, accuse forest officials of corruption and illegal sale of forest produce. Many programmes of Joint Forest Planning and Management are imposed from above, while existing local rights in the forest—of which people tend to be unaware—are ignored (Jeffery 1998: 13). Villagers are often ignorant or cynical about the long-term benefits promised by development projects, while government officials have at the best a paternalistic attitude towards them. Their knowledge is usually ignored, or sometimes construed as the ecological wisdom of noble savages, opposed to instrumental modernity. They are usually seen as deprived, and so can be moved, regardless of ethnic, class or gender equity (Behera and Patel, this volume).

With the ebb and flow of central powers, forest communities have been alternately dominant and dominated. In kingdoms where tribes formed the military workforce such as in Koraput (Pfeffer and Otten, both this volume), economic and ritual exchanges between king and tribe forged a complementarity which in turn shaped ethnic identities. The contacts tribes had with artisans and other specialists also contributed to construct cultural difference (Andersen, Carrin, Hadders, all this volume). Today, whatever their past, peripherals have become subalterns. Some, like the Mundari-speaking tribes, have effectively become labour reserves for industry and plantations ever since the expansion of the colonial economy (Ghosh 1999). Displacement by hydro-electric projects strengthens this trend (Behera and Patel, this volume).

It is in the periphery that confrontations between development projects, conservation efforts, and local populations have been most marked. In these exchanges, the centre is the locus of power, while peripheral groups are opposed to central control. What peripheral populations in South Asia share is their strategic position with regard to the centre, and not a common culture. Thus we find ethnic groups that are markedly distinct, in language, religion and social organization, from surrounding societies, as well as others who share a great deal of their culture with people of the centre, integrated in a caste order (Carrin 1996).

THREE TYPES OF PERIPHERAL GROUPS

The three types of subaltern groups found in this work—tribes, low castes and pastoralists—are peripheral in different ways, with important variations between regions and between specific groups.

The groups usually referred to as tribes are culturally linked to their own territory in the periphery, and stress their cultural distinction from the centre. They have been characterized as multifunctional groups (Sahlins 1968; Godelier 1973), as opposed to castes whose boundaries tend to coincide with occupational specialization (Mayer 1960: 34). This does not mean that other groups are entirely absent from tribal territory. The Santals (Andersen, Carrin, both this volume) were served by several types of specialists—the jadopatias (Hadders, this volume) being but one—and a large number of Santals have, at least since the nineteenth century, been working and/or living outside Santal territory. Their autonomy has probably always been limited in that we have no proven account of Santal State formation. The Todas did not have a state either, but they controlled the land and played a dominant role in relation to other settlers on their territory such as the Badagas (Cederlöf, this volume). Other tribes did form states, or were subject to a raja coming from the outside but basing his power on the tribal population. The domain of such rajas might include several tribes each linked to part of the territory, as was the case in Bastar (Sundar 1997) or in the present Koraput district (Pfeffer, Otten, both in this volume). Tribes were more or less similar to each other, forming tribal complexes (Pfeffer 1997). Such multi-tribal areas might develop inequality between tribes (Sinha 1968). Still, tribal society may be defined by its relative lack of centralized political organization (Pfeffer, this volume).

Much of the reason for assigning the term tribe to a population must lie in its perception of itself. Many tribes tend towards egalitarianism. Though rank differences may be acknowledged, tribes commonly oppose their egalitarian values to those of hierarchical caste society (Carrin, this volume). Thus there is an ideological frontier marked by insistence on different values, the very essence of an ethnic boundary in Barth's (1969) terms.

Low castes on the close periphery of village society represent a different type. Here, a cultural stigma (Eidheim 1969), a negative self-image, is internalized, and hegemonic ideas of rank are brought to play. But to be aware of a negative evaluation of oneself does not necessarily imply sharing it, as Berreman (1973), and Khare (1984) show. For the Kuravas of Kerala (Uchiyamada, this volume), their low status emerges as only one element in a complex identity. Another is based on the powers of Kurava deities, rooted in their sacred groves. Like many gods and goddesses of untouchables in India, they are impure to higher castes, but they are powerful, and their power is not restricted to their own community. Nor are these deities simply inversions of high-caste values (Dumont 1966), as is shown when their sacred groves are invaded by outsiders. Then, the Kuruva gods tend to be replaced[9] by fierce versions of pan-Hindu deities, negating the relative autonomy needed for this pillar of Kuruva identity. Yet, while Kuruva deities are different from all-Indian deities, their pantheon is not as autonomous in relation to Hinduism as that of most tribals. There is a complex dialectic here, between the rejection of the 'impure' by caste society, shown by the location of untouchable quarters outside the village walls (in the real or figurative sense) and a tendency for untouchables themselves to retreat from the village proper to 'unsettled' lands. It is this feature of low-caste adaptation which leads us to include them among the 'people of the *jangal*.'

A third type is represented by the pastoralists (Tambs-Lyche, this volume). Their adaptation makes them relatively independent of the judgements of villagers. But unlike tribals, they see themselves as Hindus and their deities as parallels to those of settled people. Interaction with villagers turn on the symbiotic relationship between adaptations, but implies different interpretations of central values. Pastoralists do not so much reject hierarchical values as they underline differences in evaluation: consistently, they allot themselves higher rank than villagers accord them. This relative autonomy does, however, become increasingly difficult to maintain in present conditions, so that the least autonomous pastoralists, staying close to village society, tend to improve their status, relative to the long-range nomads.

THE CONTESTED CONCEPT OF TRIBE

The people of the *jangal*, as peripheral populations, do not coincide with the category of tribe. Still, the debate concerning tribes is crucial to our purpose. Central here is the debate between Elwin

(1944) and Ghurye (1943). Ghurye read centre-periphery relations in evolutionary terms: tribes were not yet incorporated by the inevitable expansion of mainstream Hindu caste society (1963). Protection of their culture was both reactionary and futile: assimilation should be assisted. In assuming a general trend where peripheral populations adopt traits of the 'Sanskritic' culture of the brahmin elite, Srinivas (1952, 1962, 1967) introduced another paradigm, contested whenever tribals or dalits claim cultural autonomy.[10] This idea still underlies efforts at 'uplifting' or 'civilizing' the tribes. Elwin, who admired the tribal cultures, wanted protection to allow the tribes to face modernity on their own terms (Ramachandra Guha 1999).

The debate, then, tended to reify the category tribe as an object of an ideological and political discourse. Stressing the modernity and artificiality of the term tends to serve the dominant Hindu discourse, while adivasis, in their turn, tend to capitalize on the ethnic minority issue, and to associate their efforts with international movements of indigenous peoples. To ask whether 'tribes' are more 'indigenous' than other Indians (Béteille 1998) tends, we feel, to side-track the issue, which is not to debate cultural history but to legitimize claims for cultural autonomy (Brosius 1999). To discard the category of tribe is, therefore, in itself a political act.

The evolutionist agenda of nineteenth-century scholar-administrators was essential to constructing the tribal as primitive. The evolutionist overtones are evident. The colonial census served to classify Indian populations by castes and tribes, and to produce information about them. Historians like Bates (1995) have linked the construction of the division between tribe and caste with such structuring of colonial hegemony, reifying the differences between groups. As Susan Bayly (1995) notes, however, the term was not used, by the early authors of caste compendia and gazetteers, with the sociological distinctiveness it was to acquire later. The terms tribe and caste were often used interchangeably, and the word tribe was used, in the same period, to describe ethnic strains in European populations. Only gradually did a structured dichotomy of caste versus tribe develop in the colonial discourse. In early twentieth-century usage, the tribe/caste dichotomy became substantialized, reflecting the use of tribe as a general concept in academic ethnology.

To criticize this usage, however, does not alter the opposition between central and peripheral populations in Indian society: the meaning we give to the term tribe must be related to the ethnographic setting we are dealing with (Pfeffer, this volume).

In the Indian context, this dichotomy built on the indigenous tradition where various terms were used to distinguish forest-dwellers or others living outside the caste society of the plains. Such distinctions were often pejorative (S. Guha 1999). Yet the use of contrasting categories reflect the importance of centre-periphery relations to indigenous perceptions of social reality.

We stress, here, the perception peripheral groups have of themselves. The Santal and other Mundari-speaking groups, for example, draw a clear line between themselves and the *diku* or foreigners represented by village and urban caste society (Carrin, Andersen, Hadders, all in this volume). The fact that terms like adivasi or tribe are modern terms cannot dissimulate, for the Santals, the fundamental differences in language, religion and kinship that sets them off from the majority population. These differences are surely old enough to disprove any thesis of a wholesale creation of tribal culture during colonial times, and the Santals were clearly as aware of these differences when their great rebellion broke out in 1855, as they are today. The numerous documents written by Santals at the instigation of Lutheran missionaries from 1870 onwards show an active effort at redefining and locating Santal tradition in a new context, but the myths and traditions on which it is based are evidence of an older sense of cultural particularity (Andersen, this volume; Carrin and Tambs-Lyche, 2008).[11] Similar arguments clearly apply to the Toda as well as to the tribes of Koraput (Cederlöf, Pfeffer and Otten, all this volume).

The use of the term tribe is not restricted, however, to cases where linguistic and cultural particularities are as marked as they are in these cases. Thus when pastoralists were referred to as tribes, the rationale would seem to be their life outside 'civilized' village society—borrowing, in fact, from the indigenous identification of peripheral populations—rather than from contemporary academic discourse. A similar rationale probably operated when low castes were deemed to be of tribal origin: they were not civilized in the eyes of their Hindu neighbours, so they were deemed 'primitive'.

Pastoralists are certainly 'people of the *jangal*' to villagers, while tribes like the Bhil may include members who live separately in 'tribal' territory as well as others who stay in villages and are seen there as a 'caste', usually low in the local hierarchy. The way the term tribe is commonly used, therefore, provides a continuum between clear and doubtful cases, where the latter might equally be referred to as castes.

Yet from colonial times, both tribes and castes based much of their politics, as interest groups, on such classificatory categories. Many caste associations were formed to make demands in terms of reservations (quotas) both with regard to educational institutions and to the administration (Jaffrelot 2003). In 1928, these different movements achieved the classification of underprivileged groups as depressed classes, aboriginal and hill tribes, and other backward classes. In 1935, the term scheduled castes replaced depressed classes, while for the aborigines, the category of scheduled tribes was created.

These two scheduled categories, listed by the Central Government, correspond to some 15 and 8 per cent, respectively, of the population. The untouchables call themselves *dalit*, while the tribes use the term *adivasi*. Though they form an important part of the labour force, the dalits and adivasis remain poor and have no control over the means of production. Yet the revendications of these exploited groups imply a new consciousness, which incites subalterns to reject the values of the dominant and seek paradigms of identity alternative to a colonized conscience, though it does not necessarily result in the autonomy claimed (Carrin and Jaffrelot 2003).

THE QUESTION OF DOMINANCE

In brief, domination has shaped the lives of adivasis in the hills, and contributed to an identity which distinguish them from people in the plains. Whenever they have been able to maintain their hold on the periphery, they have kept their language and symbolic systems. This sets them apart from Hindus, even if some have borrowed Hindu features and been influenced by hierarchical values. The Hindu influence is often ambivalent as it contradicts the egalitarian ethos expressed in the tribal community (Carrin; Behera and Patel, both this volume).

Resistance to dominance leads to reformulations of identity, with the problem of autonomy for the dominated (Guha 1999). Dominance depends on controlling land, trade and—we insist on this point—knowledge. Any discussion of hegemony in India must account for the importance of the Brahman in this field. The quest for knowledge among tribals is equally clear, as shown by the eagerness with which the Santals have embraced writing (Andersen, this volume).

Identity, of course, also relates to culture seen as a way to see and do things (Goodenough 1961: 522); the way people deal with the problems of their adaptation is a central issue in identity formulation. But, as perspectives from ethnicity theory and cultural ecology indicate (Barth 1956, 1964, 1969), cultural adaptation and identity relate as much to other human groups as to nature: external power and pressures are very much part of these relations. Ethnicity is not a simple manifestation of primordial solidarities. Accounts of traditional societies tend to essentialize ethnicity as rooted in a particular territory. They, we are told, have a holistic approach to environment, which creates links between nature and society and endows hills or pastures with religious significance. But such links are also invoked strategically to legitimate territorial rights (Cederlöf, this volume). Such legitimizing accounts generate invented traditions expressing ethnic claims in a political context, as Prakash (1991) shows for the Bhuinya.

For the Jadopatias (Hadders, this volume), the tribal environment is their niche, in the sense of an earlier ecological anthropology (Barth 1956, 1964). In the Indian subcontinent, no group can be seen as isolated, and strategies for dealing with the external world form part of local cultures from very far back, as we can see from history (Carrin, Andersen, all this volume). Thus resistance is not just a reaction to contemporary pressures, but an integral part of tradition, and political consciousness is not a simple product of the present situation. This is true even when the strategy has been one of withdrawal, as is the case for the Bondo (Pfeffer, this volume).

The appropriation of nature and labour is intrinsic to industrial development, and marginalizes outsiders to the national mainstream. Elites in their turn refuse to acknowledge that development profits the urban middle class rather than the rural poor, and tend to see local activists as eco-fundamentalists. There has been a tendency, in India, for the dominant discourse on development to dismiss ecological problems as minor concerns, as 'tigers and trees' (Arnold and Guha 1995). Displacing a population is a brutal move with serious consequences for identity. The Narmada conflict has been important in India and elsewhere in showing the 'inseparability of ecological sustainability and social justice' (Baviskar 1995: 236).[12] The Indravati project did not incite similar national and international interest and the displaced did not receive the same consideration. Behera and Patel (this volume) show how the innovative idea of forcing the evictees to buy land, aborted. Here, as in the Narmada valley, no consultation was made with the affected populations before the work started, and the Pengs realized too late what was happening to them.

In the Narmada conflict, as in the Jharkhand issue, the articulation of resistance with an environmental discourse has been inspired by intellectuals from outside. Here, the opposition between centre and periphery is repeated within the movement itself. Adivasis are certainly able to understand environmental issues, but often conflate them with their concern for autonomy. The idea that intellectuals have, that adivasis live in a sustainable manner tends to romanticize subaltern forms of experience and culture.[13] Baviskar argues, rather convincingly, that adivasis are 'environmentalists by default'.[14]

CONSCIOUSNESS, AUTONOMY AND HEGEMONY

This does not imply a lack of political consciousness. Baviskar (1995) shows how in the Narmada valley the notion of community is transformed by the work of a tribal association, the Bhil Sangathan, which unites people as adivasis against the state to secure access to land and forest. Yet, as Cederlöf (this volume) stresses, local politics have their own dynamics. In the Jharkhand case, responses are intimately linked to identity maintenance, so that the role of environment and adaptation as bases for identity becomes central. This is true even for Santal steelworkers or urban pastoralists (Carrin and Tambs-Lyche, both this volume). Hindus (*dikus*) have become Jharkhandis when they realized that they shared their history of exploitation with the adivasis (Carrin and Hadders, this volume). Whenever adivasis or low castes come together, they share a subaltern experience of exploitation and exposure to cultural hegemony.

Are subalterns able to forge their identity regardless of dominant surveillance, in contexts where the dominant symbols of power and authority become objects both of envy and rage?[15] The central question here, brought up by the subalternist school of historians, is the relative autonomy of the subaltern subject. Guha (1983) sees a paradox here, which traps and splits subaltern consciousness, focusing on their own dominated position as well as that of the dominant which they want to appropriate. The problem lies, says Guha, in being unable to imagine other possible relationships.

We oppose O'Hanlon's view (1988) that the concept of consciousness is eurocentric, and that subalterns are unable to create their own values. Like Gold and Gujar (2002) we cannot experience our Indian informants as devoid of subjectivity or consciousness, and social action to us is always mediated through an actor. The Bharwad activist who talks pastoralist politics (Tambs-Lyche, this volume) certainly is a conscious political actor. Why should adivasis be different ? As Baviskar puts it:

> It is adivasis—not agents in the abstract, but definite socially and historically located individuals—who have ideas, whose subjective understanding guides their collective action and gives it meaning, and shapes their world. We cannot simultaneously hail adivasis as agents of history while dismissing their consciousness and their everyday lives. (1995: 237)

The very idea of the actor implies, to us, not absolute autonomy as O'Hanlon seems to think, but a sharing of values and categories known to himself and his entourage (Barth 1966). As Keesing argues (1992), this does not imply that actors in the same milieu are alike, since 'culture' is always inequally distributed. Thus hegemony is necessarily relative, and the question of ideological dominance must admit different answers in different situations. As Haynes and Prakash (1991) note, subaltern resistance does not need to express itself in a conscious political agenda since the context furnishes a contesting meaning. They argue that resistance pervades subaltern traditions, and this, we feel, is what the cases presented in this volume show.

The external pressures that act on peripheral populations range from projects advanced by the centre, such as the mega-dam of Behera and Patel's contribution, to the encroachment of untouchables' lands by local high-caste people in Uchiyamada's account. Pfeffer reports pressures that subtly sap a culture's foundations, as when tourists flock to photograph the exotic Bondos for a fee. The Jadopatias, who cater to tribal clients, have been denigrated as 'magicians' while the Patuas in the plains qualify as folk artists (Hadders, this volume). The Ronas, however, as Otten tells us, adapt and integrate foreign medical technologies in their own culture, while the pastoralist responses to environmental and socio-political pressures are as diverse, in Tambs-Lyche's view, as the outside influences. Andersen shows how the use of writing among the Santals opens new ways of reinventing tribal identity. Carrin's contribution analyses creative Santal responses to a whole complex of pressures from without.

The cultural autonomy of subalterns has often been identified with rebellion rather than everyday gestures having a contesting potential (Scott 1985; Cederlöf, this volume). In the context of domination and resistance, language itself has been developed into an oppositional tool, allowing the reinvention of tradition (Hobsbawm and Ranger 1983; Ranger 1993). The reactive process is a complex dialectic in which the categorical structures of domination may be deployed in a counterhegemonic discourse as shown by the recasting by Solomon Islanders of themselves as Christians, and European tourists as heathens (Keesing 1992: 237).

Through the struggle, old forms and myths acquire new meanings. These reinterpretations which emerged in the nineteenth century, generate constructions in which indigenous values—such as egalitarianism—are forged into objects of discourse, becoming the tools of creative ideological constructions. The subaltern project which aims at retrieving the subaltern's reflexivity and autonomy of thought and action, is limited by the nature of its sources: myth and storytelling, as in the Santal case (Carrin, this volume) access indigenous consciousness in a way that official archives, even when reinterpreted, only occasionally do.[16] Yet, fascinated by the symbolic ability of adivasis to redefine their link to territory and identity, anthropologists too often seem to assume that subalterns are able to transform their objective conditions of domination. While insurgent consciousness expresses resistance to domination, changing these conditions requires a capacity to pose an alternative policy.[17]

Cultural traditions alone are inadequate to formulate a new policy capable of imposing itself on the State or on public opinion in India. Subalterns are not equal. Some may succeed in expressing their claims (Andersen, Carrin, Cederlöf, Tambs-Lyche, all this volume), and Pfeffer shows how Bondo violence is an effective way of keeping intruders out. Yet people like the Saora (Vitebsky 1998) or the Kurava (Uchiyamada, this volume) seem deprived of this symbolic potential. Peripheral groups may need the aid of activists who are able to locate the channels of negotiation necessary in the national and international context (Behera and Patel, this volume). Resistance helps them only to develop an alternative culture, which must then find the support of a political party or movement such as the Jharkhand. Such movements have compelled adivasis to formulate a strategy, using channels of non-violent collective action.

Our argument against giving too much weight to the hegemony of the centre, is rooted in the specific South Asian context. Certainly, sanskritic Hinduism and the ideology of caste are important ideological forces. But Hinduism is notoriously diverse, embracing many strains that conflict with each other, and the empirical form that caste constellations take, vary considerably from one region to another. Moreover, the history of these forces show that the spread of these Sanskritic ideas is and has been opposed by local and specific notions.

Thus at least since Berreman (1961) scholars have stressed the use untouchables make of Hindu mythemes in reversing the 'moral' of the myth (Narayan 2002), while pastoralists have maintained for centuries an ambiguous relationship to the evaluations of settled populations. Tribals, of course, are more independent of Hindu values than both these groups, whenever they have retained their own religion and social organization. In much of tribal India, it is the Hindu influence which must adapt to an indigenous world-view (Otten and Carrin, both this volume). In all cases, the strategies developed by the various peripheral groups are rooted in a consciousness which is only partly shared with the bearers of ideological hegemony. Thus there is room for developing strategies based in the subaltern's own perception of the encounter, with at least a relative autonomy in regard to the hegemonic world-view—though the degree of autonomy varies from case to case.

Chatterjee (1993), maintains that the dominated in Indian society are capable of constructing their identity through struggle. Since the nineteenth century, subaltern resistance has expressed itself through collective action such as burning forests claimed by the state or forcibly harvesting the landowners' crop (Pouchepadass 1990, Devalle 1992). When and how resistance becomes consciously political, must remain a matter of judging each situation. Subaltern groups in India have forged their identity through their struggle for survival, and continue to do so.

NOTES

1. The various studies presented here grew out of a panel held during the 16th European Conference on Modern South Asian Studies, Edinburgh, 6-9 September 2000.
2. Ritually, the link to the forest was established by a war or hunting expedition, which later became increasingly symbolic in character.
3. *Adivasi*—'original dweller' is a term coined by and for the people commonly regarded as 'tribal' in India and officially classed as 'Scheduled tribes' (Carrin, this volume).
4. Maybe, as Grove (1995) argues, it was the confrontation with new ecological settings which produced, through a complex history, both the present environmentalist discourse and the Western scientific

approach to natural history. Peripheries, then, would seem to be at the origin of the environmental conceptions that guide policy at the centre, while they remain the laboratory where these conceptions are tried out.

5. The question of ecological regulation through ritual obviously evokes the debate concerning R.A. Rappaport's *Pigs for the Ancestors*. In a later comment to that debate, Rappaport admits that 'a charge of ecological rationality' might be made against the Maring—though he goes on to stress that 'the conscious purposes of the Maring were not ecological, that is, the ecosystemic regulatory functions of the ritual cycle were mystified by its sacred aspects, though some Maring were surely aware of them' (1979: 47). Elsewhere in the article, he is careful to point out that rationality, in his view, is a property of individual thinking, not collective action. Behera and Patel's statement should be read on the same terms.
6. He describes the ecological warfare which tended to oppose forest wanderers, graziers and traders, especially before 1350.
7. Their strategies have been analysed for nineteenth-century Madhya Pradesh (Rangarajan 1996), and, in a longer time perspective, for Himachal Pradesh (Ramachandra Guha 1989), and Maharashtra (S. Guha 1999). For Rajasthan, Gold and Gujar (2002) have shown how a local ruler protected the forest in face of the opposition of his own subjects.
8. This policy of privatization was urged by Munro and was related to his ideas on *ryotwari* land tenure and respect for private property.
9. For example, Fürer-Haimendorf (1982) shows how the cult of a clanic deity of the Raj Gonds is transformed into a variant of a pan-Hindu goddess cult. The identity of local goddesses may be the object of contention between brahmans and low castes, as Tambs-Lyche (2002: 286) has shown for Gujarat.
10. Ghurye was also Srinivas' teacher.
11. A translation of some of these texts is being prepared for publication (Andersen, Carrin and Soren forthcoming).
12. Citing various studies (Morse and Berger 1992; Ram Rahul 1993) Baviskar pointed out that 'resettlement has considerably worsened the lives of the few families that have shifted so far; there is every indication that satisfactory rehabilitation is impossible even for those officially classified as "project-affected" people' (Baviskar 1995: 199-200).

13. We cannot 'read into the everyday experiences of *adivasi* life an ideology that is derived from an external critique of development' (Roseberry 1989: 46). The problem of granting ecological consciousness to any group, is that cultural practices cannot be explained by hidden ecological imperatives.
14. 'Their present resource use can be called sustainable only if we compare it with the vastly more destructive practices of the state and the market' (Baviskar 1995: 239).
15. Arnold (1982), describing the revolts of 1839-1924 among Hillmen of Andhra Pradesh argues, like us, that subalterns are able to do so.
16. Cederlöf's material provides one of these rare exceptions.
17. Ecological consciousness requires imagining new social relationships and may lead to internal reform: women have occupied the front scene in many ecological movements not just because feminity and land are associated in adivasi symbolic systems but also because environmental crisis allowed the emergence of individual will, transcending traditional oppositions of class and gender.

REFERENCES

Arnold, D. (1982), 'Rebellious Hillmen: the Gudem Rampa Risings, 1839-1924', in Ranajit Guha (ed.), *Subaltern Studies,* vol. 1, Delhi: Oxford University Press, pp. 88-142.

Arnold, D. and Ramachandra Guha (eds.) (1995), *Nature, Culture, Imperialism,* Delhi: Oxford University Press.

Barth, F. (1956), 'Ecologic Relationships of Ethnic Groups in Swat, North Pakistan', *American Anthropologist,* vol. 58, 6, pp. 1079-89.

———(1964), 'Competition and Symbiosis in North East Baluchistan', *Folk,* vol. 6, 1, pp. 15-22.

———(1966), *Models of Social Organization,* Occasional Paper no. 23 of the Royal Anthropological Institute, London.

———(1969), 'Introduction', in F. Barth (ed.), *Ethnic Groups and Boundaries,* Oslo: Universitetsforlaget, pp. 9-38.

Bates, C. (1995), 'Lost Innocents and the Loss of Innocence', in R.H. Barnes, A. Gray and B. Kingsbury (eds.), *Indigenous Peoples of Asia,* Ann Arbor, Michigan: American Association for Asian Studies, pp. 103-19.

Baviskar, A. (1995), *In the Belly of the River: Tribal Conflicts over Development in the Narmada Valley,* Delhi: Oxford University Press.

Bayly, S. (1995), 'Caste and Race in Colonial Ethnography', in P. Robb (ed.), *The Concept of Race in South Asia*, Delhi: Oxford University Press, pp. 165-218.

Benton, T. (1994), 'Biology and Social Theory in the Environment Debate', in M. Redclift and T. Benton (eds.), *Social Theory and the Global Environment*, London: Routledge, pp. 28-50.

Berreman, G.D. (1961), 'Caste in India and in the United States', *American Journal of Sociology*, vol. 66, pp. 120-7.

———(1973), 'Self, Situation and Escape from Stigmatized Ethnic Identity', in J. Brögger (ed.), *Management of Minority Status*, Oslo: Universitetsforlaget, pp. 23-46.

Béteille, A. (1998), 'The Idea of Indigenous People', *Current Anthropology*, vol. 39, 2, pp. 187-91.

Biersack, A. (1999), 'Introduction: From the "New Ecology" to the New Ecologies', *American Anthropologist*, vol. 101, 1, pp. 5-18.

Brosius, J.P. (1999), 'Analyses and Interventions: Anthropological Engagements with Environmentalism', *Current Anthropology*, 40(3), pp. 277-309.

Carrin, M. (1996), 'Les tribus de l'Inde: repli identitaire et mouvements insurrectionnels', in C. Jaffrelot (ed.), *L'Inde contemporaine de 1950 à nos jours*, Paris: Fayard, pp. 421-40.

Carrin, M. and H. Tambs-Lyche (2008), *An Encounter of Peripheries: Santals, Missionaries, and Their Changing Worlds, 1867-1900*, Delhi: Manohar.

Carrin, M. and C. Jaffrelot (2003), 'Introduction', in M. Carrin and C. Jaffrelot (eds.), *Tribus et Basses Castes: Résistance et Autonomie Dans la Société Indienne*, Purusartha, 23: Paris, EHESS, pp. 11-32.

Chatterjee, P. (1993), *The Nation and its Fragments: Colonial and Postcolonial Histories*, Princeton: Princeton University Press.

Descola, P. and G. Pålsson (1996), *Nature and Society: Anthropological Approaches*, London: Routledge.

Devalle, S.B.C. (1992), *Discourses of Ethnicity: Culture and Protest in Jharkhand*, Delhi: Sage.

Dove, M.R. (1992), 'The Dialectical History of "Jungle" in Pakistan: An Examination of the Relationship Between Nature and Culture', *Journal of Anthropological Research*, 48, pp. 231-54.

Dumont, L. (1966), *Homo Hierarchicus*, Paris: Gallimard.

Eidheim, H. (1969), 'When Ethnic Identity is a Social Stigma', in F. Barth (ed.), *Ethnic Groups and Boundaries*, Oslo: Universitetsforlaget, pp. 39-57.

Elwin, V. (1944), *The Aboriginals*, London: Oxford University Press.

Freeman, R. (1994), *Forest and the Folk: Perceptions of Nature in the Swidden Regimes of Highland Malabar,* Pondicherry: French Institute of Pondicherry.

———(1998), 'Folk-Models of the Forest Environment in Highland Malabar', in R. Jeffery (ed.), *The Social Construction of Indian Forests*, Delhi: Manohar, pp. 55-78.

Fried, M. (1975), *The Notion of Tribe*, Menlo Park, CA: Cummings.

Fürer-Haimendorf, C. von. (1982), *Tribes of India: The Struggle for Survival*, Berkeley: University of California Press.

Gadgil, M. and Ramachandra Guha (1992), *This Fissured Land: An Ecological History of India,* Delhi: Oxford University Press.

———(1995), *Ecology and Equity: The Use and Abuse of Nature in Contemporary India*, London: Routledge.

Gadgil, M. and K.C. Malhotra (1989), 'Adaptive Significance of the Indian Caste System: An Ecological Perspective', *Annals of Human Biology,* 10, pp. 465-78.

———(1994), 'The Ecological Significance of Caste', in Ramachandra Guha (ed.), *Social Ecology, Oxford in India Readings in Sociology and Social Anthropology,* Delhi: Oxford University Press, pp. 27-41.

Gadgil, M. and V.D. Vartak (1976), 'The Sacred Groves of Western Ghats in India', *Economic Botany,* 30, pp. 152-60.

———(1981), 'Studies on Sacred Groves along the Western Ghats from Maharashtra and Goa: Role of Beliefs and Folklores', in S.K. Jain (ed.), *Glimpses of Indian Ethno-Botany*, Delhi: Oxford University Press.

Ghosh, A. (1999), *Jharkhand Movement: A Study in the Politics of Regionalism,* Calcutta: Minevva Associates.

Ghurye, G.S. (1943), *The Aboriginals so-called and their Future,* Bombay: Popular Book Depot; reedited and revised 1959 as *The Scheduled Tribes,* Bombay: Popular Book Depot.

Gold, A. Grodzins (1999), 'From Wild Pigs to Foreign Trees', in S. Toft Madsen (ed.), *State, Society and the Environment in South Asia*, Richmond, Surrey: Curzon, pp. 20-58.

Gold, A. Grodzins and B.R. Gujar (2002), *In the Time of Trees and Sorrows: Nature, Power, and Memory in Rajasthan,* Durham and London: Duke University Press.

Godelier, M. (1973), 'Le concept de tribu: crise d'un concept ou crise des fondements empiriques de l'anthropologie ?', in M. Godelier, *Horizon, trajets marxistes en anthropologie*, Paris: Maspero, pp. 93-131.

Goodenough, W.H. (1961), 'Comment on Cultural Evolution', *Daedalus*, 90, pp. 521-8.

Grove, R.H. (1995), *Green Imperialism: Colonial Expansion, Tropical Island Edens and the Origins of Environmentalism, 1600-1860*, Cambridge: Cambridge University Press.

Guha, Ramachandra (1989), *The Unquiet Woods: Ecological Change and Peasant Resistance in the Himalaya*, Delhi: Oxford University Press.

Guha, Ramachandra (1999), *Savaging the Civilized*, Delhi: Oxford University Press.

Guha, Ranajit (1983), *Elementary Aspects of Peasant Insurgency in Colonial India*, Delhi: Oxford University Press.

Guha, S. (1999), *Environment and Ethnicity in India, 1200-1991*, Cambridge: Cambridge University Press.

Habib, Irfan (1974), 'The Social Distribution of Landed Property in Pre-British India', in R.S. Sharma and V. Jha (eds.), *Indian Society: Historical Probings*, Delhi: People's Publishing House, pp. 264-316.

Hardiman, D. (1994), 'Power in the Forest: The Dangs, 1820-1940', in D. Arnold and D. Hardiman (eds.), *Subaltern Studies VII*, Delhi: Oxford University Press, pp. 89-147.

———(1999), *Feeding the Baniya: Peasants and Usurers in Western India*, Delhi: Oxford University Press.

Haynes, D. and G. Prakash (1991), *Contesting Power: Resistance and Everyday Social Relations in South Asia*, Delhi: Oxford University Press.

Heesterman, J.C. (1978), 'The Conundrum of the King's Authority', in J.F. Richards (ed.), *Kingship and Authority in South Asia*, Madison: University of Wisconsin, pp. 1-18.

Hobsbawm, E. and T. Ranger (1983), *The Invention of Tradition*, Cambridge: Cambridge University Press, pp. 1-27.

Inden, R.B. (1990), *Imagining India*, Oxford: Blackwell.

Ingold, T. (1992), 'Culture and the Perception of the Environment', in E. Croll and D. Parkin (eds.), *Bush Base: Forest Farm – Culture, Environment and Development*, London: Routledge, pp. 39-56.

Jaffrelot, C. (2003), 'Mobilisation Dalit en Inde du Nord et contre-offensive nationaliste hindoue', in M. Carrin and C. Jaffrelot (eds.), *Tribus et Basses Castes: Résistance et Autonomie Dans la Société Indienne*, Purusartha 23, Paris, EHESS, pp. 329-63.

Jeffery, R. (1998), 'Introduction', in R. Jeffery (ed.), *The Social Construction of Indian Forests*, Delhi: Manohar, pp. 1-16.

Kalam, M.A. (1996), *Sacred Groves in Kodagu District of Karnataka (South*

India): A Socio-Historical Study, Pondicherry: French Institute of Pondicherry.

———(1998), 'Sacred Groves in Coorg, Karnataka', in R. Jeffery (ed.), *The Social Construction of Indian Forests*, Delhi: Manohar, pp. 41-54.

Karlsson, B.G. (2000), *Contested Belonging: An Indigenous People's Struggle for Forest and Identity in Sub-Himalayan Bengal*, London: Curzon.

Kaviraj, S. (1993), 'The Imaginary Institution of India', in P. Chatterjee and G. Pandey (eds.), *Subaltern Studies VII*, Delhi: Oxford University Press, pp. 1-39.

Keesing, R. (1989), 'Theories of Culture Revisited', paper presented at the American Anthropological Association Annual Meeting.

———(1992), *Custom and Confrontation: The Kwais Struggle for Cultural Autonomy*, Chicago: University of Chicago Press.

Khare, R.S. (1984), *The Untouchable as Himself*, Cambridge: Cambridge University Press.

Kosambi, D.D. (1975), *An Introduction to the Study of Indian History*, Bombay; Popular Prakashan.

Kottak, C.P. (1999), 'The New Ecological Anthropology', *American Anthropologist*, vol. 101, 1, pp. 23-35.

Kulke, H. (1993) *Kings and Cults: State Formation and Legitimation in India and Southeast Asia*, Delhi: Manohar.

Lattimore, O. (1962), *Inner Asian Frontiers of China*, Boston: Beacon.

Leach, E.R. (1954), *Political Systems of Highland Burma*, London: Athlone.

Madsen, S. Toft (1999), 'Introduction', in S. Toft Madsen (ed.), *State, Society and the Environment in South Asia*, Richmond, Surrey: Curzon, pp. 1-19.

Malamoud, C. (1996), 'Cooking the World: Ritual and Thought in Ancient India'. This particular essay originally published 1976: 'Village et forêt dans l'idéologie de l'Inde brahmanique', *Archives Européennes de Sociologie*, XVII, pp. 3-20.

Mayer, A.C. (1960), *Caste and Kinship in Central India*, London: Routledge & Kegan Paul.

Morse, B. and T. Berger (1992), *Sardar Sarovar: The Report of the Independant Review*, Resource Futures International: Ottawa.

Narayan, B. (2002), 'Caste (Hi)stories Among Dalits', in M. Carrin and C. Jaffrelot (eds.), *Tribus et Basses Castes: Résistance et Autonomie Dans la Société Indienne*, Purusartha, 23, Paris: EHESS, pp. 159-80.

Njammasch, M. (1992a), 'Die Dorfgemeinde in Maitrakareich', *Beiträge des Südasien-Instituts, Humboldt-Universität zu Berlin*, 1, pp. 1-49.

———(1992b), 'Die Flur-und-Besitzverhältnisse im Dorf Madasara auf Kathiawar im Jahre 675 n. Chr.' Beiträge des Südasien-Instituts, Humboldt-Universität zu Berlin, 2, pp. 27-68.

———(1993), 'Freie Bauern und Pächter im Frühmittelalderlichen Indien', Beiträge des Südasien-Instituts, Humboldt-Universität zu Berlin, 5, pp. 1-61.

O'Hanlon, R. (1988), 'Recovering the Subject: Subaltern Studies and Histories of Resistance in Colonial South Asia', *Modern Asian Studies*, 22, 1, pp. 189-224.

Pfeffer, G. (1997), 'The Scheduled Tribes of Middle India as a Unit: Problems of Internal and External Comparison', in D.K. Behera and G. Pfeffer (eds.), *Contemporary Society: Tribal Studies. I: Structure and Process*, Delhi: Concept, pp. 3-27.

Pouchepadass, J. (1990), *The Ecological History of the Central Western Ghats in the Modern Period: A Preliminary Survey*, Pondicherry: French Institute of Pondicherry.

Prakash, G. (1991), 'Becoming a Bhuinya: Oral Traditions and Contested Domination in Eastern India', in D. Haynes and G. Prakash, *Contesting Power: Resistance and Everyday Social Relations in South Asia*, Delhi: Oxford University Press, pp. 145-74.

Ram, Rahul N. (1993), *Muddy Waters: A Critical Assessment of the Benefits of the Sardar Sarovar Project*, Delhi: Kalpavriksha.

Rangarajan, M. (1996), *Fencing the Forest: Conservation and Ecological Change in India's Central Provinces, 1860-1914*, Delhi: Oxford University Press.

Ranger, T. (1993), 'The Invention of Tradition Revisited: The Case of Colonial Africa', in P. Kaarsholm and J. Hultin (eds.), *Inventions and Boundaries: Historical and Anthropological Approaches to the Study of Ethnicity and Nationalism*, Roskilde: Roskilde University, International Development Studies, pp. 9-50.

Rappaport, R.A. (1979), *Ecology, Meaning and Religion*, Berkeley: North Atlantic Books.

Said, E. (1978), *Orientalism*, New York: Pantheon.

Roseberry, W. (1989), *Anthropologies and Histories: Essays in Culture, History and Political Economy*, New Brunswick: Rutgers University Press.

Sahlins, Marshall D. (1968), *Tribesmen*, Englewood Cliffs: Prentice Hall.

Scott, James C. (1985), *Weapons of the Weak: Everyday Forms of Peasant Resistance*, New Haven: Yale University Press.

———(1990), *Domination and the Arts of Resistance: Hidden Transcripts*, New Haven: Yale University Press.

Sinha, D.P. (1968), *Culture Change in an Intertribal Market*, Bombay: Asia Publishing House.

Sivaramakrishnan, K. (1999), *Modern Forests: Statemaking and Environmental Change in Colonial Eastern India*, Delhi: Oxford University Press.

Skaria, A. (1999), *Hybrid Histories: Forests, Frontiers and Wilderness in Western India*, Delhi: Oxford University Press.

Srinivas, M.N. (1952), *Religion and Society Among the Coorgs*, Oxford: Oxford University Press.

———(1962), 'Sanskritization and Westernization', in M.N. Srinivas, *Caste in Modern India and Other Essays*, Bombay: Asia Publishing House, pp. 42-62.

———(1967), *Social Change in Modern India*, Berkeley: University of California Press.

Sundar, N. (1997), *Subalterns and Sovereigns: An Anthropological History of Bastar 1854-1996*, Delhi: Oxford University Press.

Tambs-Lyche, H. (1997), *Power, Profit and Poetry: Traditional Society in Kathiawar, Western India*, Delhi: Manohar.

———(2002), 'Townsmen, Tenants and Tribes: War, Wildness and Wilderness in the Traditional Politics of Western India', in G. Pfeffer and D.K. Behera (eds.), *Contemporary Society: Tribal Studies*, vol. 5: *The Concept of Tribal Society*, Delhi: Concept, pp. 186-207.

———(2003), 'Koli, Rajput, Kanbi, Patidar: revendications identitaires au Gujarat, hier et aujour d'Hui', in M. Carrin and C. Jaffrelot (eds.), *Tribus et Basses Castes, Résistance et Autonomie Dans la Société Indienne*, Purusartha 23, Paris, EHESS, pp. 265-96.

Vitebsky, P. (1998), 'A Farewell to Ancestors ? Deforestation and the Changing Spiritual Environment of the Sora', in R.H. Grove, V. Damodaran and S. Sangwan (eds.), *Nature and the Orient: The Environmental History of South and South-East Asia*, Delhi: Oxford University Press, pp. 967-82.

Zimmerman, F. (1987), *The Jungle and the Aroma of Meats: An Ecological Theme in Hindu Medicine*, Berkeley: University of California Press.

1

Between the Desert and the Sown: Pastoralists of Western India through the Centuries[1]

HARALD TAMBS-LYCHE

INTRODUCTION

Throughout the dry zones of western India, pastoralists have occupied, at least since early medieval times, a niche between the desert and the sown. A crisis, ecologically defined, is commonly claimed for this adaptation: desertification on the one hand, expansion and intensification of agriculture on the other, are seen as reducing the capacity of the niche pastoralists occupy. Yet total cattle stocks are, in fact, increasing, which seems to indicate that more fodder is becoming available. We are dealing, here, with developments in the relation of pastoral adaptations to husbandry in general, as well as changing relations between settled and migratory populations. The problem, then, is political and cultural as well as ecological.

Sedentarization of pastoralists has gone on for centuries in western India. When nomads were offered land by a ruler, they seldom refused. But settlement often served only as a base for the annual migrations. While the importance of agriculture in such mixed adaptations tends to grow, this does not imply giving up pastoralism altogether. As Fisher points out, for western Rajasthan, census statistics seriously underestimate the pastoral component of the mixed adaptations typical of the area. While the census tends to stress agriculture as 'gainful employment', a much larger part of the actual work performed in the villages he studied, was devoted to pastoral activities (Fisher 1997: 36-40). Henderson's account of a single village (1994) substantiates this point, true, apparently, for most semi-arid regions of western India: settled and migratory adaptations are combined in ways that defy present statistical categorization. Yet planning and politics, pastoralists and husbandry still takes a back seat to agricultural activity.

At the ideological level, parallel processes have been at work. Bhattacharya has shown, how for the Punjab, colonial discourse and legislation changed the view of pastoralism. Land rights were tied to agricultural use, 'the extension of cultivation was synonymous with progress', and grazing territories were seen as wastelands (1995: 72). With the Criminal Tribes Act of 1871, 'wanderers'—including pastoralists—might be classified as criminals (ibid.: 83). Such attitudes were largely inherited by officials of independent India, and are today felt particularly in confrontations between pastoralists and the Forest Department. Recent attempts at settling pastoralists have met with little success. Certainly, in parts of Rajasthan,[2] worsening ecological conditions have led herdsmen to settle on the outskirts of villages, often where famine relief was originally offered to them. But the general situation in Gujarat and Rajasthan vindicates Bhattacharya's conclusion that there is no 'simple, smooth process of displacement and dispossession' (ibid.: 85). More complex processes are at work.

HISTORICAL PERSPECTIVES

Modernity has cast pastoralists as subalterns. Yet they have not always been so, and their reduction to subaltern status in western India starts with the growth of the modern state—in the case of Saurashtra from the sixteenth century—rather than with the coming of the British. Yet even the modernized indigenous order did not marginalize pastoralists to the extent that British policy did. The fact that so much of western India remained under princely control, escaping many of the measures of the colonial state, is important here.

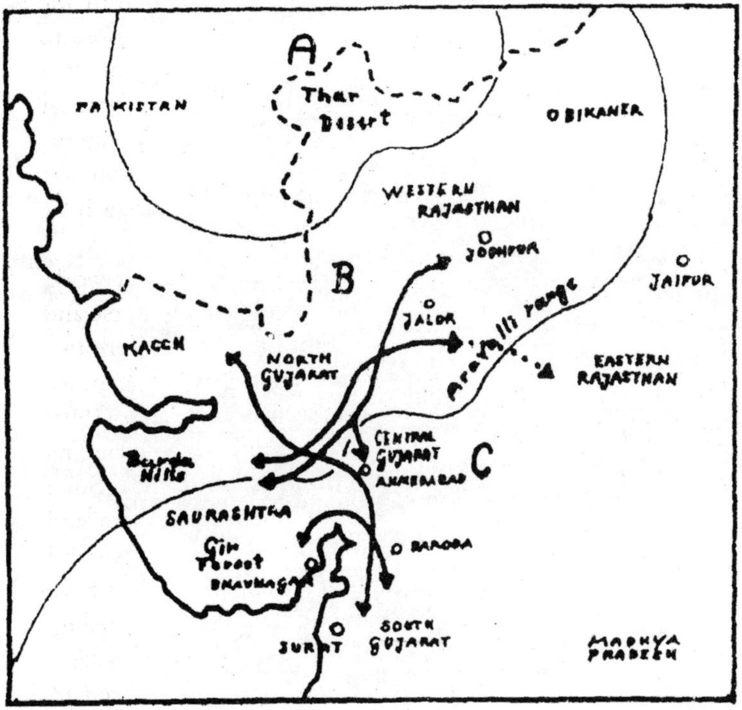

Sketch map of the Rajasthan/Gujarat area, showing precipitation zones (A, B, C) and some of the migration routes (double arrows) mentioned in the paper. Zone A has less than 100 mm annual rainfall, zone B 100-500 mm, and zone C more than 500 mm. Geographical names are given reference only. Approximate scale 1: 10 million.

Adopting a long-time perspective, we must avoid environmental determinism and deal with the pastoralists' place in the symbolic landscape of the region, as well as in physical space. Indeed, until the second half of the twentieth century it is hard to describe the pastoralists of western India as 'peripheral' to a central, agricultural base. Pastoralists are seen as representing traditional culture and certain aspects of religion. Krishna, of course, is one of them, though the pastoral castes of the region are mainly devotees of the various forms of the Goddess. The Charan bards, important in the old Rajput kingdoms and central to the present revival and reinvention of tradition (Tambs-Lyche 1996b) are also seen as having pastoral origins.

Westphal-Hellbosch (1974, 1976) has tried to establish when each of the pastoral communities came to Saurashtra.[3] Her conclusions are that several waves of immigrants—among them the present pastoralist castes—came to Saurashtra from the eighth century onwards, and during the gradual establishment of the Rajput-dominated traditional order from the eleventh to the fifteenth century (Wilberforce-Bell 1916; Tambs-Lyche 1997). Immigration to Rajasthan probably followed a similar course, possibly predating events in Saurashtra by a century or two.

It is likely that the Vallabhi kingdom, like the preceding Gupta empire and the states of classical India, should be considered on a 'grid' pattern: towns and cities surrounded by a periphery of agricultural exploitation as nodes bound together by roads, which remained, more or less, under government control.[4] Between these nodes and lines there must have been large 'blank' areas, inhabited by people we would call 'tribal', largely beyond the control of the state. Immigration of the groups now known as pastoralists must have contributed to transform these interstitial areas, and we may read the earliest myth of the goddess Khodiyar as the story of how the Vallabhi kings failed to come to terms with the newcomers, causing their fall. Here, Khodiyar and her sisters curse the king Shiladitya so that his heirs will have no offspring, then qualify their curse—'unless they shall marry a woman of the people'. Commentators note that one Vallabhi ruler is indeed said to have married a woman from the Kathi community, among the new immigrants (Tambs-Lyche 1996a, 1997).

Two or three centuries later, when the Gujarat kingdom had conquered Junagadh, Khodiyar and her pastoralist Ahir followers helped prince Naughan to regain the Chudasama throne. Naughan received the *tika*[5] from his Ahir foster-sister, daughter of the chief who sheltered and supported him. These events forged a lasting alliance between his dynasty and the Ahirs (Tambs-Lyche 1991, 1997). Just as the Ahirs used to put the *tika* on the Chudasama king-to-be, so the Mers—immigrants, apparently, from the same period—did the same for the Jethwa kings of Porbandar. They, however, also received a *tika* from the hands of a Rabari—another pastoralist caste—if some sources are to be believed (Westphal-Hellbosch 1974). The kings of Mewar received the *tika* from a Bhil tribesman.[6] The ceremony of the *tika* was common all over western India, and usually performed by the chief's main vassal. But in the states mentioned, all established before the twelfth century, the act is carried out on behalf of an ethnic group by one of its members. If we assume that migrations in the early medieval period, along with the collapse of the old urban centres, displaced the political centre of gravity towards the countryside, authority must have been based on an alliance between the new rural groups and the king. In the early medieval period, then, kingship in the region rested on an alliance in which pastoralists were the main military resource of the budding state (Tambs-Lyche 1997: 33-41).[7]

The emergence of a feudal system was accompanied by technical improvements in agriculture, mainly in north and central Gujarat, where the period from the eleventh to the twelfth century is that of the beautiful step-wells and a number of large tanks. What was to become the Rajput-dominated area of western India was the periphery to this central Gujarat kingdom and later the Sultanate. Rajput dominance spread gradually through this periphery, and as we approach the age of the 'Rajput Great Tradition' (Kolff 1991), pastoralists ceased to be king-makers. They became peripheral to a political order built on the control of agriculture, more so, as trade again became an important element in state formation, as in Saurasthtra from the sixteenth century onwards. Even when no longer central to state building, however, pastoralists remained important to regional culture and identity. The opposition between peasants and pastoralists was certainly present in oral tradition—as in the Punjab (Bhattacharya 1995: 80-3)—and in ideology. Yet pastoralists were, in Saurashtra, always included in the 'thirteen castes' (*ter tansali*)[8] that formed the core of political community in the villages (Tambs-Lyche 1997: 112-13). Similar inclusion of pastoralists in the village community is reported by Rosin (1994: 41) for the Aravallis and by Mayer (1960: 33-60) for Malwa.

CASTES OF PASTORALISTS

In Gujarat, the pastoral castes are Rabari, Bharwad, and Charan. In Rajasthan, there are also the pastoral Jats. There, and in south Gujarat, we must add the caste known as Ahir or Gujar. Both the Ahirs/Gujars and the Charans have settled, in various regions, as agriculturalists. While Charans dominate several villages of western Rajastan, settled Ahirs and Gujars are found in pockets over much of western India, as well as the north and north-west. In Kutch, some Rabaris have even become farmers, and wherever pastoralists have land, they cultivate it in addition to their main occupation.

At the apex of the traditional Rajput order—from the fifteenth to the eighteenth century—pastoralists were peripheral, but through the Charan bards and genealogists at court, Maldhari cultural influence remained significant (Qanungo 1969; Tambs-Lyche 1997). These courtiers were no longer active pastoralists, but some Charans were caravan traders, and as some of them dealt in cattle, the line between trade and pastoralism was not easy to draw. Today, Charans form a small but extremely diversified community. Families of the old court bards may still be important landowners; not a few have become intellectuals; but some are still pastoralists. The pastoral Charans specialize in buffaloes, and in the Gir forest were still practising the rite of buffalo sacrifice as late as the seventies (Westphal-Hellbosch 1976). I have also met Charan families living on the outskirts of towns, selling their milk products, and sharing the niche of some Bharwads.

Traditionally, the Rabaris are associated with camel herding. In Rajasthan, they were known as Raikas and were purveyors of camels—strategically important animals of great value—to the various courts. Sometimes, they formed an entire camel corps of the rulers' armed forces. Many Rabaris are still nomadic, and they remain the most traditional of the pastoral castes, as well as enjoying the highest position among the nomads of the region. Their large annual fair at Pushkar has become a tourist attraction; another, less known, is at Jalor in south-western Marwar. As nomads based in the periphery, they are outside rather than being submitted to the rank order of the village.

Bharwads cannot remain outsiders in the same way. More and more, they become the 'village herdsman', placed, in the local hierarchy,. below the farmer, whose production surplus was the Rajput's main source of income. Bharwads generally herd sheep or goats (though quite a few also have cows), and are traditionally seen as the lowest among the pastoral castes. They are also the most urbanized group, and monopolize the niche of milk merchants. They have proved capable of adapting themselves to present changes, and tend, at least in Saurashtra, to rise in the hierarchy.

The Ahir/Gujar group is the largest pastoral community in India, and their status varies according to adaptation and region. Typically, however, they used to herd cows rather than sheep or goats, and thus traditionally occupied an intermediate position between Rabaris and Bharwads. But many have (sometimes for centuries), been settled as agriculturalists, and the Ahirs of Saurashtra—said to be Krishna's own people and proud of their pastoral origins—are today, basically farmers. As noted, they figure prominently in myths surrounding the early years of the Chudasama dynasty of Junagadh, founded in AD 875 and conquered by the Sultanate of Gujarat in 1470. Most myths concern king Naughan, who can be placed in the eleventh century. Here, Ahirs play the role of king-makers and the Chudasama ruler was conventionally described as the king of Ahirs (Amarji 1882). In these myths the Ahirs are clearly seen as pastoralists who live in the *jangal*, and we may assume that their sedentarization took place during the subsequent centuries of Chudasama rule. Today, Ahirs are often seen as the dominant caste (Srinivas 1952, Mayer 1958) in the villages around Junagadh, a view clearly related to times when their alliance with the king formed the basis for the kingdom; for under Muslim rule, villages were taken over by zamindars, and the Ahirs lost their earlier power and influence. Yet even today they are clearly distinguished, by themselves and others, from the peasant castes of Kanbi and Koli.

The consciousness of belonging to a distinct subculture is common to members of all the pastoral communities. Those still on the move are *daghlabhai*, 'brothers of the blanket', who share a common appreciation of the migratory life and of the *jangal*—wilderness. It is striking how pastoralists and Ahirs both tend to confirm the pastoralist origins of the latter—sometimes including them with the *daghlabhai*, though they no longer wander. Thus the Ahirs may serve as a pointer to the feeling of cross-caste community that, in Saurashtra, unites them with Charans, Rabaris and Bharwads. Typically, Saurashtra Ahirs share with Rabaris and Bharwads a traditional style of dress, all of them slightly but visibly distinguished from that of the peasants. Thus all pastoralist women share the long skirt and the *odhani*,[9] in black and red, though the combination of the colours differ between the castes. Similarly, males of all three castes have red stripes in their turbans, though these, again, differ. The Ahirs may be farmers, but they are not *chapatiwalas*, a word used by herdsmen and fishermen alike to denote 'peasants' in a derogatory sense.

In the traditional order Rabaris were, so people say, the right side of Krishna's body, of which the Bharwads formed the left side. Rabaris were superior to Bharwads, with Ahirs in between, whenever they were cited as a pastoral caste. Charans, as bards, were certainly superior to the others.

This order is getting reversed today, at least in the eyes of townsmen and peasants. The old order equated 'wildness' with claims to authority—I feel here, that Skaria's perception of 'tribal' wildness (1999) may more fruitfully be extended to the entire Rajput order (Tambs-Lyche 2002)—but today, the people of the *jangal* are simply seen as *jangli*.[10] In this context, Rabaris are uncivilized, whereas Bharwads, through their many novel strategies of adaptation, are much less so.

In terms of the caste system, the position of the pastoralists is ambiguous.[11] In a sense, they are both inside and outside the system. They are insiders when villagers place them in relation to their own order: yet remain outsiders relatively independent of village society. Thus there is room for divergence between their self-image and the view villagers have of them. In Gujarat, they are known as Maldharis,[12] and regarded with some of the suspicion, mixed with exotic appreciation, that Europeans reserve for Gypsies (Enthoven 1920-2; Pocock 1972; Westphal-Hellbosch 1974, 1976; Tambs-Lyche

1997). They are closely associated with the *jangal,* wilderness, which in this part of India is not the forest but the area beyond cultivation and village control (Tambs-Lyche 2004). Typically, pastoralists are seen as close to forces that Westerners would see as 'nature': in western Saurashtra, villagers turn to Momai Mata, the goddess of the Rabaris, to pray for rain (Trivedi 1961).

THE ECOLOGY OF THE REGION

The ecology of the region is complex, partly because of its geological instability, as manifested in the 2001 earthquake. In general, the land has tended to rise, which explains both the peculiar character of the Rann of Kutch and the saline soils along its coasts as well as that of the Gulf of Cambay.[13] The sand dunes of the Thar desert constitute another factor of natural instability (Haynes 1998: 738-40).

The region presents strongly contrasting ecological zones. Moving east and south, the desert gradually gives way to dry bush till we reach the agricultural area. The boundaries between these three zones are both gradual and historically shifting.

The Aravalli range, forming a natural boundary between western and eastern Rajasthan, 'is one of the most densely populated arid and semi-arid regions of the world' (Rosin 1994: 30; Malhotra 1977: 302). The southern part of the chain is still forested, and borders on the woods of eastern Gujarat, while the northern Aravallis have a long history of artificial irrigation and settled agriculture (Rosin 1994). Eastern Rajasthan is generally less dry than the western part of the state, and its southern boundaries merge with the forests of Madhya Pradesh.

In Gujarat, too, the north-west is dry. Kutch and Saurashtra (Kathiawar), geologically distinct from the mainland, have shallow soils and rocky outcrops making for considerable local variations. They are part of tectonic plaques which originally formed part of the African continent. In southern Saurashtra, only the small, dry deciduous Gir forest remains, of what was recently a much larger wooded area: hunting lodges of the old princes are found today in areas where no forest can be seen. Similar observations were current in the late nineteenth century (Watson 1884: 94). But Central

Gujarat, the main political and agricultural centre of the region since early times, has deep sedimentary soils, and to the east we find black soils bordering on the Deccan lava trap. South Gujarat receives much more rain, and towards the state's south-eastern border, there are deep forests.

ECOLOGICAL CHANGES

Economically and in terms of population, agriculture is the dominant adaptation in the region. The expansion of arable land during the last century is considerable: from 32 per cent of Gujarat's present area in 1890 to 43 per cent in 1930 and 52 per cent in 1970. One might well conclude that this expansion would reduce the grazing area available to pastoralists by the same amount, a total reduction of 3.9 million hectares. Yet Haynes notes that grasslands and shrub, the most obvious land for grazing, have both declined by some 421,000 hectares between 1910 and 1970, only some 11 per cent of what we would expect from the increase in arable. Clearly, only a small part of the agricultural expansion has been at the cost of this type of vegetation (Haynes 1998: 742).

Instead, the area under forest has declined radically, from some 31 per cent in 1890 to 9 per cent in 1930 and to 6 per cent by 1970 (ibid.: 747). Deforestation has indeed been radical in Gujarat. In Saurashtra, the Gir forest, the only one left, is deteriorating.[14] In spite of the common allegation that this is a result of colonial policy, most of the decline took place when a very large part of Gujarat—including Kutch, Saurashtra (Kathiawar) and much of the East Gujarat forest—was still under princely rule. Large-scale clearing of forests must have taken place in the princely states, as well as in British territory, between 1890 and 1930, even if some forest reserves were protected by the princes, who monopolized hunting. As late as the 1920s, several forest areas in Saurashtra were still fit for hunting tiger or deer. Since 1930, a third of the remaining forest area has gone. The forests of Rajasthan, too, have been depleted: while about 5.4 per cent of its area was covered by forest in the 1860s, this had declined to 2.1 per cent by 1980.

Contrary to common assumptions, the total area of desert has declined these last hundred years—from 17.3 to 11.4 million hectares. But the unvegetated desertic zone has expanded by 53.6 per cent, so there has been a radical decrease in semi-desert scrub and 'desertic communities' of plants—a situation which no doubt largely explains the difficulties of camel herders. In brief, the zone between the desert and the sown, which is of primary interest to herdsmen, has declined radically. The Thar desert is said to be advancing eastwards in spite of attempts at soil conservation. Fisher (1997) does not accept this, but underlines that ecological conditions have worsened within the desert itself. What seems to happen, according to Haynes (1998), is that the sand dunes advance on the dry shrub, while cultivation expands to approach the advancing sand.

While pastoralists may be wrongly accused of destroying Saurashtra's forests, there is no doubt that efforts at conservation in Rajasthan are countered by the desperate efforts of pastoralists to use any grazing available. The situation was vividly described by Dr. Kothari, the director of the Folklore Research Centre at Borunda (Marwar). 'There is a fence', he said, 'put up by the Forest Department. Suddenly a Maldhari approaches, cutting a hole in the fence. No animals were to be seen: suddenly there are cows everywhere'. The effectiveness of the modern state in protecting forests against depletion as well as herds, should not be overestimated. As one of Gold's informants tells us: 'In the time of the *raja maharaja* there were twenty forestry guards; and now the government sends only one man' (1999: 34).

The expansion in arable has been even more radical, over the last century, in Rajasthan than in Gujarat—182.6 per cent from 1880 to 1980, as against 47.4 per cent for Gujarat. The increase was 108.8 per cent for the region as a whole. Conversely, there is a steep drop in what Haynes calls 'resource areas' (the sum of forest and woodland, interrupted woods, grass or shrub complexes, major wetlands and semi-desert scrub) almost to half—from some 21.5 million hectares, to about 13 million in Rajasthan, and from about 8 million hectares to 4.5 in Gujarat (Haynes 1998: 747 and 772). These areas are clearly important to pastoralists.

Yet this is not the full picture. While modern irrigation, as in central Gujarat, may intensify agriculture and increase the number of annual crops so as practically to exclude grazing on the fallow, irrigation does not necessarily have this effect. Thus for the Northern Aravallis, Rosin stresses that 'the necessity of animals for draft, and the year-round maintenance of cattle made possible by the abundance of fodder available from two crops a year, makes the activities of crop cultivation, irrigation and animal husbandry highly interdependent' (1994: 37). As for the drier zones of western Rajasthan, the same author points out that

> extensive cultivation of a rain-fed crop . . . directly supports pastoralism in the region. Crops of millet, sorghum, pulses and melons, seeded over as much land as possible, add fodder to supplement the jungle grasses, leafy bushes and trees on which the animals graze. Even in rain-scarce years, crops that do not mature to grain are valuable for the chaff and straw they provide for livestock feed. Improvements in water, feed and human food reserves permit half-year settled residence in a home village or hamlet in the savanna, a pattern which today characterizes a vast number of pastoral families (whether Jaṭ, Gujar or Rebari). The extensiveness of crop cultivation by a people often classified as pastoral is evident today in the high percentage of land brought under single crop cultivation in the regions identified with pastoralism. (1994: 33-4)

Thus extension of agriculture is not necessarily detrimental to livestock herding and pastoralism. One trend seems to be that pastoralists, excluded from the areas of most intensive multi-crop agriculture, are transforming grasslands and shrub into single-cropping areas, thereby reducing the area of non-cropped 'resource areas' but also their own dependence on migration and access to other lands. Another plausible trend, not documented in the literature, is that extensively single-cropped lands become irrigated, to produce two crops with fallow in between, thus opening a new niche for grazing as an older one is closed. Thus we are faced with some trends that increase, and others that decrease, the total availability of fodder and pasture. To calculate the net loss or gain of these concurrent processes is no easy task, and has not, to my knowledge, been attempted.

LANDSCAPES AND *MALDHARI RESTO*—ROADS FOR HERDSMEN

The semi-arid landscape becomes extremely complex from a Maldhari point of view. In my exploratory fieldwork, I spent much time trying to learn something of this view, as expressed in the term *maldhari resto*—roads for the herdsmen. They may be defined quite simply as ways along which a herd may pass, with access to a reasonable quantity of grazing and water, as the herd proceeds. Some notes from the bus window:

(16/2/91) . . . As we leave Jalor on the Abu Road bus, we see a number of dwellings looking like those of Rabaris on this side of the town, too (towards SE)—and we also pass a Rabari leading a flock of about 40 sheep here. Further on we meet 4 camels—and there are also quite a few dwellings of the same type a little farther from the town—thinning out, it seems, as we go further. The landscape here is still a mix between dry shrub-land (sandy) and irrigation fields—even quite some distance from Jalor—without any clear break. It seems evident that all extension of irrigation here affects grazing, for there is no 'ecological boundary' (zone) save that created by the pumps.[15]

Here there was grazing for sheep and goats, at least, in a zone extending some distance from the town: there is a population of shepherds living on its outskirts and taking their herds grazing outwards towards the periphery during the day. Farther out, however, the shrub seems too poor for grazing, and the boundary towards the irrigated fields is too sharp so there is no 'road' for herdsmen here between the desert and the sown. It is plausible that irrigation here has harmed grazing by lowering the ground water level. In such places there may be a 'road' at other times, if there is enough of a time-lag between the harvesting of one crop and the sowing of the next to make the stubble available for grazing. Thus, one can see that the Jalor-Sirohi route is not usually a 'road for herdsmen', unlike that from Jalor towards Radhanpur, passing west of Mount Abu, passing through a drier area but with much less cultivation. Yet in an exceptionally rainy year, a good growth of the shrub may 'open a road', while a bad year may close another.

Thus the *maldhari resto* are not fixed 'wandering routes', such as the Basseri, for example, are used to (Barth 1964). This explains why herdsmen of western India, in general, cannot build an organization around the use of territory, as the Basseri have done. Much of the day's work, for a wandering Maldhari, is spent in scouting, prospecting, and gathering information. This was obvious to me when I toured Saurashtra and central Gujarat on my motorcycle. Maldharis were easy to observe but not, generally speaking, talkative: but whenever I came from the direction they were heading, contact was easy, as they eagerly tried to get information on the conditions ahead. Was there a road? The question involved the state of vegetation, the number of Maldharis and animals seen, whether the land was open or enclosed, whether it was in crop or lying fallow. During the crisis of 1991 the cowherds' range of questions was much wider: 'had I been to the West, towards Rajkot? Were the fields already "used up" towards Cambay? Did I have news from the Rajpipla area? What about the Gir forest?' These were long-range nomads, spending the rains in their homes in the Little Rann of Kutch and normally following a standard route, taking them south through the borderlands between Gujarat and Saurashtra, across central Gujarat, and then south-east towards the forest around Rajpipla. Questions about Rajkot or the Gir, places far from their usual route, was an attempt to establish possible crisis strategies.

That year, such solutions were hard to find. Drought seemed to be everywhere—except at the goal of their journey, the south-eastern forests. Typically, near Rajpipla I met a Bharwad shepherd, hailing from the Bhavnagar area in eastern Saurashtra. Like many Bhavnagar Bharwads, he used to migrate north to Cambay, across central Gujarat, and down to Rajpipla. But now he had chosen to stay there permanently, supplementing his own small herd of goats by herding the bovines of other villagers. As he put it: 'the road has gone bad' (*kharab*). He was one of many, but quite different, cases of sedentarization.

Drought has certainly led to a decline in some pastoral adaptations of the region,[16] and the crisis I observed during the winter of 1991 is but one in a long line of such events. But Fisher, who has studied records of drought and famine in western Rajasthan dating back to 1804, stresses the local differences between these records (1997:

31-2). A year characterized as severe famine in one account may be seen as a moderate drought in another. This may be due to sub-regional variations as well as the fact that a particular crisis may hit one adaptation harder than another. Thus 1991 seems to have been particularly hard on cows, while sheep, goats and camels fared better. Fisher also notes that a crisis for those who herd one species may subsequently open up new grazing lands for others. During the years 1985-7, many cowherds of Marwar settled in cattle camps; by 1990-1 they were still there, in very poor dwellings. This certainly hurt the prospect for goatherds near these settlements; but the opposite may be true of the areas the cowherds had left. Such changes may well be reversible: one cannot exclude the possibility that a series of good years might lead the cowherds to take up migration again. Certainly such returns to a migratory adaptation must have happened in the past.

CURRENT PASTORAL ADAPTATIONS: LONG-RANGE NOMADS

Pastoral adaptations are manifold in western India. Some are long-distance nomads, travelling as far as a thousand kilometres. The most obvious example today, in Gujarat, are the Rabaris from the north-eastern edge of the Rann of Kutch, who in the wet season retire into the desert or semi-desert areas. They stay there in their villages during the rainy season, and spend the dry season in the forest belt of south-eastern Gujarat, around Rajpipla. They specialize either in camels or bovines,[17] in both cases keeping a few camels for transporting their tents and other gear. Migrating with flocks of a hundred animals or more, several families together, they graze their animals on the stubble of the barren fields. In north and central Gujarat, these nomads had customary contract relations with particular farmers along their route, so they would visit the fields of the same farmer year after year. This type of relation has suffered badly from irrigation and intensified agriculture, as the farmers have no place for the visiting nomads any more.[18]

From Marwar and other districts of western Rajasthan, a considerable number of pastoralists migrate into Gujarat during the dry period, entering the state through the plains to the west of Mount Abu, then move on past Palanpur to central Gujarat and, in smaller numbers, into Saurashtra. Reciprocally, Gujarat shepherds, mainly from Saurashtra, migrate into the districts of Kota, Sirohi, Jalor, Pali, Jodhpur and even Barmer (Kavoori 1999: 27-9).

Many Rabaris of western Rajasthan (Marwar) have settled, in or near villages and towns, changing from camels to sheep and goats. The change provides for survival at the loss of traditional rank. In the north, in Bikaner and Jaisalmer districts, camel nomads are still travelling; the fair at Pushkar will not disappear just yet. But at the similar fair at Jalor in the south, in 1990, the change to sheep and goats was clear. Only the nomads from Kutch continued to bring their camels in any number. In general, however, the Rabaris cling to their traditional adaptation as far as possible. This is true both of camel and cow herders. If they give up pastoralism, they tend to take jobs in town; quite a few are employed as watchmen or guards, as, for example, in Dhrangadhra.

An old pastoralist niche that has practically disappeared is trade. Banjara caravan traders, often from the Charan caste, led very large caravans of pack oxen from Gujarat to Agra, Delhi, the Punjab, or Sindh. This trade succumbed to the competition of railways and truck transport, and many old trading families are landlords today, for example, in Marwar. Some informants hint at smuggling across the Indo-Pakistani border as the last remaining element of this trade, and the Raikas in Rajasthan are still said to engage in transport where roads are bad or non-existent.

MIDDLE-RANGE MIGRATORY ADAPTATIONS: SEMI-NOMADS

Then there are the Bharwad goatherds of Bhavnagar district—some of whom have cows, but the proportion of bovines is diminishing—who stay in the salty Khar plains along the Gulf of Cambay during the rains, then go by Cambay to winter in the Rajpipla area. These migrations do not involve the whole Bharwad population: some stay close to home, some choose shorter migration routes into the more fertile areas of the district. There are also semi-nomads, living in a village of farmers or in their own hamlets, but leaving during the wet season to find grazing elsewhere. They then effectively exploit the grazing which other transhumant groups have left. Thus there are almost always animals and herdsmen to be seen in the open Saurashtra landscape: but they are not necessarily the same from one season to another.

Like the long-distance nomads, the semi-nomads enter into a variety of contractual agreements with farmers as to grazing and manure. But they wander in small groups, often a couple of brothers or a father and son, with smaller flocks. They are mostly sheep- and goatherds, though some keep cows. Typically, the Maldharis of Surendranagar district—near the Gujarat border—cross into Mehsana or Ahmedabad district towards the end of the dry season, travelling perhaps 100 to 150 km in all. Some Bharwads go farther than that, and the line between 'nomads' and 'semi-nomads' is as fuzzy as most other distinctions I make here.

Fundamental to such migration, of course, is its adaptive value in a dry zone where climatic variations are both radical and unpredictable. Pastoralism, as Rosin puts it, 'stores mobile wealth on hoof, which can be shifted to other areas with adequate grazing and browsing resources'. He also stresses the fundamental role of the livestock fairs in assuring liquidity through redistribution by sale, as well as craft specialization and labour migration to augment or replace income from land and animals (1994: 43).

SETTLED HERDSMEN

All herdsmen do not migrate. Village herdsmen, settled for generations, herd the animals of other castes along with their own, and form part of the local caste system. Such families, most of whom are Bharwads, are found all over the region. They herd sheep, goats or bovines, and for herding the animals of others they receive payment in cash or kind. Another sideline is the sale of dung, either by grazing their animals on the stubble of the dry fields or by selling, in bulk, the mixture of dung and straw from their compounds.[19] Settled pastoral communities seldom specialize in raising camels for sale, but I did meet one such group near Bhildi in north Gujarat.

In certain areas, hamlets of pastoralists cover pockets where no farmers settle. I visited one such hamlet in north Gujarat in the 1970s. This was effectively a small village, with most village institutions, yet essentially a one-caste Bharwad community. They had lands, but were mainly herdsmen, and did not distinguish themselves culturally from Bharwads in other adaptations. Ecologically, theirs was a sector of non-irrigated land surrounded by irrigated villages dominated by the Patidar caste. They were not really poor, though certainly 'backward': yet they had just succeeded in getting their own school, where a young, educated Bharwad was teaching. They had tried other teachers earlier, but none had stayed: the young teacher doubted that anybody but a Bharwad would stay there. For him, it was another matter: he hailed from there.

One of the areas where pastoralists live permanently apart from other people is the Gir forest. These groups participate in the market economy only peripherally. Westphal-Hellbosch (1976) has described a small Charan community here, while I visited a compound of Rabaris. They had arrived recently, by 1986 or 1987, in search of water and grazing, and decided to stay.[20] Of earlier moves, they only told me that they had been 'here and there—everywhere'. Yet the woman who was their spokesman hailed from Marwar, and had married her husband at the annual marriage fair at Jalor. Long-range networks are certainly common among pastoralists in the area, even when settled. Affinal ties clearly have an adaptive function, linking drought-stricken families to places where water and pasture may still be found (Henderson 1994; Rosin 1994).

In 1980, the forest department drove away many pastoralists from the Gir forest, since their presence was thought to contribute to the steady deterioration of the vegetation. This view is debatable (Berwick 1976). The hamlet we saw was part of a subsequent process of resettlement of the forest by pastoralists. There has been, too, an increase of cowherds in the area surrounding the forest, between the cultivated fields and the wood. They must have come from drier areas to profit from the shrinking of the forest, grazing on Forest Department lands on which peasants cannot encroach, an example, in fact, of the new opportunities that deforestation may offer to herdsmen. Generally, Bharwads do not come near the forest with their goats, fearing lions and other wild animals.

Yet another retreat, unsuited to agriculture, is the area around the salty Nal lake on the border of Saurashtra and Gujarat, which has long had a steady population of Charans.[21] It is seen locally as 'badlands', and is relatively inaccessible.[22]

The Barda hills, between Jamnagar and Porbandar, used to offer similar vegetation but this has declined considerably during the last century or so, so that the area no longer functions as a retreat for pastoralists. One well-documented hamlet near this area is Pacchatardi, a Rabari hamlet described in a village monograph of the 1961 census. Pacchatardi may certainly be seen as situated in the *jangal*, though it is on the outskirts of the ruins of Ghumli, a capital of the Jethwa Rajputs until it was destroyed, probably in the thirteenth century. At one time, then, this grazing land must have resulted from depopulation and declining agriculture in the vicinity. Now, the Rabaris have a little land here: they keep buffaloes, cows and goats. In 1960 they were the only Rabari village in the neighbourhood engaged in agriculture. They take their animals into the hills during part of the dry season, but are transhumant rather than migratory.

Then, there are urban Maldharis, living on the outskirts of the towns. They subsist on selling milk to townsmen, grazing their cows on unoccupied land (including parks) as well as buying fodder in the market. This adaptation has become more important these last generations. Some have lately become businessmen, buying milk on the outskirts of town and selling it in their own milk shops.

PASTORAL VOICES: ADAPTING TRADITION TO MODERNITY

In Bhavnagar, I visited a family of such urban pastoralists. They were Bharwads, and owned a small compound, where they had built their own hut of some 8 by 5 m, of two rooms. They were just busy adding an extension, which they would let to other Bharwads. They also owned, the wife told me, a small *pakka* bungalow, with two separate quarters, which they also let to Bharwad families. They had moved here from a nearby village, buying the plot of land: now they had four milch cows, a couple of heifers, and two young calves. The heifers were to be sold, while the calves were raised for later sale. From the cows they sold milk of two different qualities: the half-price variety being an equal mix of milk and water. Most of the fodder for their animals had to be bought in the market: yet they were clearly making a living and even doing quite well. Here, too, networks were widespread: their son was about to marry a girl from 'the Surat side'.

On the road, I met one successful Bharwad milk merchant; I was having trouble problem with my motorcycle as another Yezdi (Jawa) pulled up. This bike was highly customized, and I later learnt to distinguish such mounts as typical of the successful milkmen, among whom the motorcycle has become a symbol of status and individuality, a real cult of the machine. The helpful rider was elegantly dressed in a white cap and wore sunglasses. His father had given up herding in the sixties, to open a milk shop: now his four sons had three such shops between them, located in different towns. But not in Rajkot, he told me: 'the dairy there is too powerful'.

I met sweet-makers in Rajkot who told me they preferred to buy their milk directly from the Bharwads, since they felt the quality was better. I also met one of the technical functionaries of the dairy, Kharvabhai Rathadiya, a Bharwad, and very active. But as he put it: 'The Maldharis have no political clout. Traditional leadership exists, but it is not political. Politicians—all parties—do not care about the Maldharis. Only in the Rabari Sanshod of Mehsana is there proper leadership', he said, citing Bigabhai Rabari as an important leader. Some leaders in Baroda also had his approval. Other Maldharis praised the 'Maldhari Union' in Rajkot, where Rathadiya himself is an active member. When Kharvabhai identified lack of leadership as a main problem of the Maldharis, one felt he was not foreign to the idea that he himself might become such a leader. There is, and has been since the 1960s (Westphal-Hellbosch 1976) a sizeable community of Bharwads in the city, living on their animals. Even then they had a strong caste organization, and this has since expanded considerably. In general, the Bharwads are now a very well-organized community, successfully defending their interests.

According to Rathadiya, Maldharis adjust to new situations singly, on the household or family level. They assess the market for their products and the conditions for production. Panchayats and organizations, he says, deal with customs only; and have no say in economic decisions. 'Sometimes', he says, 'there is a market for 30 kg of milk a day, so you try to have the animals for 30 kg. If the market is diminishing, you try to adjust. If fodder is diminishing, you try to adjust'. He knows of families having other work on the side—and does not think four to five cows (like the herd of the Bhavnagar family mentioned) such a small herd for settled people: 'When there is enough grass and water, they stay: When there is not, they may try to move. All such decisions are taken by single households or kinship clusters. Caste panchayats are very important for customs and maintenance of traditional law: but they never deal with economic matters. Such choices are left entirely to the household.'

He sees individualism as typical of Bharwads: they adjust to settling or not settling, in village or town, migrating or not migrating, choice of migration routes, and since there are no fixed patterns, the question of 'customary rights' is hardly important. All this confirms what Westphal-Hellbosch (1976) and Trivedi (1961) says, that individual families of travelling Bharwads are not known to the villagers.

Rathadiya keeps close to his community in spite of working as an important functionary in a public enterprise. His blend of pastoral and urban culture was even more striking as I visited his beautiful cowstable, where he keeps some animals of selected breeds. This cowstable is open to visitors, and strategically located next to a popular outdoor restaurant on the outskirts of Rajkot. People—from many castes—combine a nice meal with the chance of seeing some fine cows.

READAPTATION AND CRISIS

It seems clear that the traditional pastoral niche, between the desert and the sown, is decreasing in capacity. But are the conditions for all pastoralist adaptations deteriorating? The answer depends not only on natural conditions and traditional ways of life, for adaptations develop constantly, deploying animal husbandry in new ways. Thus as long as the urban market for milk and milk products continues to expand, and as long as fodder is available, we may expect the number (or at least the milk production) of animals to increase. The moot question for the Maldhari communities is a different one: what is the place of the pastoralist communities, with their traditional knowledge of husbandry, in the future development of animal production?

In Rajasthan, many Ahirs and Gujars were forced to settle during the crisis year of 1988, losing or selling most of their flocks. Many have as yet had no chance to recoup their losses, but become part of the village poor, subsisting on temporary labour and their few remaining animals. Yet the critical situation is not something new to the herdsmen of western India, nor is the constant process of readaptation in itself new. For Punjab, Bhattacharya stresses the historical diversity of such processes:

> While pauperized, some nomads took to wage labour, earning small sums by digging canals or building roads. Some became part-time peasants or expanded their cultivation to supplement a declining income. Others concentrated on trading activities. And finally, there were those that continued their earlier pastoral activities even within the new regime where a legal order classified them as vagrants and criminals, forest acts appropriated their grazing grounds, and an expanding agrarian frontier colonized the tracts over which they earlier moved. (1995: 85)

Kavoori (1999), in his study of the herders of Rajasthan, even talks of pastoral expansion. Yet he also notes several points that indicate crisis, such as conflict between sedentary populations and pastoralists, and increasingly negative attitudes to pastoralism among officials and authorities. 'Pastoral interests', says Kavoori, 'are progressively seen as tangential and even contradictory to the priorities of the state' (ibid.: 186). Yet as Bhattacharya puts it, pastoral strategies towards the colonial regime were varied: 'At times, they silently defied the encroaching norms of the new order; at other times they rebelled more openly' (1995: 85). These are subaltern strategies, and open rebellion is no longer relevant or possible. But as we have seen, some pastoralist groups have recently been able to organize as interest groups within the associational framework of modern democracy. One main point of this article, then, is to show that agency rests both with the various factors that intrude on these peripheral adaptations, and with the pastoral populations themselves.

The varied adaptations allow both for 'tradition' and 'modernity'. Most Maldharis are presently involved in processes of change. Having herds in the dry, but above all, unpredictable, climate of western India has always called for strategic innovation in order to survive.[23] Thus many camel nomads of the Rann of Kutch area have switched to cows in recent years, while other pastoralists switch from cows to sheep and goats. The latter move implies shorter migration routes, but traditionally, a response to drought for bovine herders has been to lengthen the migration routes. This was certainly done by some owners of very large herds in the crisis years from 1917-20, when one rich Charan of Marwar took his herds as far as the Punjab, Delhi, and Dwarka in various years.

Recent changes are as much ideological as ecological, as modernist criteria of 'civilization', following on from colonial ideas, vie for hegemony with reinvented tradition. The first tends to exclude pastoralists while the second celebrates their cultural contribution. Basically, we observe two opposed strategies: the humble Bharwads are forging a new place for themselves inside 'civilized' society, symbolically hinting at their connections with the *jangal*, while the proud Rabaris find themselves squeezed between marginalization and proletarization. But the place of the pastoralist as an integral figure in the region's self-image has not yet disappeared, so pastoralists may still hope to avoid being excluded from the consideration of the region's future.

The Bharwads, in clear contrast to the Rabaris, have been willing and able to adapt to change. They exploit the growing market for milk and milk products in town; and their other traditional activity, making and selling woollen blankets, seems to be expanding. They have also been able to exploit a secondary effect of irrigation and intensified agriculture: the increasing demand for manure.

Traditionally, animals grazed on the stubble and their manure was left to the farmer. In 1991, however, I found some farmers providing fodder—nicely laid out in the fields—to get manure. I also heard of farmers—in the intensively cultivated region of central Gujarat—paying for manure, as well as providing grazing facilities.

Some Bharwads have engaged in reforming the image of their caste: they are the 'blue Bharwads' whose men have adopted a uniform dark blue dress, accompanied by Vaishnavism, vegetarianism and other Sanskritizing touches. This style sets them apart from other Daghlabhai and underlines the quest for a new and different identity. I met blue Bharwads mainly in southern Saurashtra in the early 1990s, but the movement may have spread since then.

Why are the Bharwads better able than the nomadic Rabaris to exploit new possibilities? I think the answer lies in the flexibility of Bharwad organization. A small flock of sheep and goats, herded by a couple of men, can use one field at a time, even if small; it can easily shift to the next village whenever there is a demand for manure there. Rabaris, travelling with a hundred or more cows, need a large part of the village lands, at one and the same time. Their negotiating position is critical, in that cows may become too feeble to walk or even die if grazing is not available quickly and in quantity. Small flocks of sheep and goats, on the other hand, need only limited grazing, are satisfied with fodder of inferior quality, and may, for shorter periods, subsist on roadside grazing. For the Rabaris, the need to negotiate may itself be new; in north and central Gujarat they used to have standing agreement with villages (not individual farmers) which they visited every year.

The crisis of 1991 pointed to a very specific problem. The Rabaris from Kutch were able to get through towards central Gujarat, and there was grazing farther south, towards Rajpipla: the main problem was to get through the 'corridor' through central Gujarat north of Cambay. Here, irrigation and intensified agriculture has considerably reduced the grazing available. The main difference between the situation that Kavoori (1999) describes for Rajasthan where there are alternative routes, and this one, is that in Gujarat, most routes of migration pass through the central Gujarat corridor, which cannot be avoided.

In 1991, the crisis was partially alleviated by charity, providing 'fodder depots' in the towns. Such depots—possibly organized by co-operative means—might constitute a solution to the problem, replacing the former contractual agreements with farmers. Another possible solution might lie in transporting animals by truck across the corridor, as was widely done during the 1987-8 crisis in Rajasthan (Kavoori 1999: 105-7). Yet this transport was largely financed by the wool merchants, who had a vested interest in maintaining the supply of this commodity. It is not immediately obvious that similar finance can be found for those who herd cows and camels, whose products are not similarly integrated into a structured market organization. This may, indeed, be one more factor that pushes pastoralists towards sheep rather than bovines.

During 1990-1, the plight of the cowherds and their animals provoked political debate in Gujarat. In spite of attempts—by the state as well as the local authorities—to provide relief, the BJP opposition accused the state government (Congress) of letting 3,000 cows die. In a traditionalist state where cow-protection is a political slogan, the situation was grave. This debate, however, brought the pastoralists firmly into the political picture in Gujarat, while—according to my accounts—the role of the Rajasthan authorities has been rather passive.[24] Even in Gujarat, however, the voices calling for support to pastoralists were not their own but those of their political advocates, as the BJP then lost no occasion to criticize the government. The BJP in Rajastan does not seem to have had similar need of the pastoralists.

CONCLUSION

The regional system, then, includes a wide range of adaptations, tending to blur distinctions between 'nomadism', 'transhumance' and 'sedentary adaptations'. Many herdsmen make their living from a combination of these different activities. In Swidler's terms, we find examples of 'dichotomized economies' co-existing with 'mixed' and 'intersecting' ones (1980: 22-30), with differential distribution as to caste and sub-region. In a long-time perspective, there is certainly an overall trend towards sedentarization, but the pastoralists' responses are various, and clearly indicates that their agency, too, must be taken into account. This variation is important not only as between groups: individuals of all castes are busy developing and evaluating strategies to counter the various aspects of the crisis. We can only hope, of course, that these will be successful and not thwarted by the bias towards agriculture that generally dominates official policy.

Barth (1964) has produced one of the most sophisticated analyses of a pastoral adaptation in his work on the Basseri of southern Iran. Among the Basseri, insufficient stock leads pastoralists to settle as village herdsmen and labourers, while those who amass excessive pastoral capital prefer to buy land, thus becoming landowners. Western India, however, unlike the Basseri environment, is not typically a dichotomized economy (Swidler, op. cit.). Thus the 'failure and fall-away' model, which Salzman (1980) identifies with Barth's work on the Basseri may be relevant in some cases, but the variety of possible strategies imply that it is difficult to fix upper and lower 'threshold levels' of herd size—as Barth does for the Basseri—unless restricted to a very particular group and place. And while individuals or couples take up sedentary occupations—such as when Rabaris serve as watchmen in Dhrangadhra district—we know little about whether, or how, such caste members collaborate economically with kin who still follow their herds. Rosin indicates that they do so in the Aravallis (1994: 43). It is likely but insufficiently documented that there are feedbacks on investment and support from the sedentary to the pastoral adaptation, which further complicates generalizations.[25]

It seems clear, then, that any adequate analysis of these processes must be on the 'adaptation and response' model, as Salzman puts it (1980: 14),[26] stressing 'the options available to actors and the institutionalized resources that largely define the options and make them possible' (ibid.). While ignoring neither ecological crisis nor coercive processes of a political or economic nature, the flexibility of this model enables it to explain the great variety of responsive strategies and adaptations.

The present crisis for the pastoralists is serious, but does not affect the different adaptations and communities equally. The future of camel nomadism may be in danger, and for groups like the Kutchi Rabaris, it is becoming harder to move long distances with the flocks. While there is a danger that long-range nomadism may disappear from western India, the semi-settled and settled 'milkmen' have been able to benefit from new possibilities. The Bharwads, especially, have been able to take advantage of this opportunity by market-based, urban husbandry and through the milk trade. But they compete, here, with groups that traditionally have been peasants. Future success for the Maldharis depends on their capacity for adaptation and readjustment, which favours those groups where decisions have been taken on the household level rather than collectively. Yet at the same time, the need for interest organizations stress the usefulness of caste solidarity and a conscience of cultural distinction, for even in the market economy, the image of the Maldhari is that of the specialist in husbandry and animal production. As long as this image is effective, there is hope that Maldhari traditions may survive and thrive.

NOTES

1. The study on which this report is based was financed by grants from the Norwegian Fund for General Research (NAVF) and from the Nordic Institute for Asian Studies, Copenhagen. Fieldwork was done during the winters 1989-90 and 1990-1, a total of six months. Other, earlier fieldwork periods (1973-4, 1979-80) contribute some of the context for this paper.
2. This information concerns the western part of Jodhpur district.
3. Her study does not include the Ahirs, but other sources (such as Enthoven, 1920-2) unanimously hold that the Ahirs were already there when the other pastoral castes arrived. The earliest myths about Charans of the peninsula are those of the goddess Khodiyar, claimed as coeval with the fall of the Vallabhi kingdom (eighth century AD). Tod placed their arrival in Kutch in the same century (1829, I: 84). The myth of Avad, Khodiyar's 'sister', gives the ninth century for their arrival in Rajasthan. Thus the Charans probably arrived in the region before the year 1000, which is the date given by Westphal-Hellbosch for the arrival

of the Rabaris in Marwar. From there, they came to Saurashtra some time between AD 1100 and 1400 (1974: 303-4). Bharwad legends tell us that in 961, they came to Banaskantha in north Gujarat, sheltering from the Muslim invasions of Sindh. Later they came to Chotila in central Saurashtra: the various groups of the peninsula spread out from there.

4. This, it seems to me, follows if we accept Kosambi's view, that the Maurya empire and its successors were based on trade.
5. A mark of blood, which comes from the finger of the person thus enthroning the king.
6. Elsewhere in Rajasthan, Mina tribesmen or Jat pastoralists were also found performing this ritual at the chief's investiture. (Tod 1957, II: 141; Saxena 1964).
7. Similar alliances between king and tribe are found in Orissa, but here the tribal who placed the *tika* was sometimes sacrificed, becoming the king's 'chosen' deity *(ista devata)*. See Kulke 1978, Carrin 2005.
8. *Ter tanṣali* literally means 'thirteen bowls' and implies interdining.
9. The *odhani* is a shawl which covers the head and reaches below the waist. The black shawl of the Ahir women is said to be worn in mourning for Krishna, though their skirts are red. The opposite combination—red shawl and black skirt—is worn by Bharwad and Rabari women, again with detail differences.
10. *Jangli* is a term used to mean uncivilized, a 'hillbilly'.
11. British writers seem to have wondered whether they were to be called castes or tribes.
12. Often translated as 'milkmen'. Another gloss is from *mal*—goods, property, capital, in this case animals; and *dhari*, holders, owners: thus, those who have animals as their main property.
13. The 1819 earthquake may have been instrumental in the formation of these phenomena.
14. Kavoori (1999: 151-2) refers to exaggerated claims, from the Madhya Pradesh government, that the forests of Gujarat and Rajasthan have disappeared due to overgrazing. While the cause is very much in doubt, there is no doubt that extensive forest tracts have vanished, in Saurashtra at any rate, since the early twentieth century, and local informants tend to assert that the decline has been much faster since the disappearance of the princely states, as do Gold's informants in Rajasthan (1999).

15. Kavoori provides detailed grazing itineraries from his observation, in 1987-8, of migrations across the Rajasthan-Haryana border. My information is far more superficial, but in both cases, the importance of prospecting in advance and concocting a migratory strategy for each herd is evident.
16. This is what emerges from my observations. Kavoori, however, shows that for western Rajasthan, pastoral migrations increase in dry years and then return to their pre-drought level (1999: 66-77).
17. Formerly, camels were much more numerous than they are today.
18. Sometimes, as Rangnekar (1993) shows for Gujarat, these traditional relationships continue in the form of contracts specifying the herd in question, the number of animals, and the length of grazing time. While such contracts may solve the problem in specific places at a given time (Kavoori 1999: 102-3), they do tend to restrict the herdsmen's choice of itinerary.
19. That such arrangements are of long standing and common in other parts of India, is shown by papers of the Revenue and Agriculture Dept. of Forests, for February 1875, B, nos. 47-50, cited by Rangarajan 1996: 68. According to these papers, agriculturists in Chanda, Seoni and Wardha (central India) paid as much as Re. 1 to Rs. 4 a night for 12 *kundies* of sheep manure.
20. Some sources indicate that the buffalo herdsmen of the Gir forest move around. These people, however, like the Charans Westphal-Hellbosch visited, were staying in their hamlet permanently.
21. These salty lands are probably another result of the rising land mass, indicating that the sea—or salt marshes like the present Rann—once separated Saurashtra from the mainland.
22. I have found no recent information on them, and the roads there were so bad that I gave up going there on my motorcycle, which broke down. The Charan pastoralists are certainly still there, however.
23. As both Fisher (1997) and Kavoori (1999), show for western Rajasthan, agriculturists having settled herds tend to adopt migration as a survival strategy in years of drought.
24. Kavoori stresses the negative attitude to pastoralists of the Madhya Pradesh authorities, but while he stresses helpful initiatives on the part of the lower ranks of the Rajasthan bureucracy (notably the Department of Sheep and Wool), he also implies that higher authorities of that state are largely neutral in their attitude (1999: 161).
25. Kavoori (1999) certainly feels there is considerable collaboration

between settled and migratory households within the context of the joint family, and his material from western Rajasthan to some extent substantiates this hypothesis.

26. The Indian situation hardly fits what Salzman (1980: 11) calls either the 'drought and decline', the 'defeat and degradation' or the 'failure and fall-away' model. The 'defeat and degradation' model, which implies forcible settlement by the authorities, has, generally speaking, little relevance in this region.

REFERENCES

Amarji, R. (1882), *Tarikh-i-Sorath,* Bombay: Education Society's Press.

Barth, F. (1964), *Nomads of South Persia,* Oslo: Universitetsforlaget.

Berwick, S. (1976), 'The Gir Forest: An Endangered Ecosystem', *American Anthropologist,* 64: 28-40.

Bhattacharya, N. (1995), 'Pastoralists in a Colonial World', in D. Arnold and R. Guha (eds.), *Nature, Culture, Imperialism: Essays on the Environmental History of South Asia,* Delhi: Oxford University Press.

Carrin, Marine (2005), 'Le sacrifice humain dans les royaumes de jungle', in J.P. Albert and B. Miclant-Reynes (eds.), *La sacrifice humain en Égypte ancienne et ailleurs,* Paris: Editions Soleb, 190-211.

Census of India (1961) vol. V, part VI, no. 1: *Village Survey Monograph: Village Pacchatardi,* Ahmedabad: Superintendent of Census Operations, Gujarat.

Enthoven, R.E. (1920-2), *Tribes and Castes of Bombay* (3 vols); rpt. 1975, Delhi: Cosmo.

Fisher, R.J. (1997), *If Rain Doesn't Come: An Anthropological Study of Drought and Human Ecology in Western Rajasthan,* Delhi: Manohar.

Gold, A.G. (1999), 'From Wild Pigs to Foreign Trees: Oral Histories of Environmental Change in Rajasthan', in S. Toft Madsen (ed.), *State, Society and the Environment in South Asia,* Richmond, Surrey: Curzon.

Haynes, E.S. (1998), 'The Natural and the Raj: Customary State Systems and Environmental Management in Pre-integration Rajasthan and Gujarat', in R.H. Grove, V. Damodaran and S. Sangwan (eds.), *Nature and the Orient: The Environmental History of South and South-East Asia,* Delhi: Oxford University Press, pp. 734-92.

Henderson, C. (1994), 'Famines and Droughts in Western Rajasthan: Desert Cultivators and Periodic Resource Stress', in K. Schomer, J.L. Erdman, D.O. Lodrick and L.I. Rudolph (eds.), *The Idea of Rajasthan,* vol. II, Columbia, Mo.: South Asia Publications, pp. 1-29.

Kavoori, P.S. (1999), *Pastoralism in Expansion: The Transhuming Herders of Western Rajasthan*, Delhi: Oxford University Press.

Kolff, D. (1991), *Naukar, Rajput and Sepoy*, Cambridge: Cambridge University Press.

Kulke, H. (1978), 'Royal Temple Policy and the Structure of Medieval Hindu Kingdoms' in A. Eschmann, H. Kulke and G.C. Tripathi (eds.), *The Cult of Jagannath and the Regional Tradition of Orissa*, Delhi: Manohar, pp. 125-37.

Malhotra, S.P. (1977), 'Socio-Demographic Factors and Nomadism in the Arid Rajasthan', in P.L. Jaiswal (ed.), *Desertification and its Control*, Delhi: Indian Council of Agricultural Research.

Mayer, A.C. (1958), 'The Dominant Caste in a Region of Central India', *Southwestern Journal of Anthropology*, 14: 407-27.

——(1960), *Caste and Kinship in Central India: A Village and its Region*, London: Routledge & Kegan Paul.

Pocock, D.F. (1972), *Kanbi and Patidar*, Oxford: Clarendon.

Qanungo, K.R. (1969), *Studies in Rajput History*, Delhi: S. Chand.

Rangarajan, M. (1996), *Fencing the Forest: Conservation and Ecological Change in India's Central Provinces, 1860-1914*, Delhi: Oxford University Press.

Rangnekar, S. (1993), 'Traditional Livestock Production Systems Among Pastoralists: Their Perceptions of the Production Systems and Attitudes to Change', in R. Cincotta and G. Pangare (eds.), *Pastoralism and Pastoral Migration in Gujarat*, Anand: IMRA.

Rosin, E. Thomas (1994), 'Locality and Frontier: Securing Livelihood in the Aravalli Zone of Central Rajasthan', in K. Schomer, J.L. Erdman, D.O. Lodrick and L.I. Rudolph (eds.), *The Idea of Rajasthan*, vol. II, Columbia, Mo.: South Asia Publications, pp. 30-63.

Salzman, P.C. (1980), 'Introduction: Processes of Sedentarization as Adaptation and Response', in Salzman (ed.), 1980, pp. 1-19.

———, (ed.) (1980), *When Nomads Settle*, New York: Praeger.

Saxena, R.P. (1964), *Tribal Economy in Central India*, Calcutta: KLM.

Skaria, A. (1999), *Hybrid Histories: Forests, Frontiers and Wildness in Western India*, Delhi: Oxford University Press.

Srinivas, M.N. (1952), *Religion and Society Among the Coorgs*, Oxford: Oxford University Press.

Swidler, N. (1980), 'Sedentarization and Modes of Economic Integration in the Middle East', in Salzman (ed.), 1980, pp. 21-33.

Tambs-Lyche, H. (1991), 'Le roi et les enfants de la déesse', *Cahiers de Littérature Orale*, 29, pp. 61-85.

———(1996a), 'Réflexions sur les mythes de fondation des royaumes

Rajput', in N. Revel and C. Champion (eds.), *Les littératures de voix: les épopées: les rites de fondation,* Paris: Centre de Recherche sur l'Oralité/ INALCO, pp. 37-54.

———(1996b), 'Une tradition orale face au postmodernisme: l'exemple des bardes de Saurashtra', in C. Champion (ed.), *Traditions orales dans le Monde Indien,* Purusartha 18, pp. 23-37.

———(1997), *Power, Profit and Poetry: Traditional Society in Kathiawar, Western India,* Delhi: Manohar.

———(2002), 'Townsmen, Tenants and Tribes: War, Wildness and Wilderness in the Traditional Politics of Western India', in D.K. Behera and G. Pfeffer (eds.), *Contemporary Society: Tribal Studies,* vol. 5, Delhi: Concept, pp. 186-207.

———(2003), 'Koli, Rajput, Kanbi, Patidar: revendications identitaires au Gujarat, hier et aujourd'hui', in M. Carrin and C. Jaffrelot (eds.), *Castes et Tribus: Résistance et Autonomie Dans la Société Indienne,* Purusartha 23, Paris: EHESS, pp. 265-96.

———(2004), *The Good Country: Individual, Situation and Society in Saurashtra,* Delhi: Manohar.

Tod, J. (1829), *Annals and Antiquities of Rajasthan,* vol. I, rpt. 1950, London: Routledge & Kegan Paul.

———(1832), *Annals and Antiquities of Rajasthan,* vol. II, rpt. 1957, London: Routledge & Kegan Paul.

Trivedi, H.B. (1961), *The Mers of Saurashtra,* Baroda: M.S. University.

Watson, J.W. (ed.) 1884, *Gazetteer of the Bombay Presidency,* vol. VIII: Kathiawar, Bombay: Government Central Press.

Westphal-Hellbosch, S. and H. Westphal (1974), *Hinduistische Viehzüchter im Nordwestlichen Indien,* I: *Die Rabari,* Berlin: Duncker und Humboldt.

———(1976), *Hinduistische Viehzüchter im Nordwestlichen Indien,* II: *Die Bharwad und die Charan,* Berlin: Duncker und Humboldt.

Wilberforce, Bell, H., 1916, *A History of Kathiawad from the Earliest Times,* London: Heinemann.

2

Bondo Violence

GEORG PFEFFER

CONFRONTED BY TRIBES

A few years ago, the late Roger Keesing recalled various forms of tribal resistance against 'processes of cultural destruction and Westernization' in Melanesian mountain regions. He saw peripheral people 'as active agents in shaping and controlling their engagement with the outside world' (1992: 2). The present paper will similarly, for an Indian region, describe active and controlling tribal agents, though their conspicuous violence is directed against external as well as internal opposites. It is a way of life, and as such a given form of resistance to administrative order, not just a summation of planned activities against outsiders who have lost themselves in the infertile mountains of 'remote' Orissa, a province called 'backward' by most other Indians.

I will introduce this Bondo case and, at the same time, promise not to subject them to further research efforts in the future, since the most relevant resistance of these hill people is exercised against my fellow anthropologists. Apart from this ambivalent Bondo role as objects of ethnographers, I shall also discuss their problematic contacts with government agencies, with immigrant caste people of the plains, and with other 'Scheduled Tribes' of hilly middle India. Furthermore, I shall try to evaluate the influence of the regular short-term visitors from other continents of the globe who have begun to transform Bondo existence into a commodity on the global market and who may be the initiators of long-term social changes.

Initially, questions of terminology cannot be avoided. Several reasons of political and academic correctness have almost completely removed the word 'tribe' from anthropological literature, the first one arising in an evolutionist debate (Fried 1965/6). Other authors noticed fuzzy tribal boundaries in Africa (Helm 1968) and a third section of critics terminated the tribal epoch with the birth of post-colonial African states (Gutkind 1970). Finally, the most far-reaching opposition may be that of the post-modern trend against any form of 'essentialization'. Concepts of tribe or caste have become discarded by an anthropology that is concerned with individual intentions and the literary style of authored texts rather than ethnography (e.g. Pels and Salemink 1999). However, beyond these textual documents, but not necessarily in contradiction to them, anyone can witness how the people of Orissa are explicitly and implicitly classifying themselves, and each other, according to certain supra-individual, obligatory and inter-generational criteria of the systematic kind. In a marketplace, in a hospital, or in a factory, the values of such specific socio-cultural systems can be discerned by anyone willing to accept ideologies beyond our familiar individualism and beyond our encompassing criterion of the political economy.

Finally, the Indian constitution provides 'protective discrimination' for nominated 'Scheduled Tribes' thus, as a compromise, the academic opponents of the term may be willing to accept the Indian administrative 'tribe' as a regional gloss or a folkloristic expression,[1] but then I would not be willing to follow this line. In the anthropological domain, the tribe should be defined by its specific features:

> The tribal structure is generalized; in this lies its primitiveness. It lacks an independent economic sector or a separate religious organization, let alone a special political mechanism. . . . The social system . . . becomes weaker where it is greater: the degree of integration decreases as the level of organization increases, and degrees of sociability diminish as fields of social relations broaden. (Sahlins 1968: 15-16)

In this context, the 'familial mode of production' (ibid.: 75) leaves the household as the only relevant economic unit. Thus members of a tribe or a major segment never unite as corporate entities in a joint action. Social cooperation beyond the village level, being of the precarious kind, requires sustained efforts. Thus the undifferentiated socio-religious complex is substantial on the local level only. Given these systematic preconditions, I maintain that Bondo violence cannot be reduced to individual idiosyncrasies or developmental dialectics.[2]

The Bondo became famous through Elwin's *Bondo Highlander* of 1950, where we can read about the violent ways of this tribe. In 1941, its homicide rate was among the highest of the world (Elwin 1950: 234). Applying the ethnic singular, the author's preface elaborates how 'the Bondo is a difficult person and his is a hard unyielding country' (ibid.: vii). Until today the five to six thousand Bondo have not been pacified. Few changes have taken place in their natural environment, the Bondo Hills of the old Koraput or the new Malkangiri district of Orissa on the border to the province of Andhra Pradesh. Bondo social contacts, however, experience new dimensions. My paper will try to show that *no crisis* has, as yet, threatened the Bondo existence in spite of the intrusion of powerful external groups at the concrete and at the symbolic level. We can speculate about future consequences of such transformations and conceive their long-term negative effects, in case we are inclined to favour peoples' self-determination. In case we would prefer a kind of education or progress towards our own or the Hindu way of life,[3] we might, as many observers do, interpret the same changes as a positive development in the struggle against 'backwardness'. For the time being, the situation as such and the symptomatic response of the Bondo will be described.

On 24 February 2000, I strolled around the weekly market of a place, we may call Chalanput. Tribal Bondo, both women and men, were the most conspicuous visitors of this *hat.* On every Thursday the women come down from their villages in the Bondo Hills carrying baskets full of rape seed on their heads, to be sold to Telugu or Oriya middlemen, just as the women try to earn a little money by selling self-made brooms and winnowing fans to petty hawkers. The bazaar was started in the 1970s and the Bondo women have only very gradually, year by year, given up some of their initial hesitation to speak to non-Bondo people. Their most important item to be sold at the weekly market is palm-wine or *salap*, tapped in the forested mountains and carried down on the narrow jungle paths in heavy brass pots, to be offered to a mixed crowd in a strange new settlement that had sprung up in the 1960s.

The customers belong to the various categories of the indigenous population or to a similar variety of immigrants from the plains who live at Chalanput. All of these castes and tribes are represented by males and females who simultaneously may be both buyers and sellers on the weekly market. Along with the wine, the Bondo women bring smaller quantities of brandy, produced out of the fruits of the *mahua* tree (*Bassia latifolia,* Gartn.). Moving in a row downhill, the women with the heavy brass pots on their heads leave their villages at sunrise. By 10 o'clock they reach the *hat* and at 12 o'clock most customers are very tipsy.

A Bondo man does not carry a heavy burden. His head is free, since he carries bow and arrows in his hands and a dagger, or a sword of about 70 cm in length, is tied around his waist. All Bondo men are lean and not taller than about 160 cm. Only younger men, or boys, move downhill to the weekly market. Since they are in search for brides, they have oiled their hair and pierced their ears with ornamental rings like the kids of Berlin. Moreover they have drawn charcoal around their eyes and decorated their hair with a number of colourful plastic combs.

The market is an opportunity for initial contacts with potential brides. In a somewhat robust manner, the male teenagers of the tribe tend to flirt with the Bondo women who, as ideal marriage partners, would be their seniors by about five years. A man or even a boy may be married to several women, the latter outnumbering Bondo males by a ratio of about two-to-one. Everywhere in India, as a major contrast to the male majority among each of the many castes, tribal women outnumber the men of their category, but the two-to-one majority of the Bondo is unique. It must be due to the male mortality rate. Bondo men tend to get killed by other men of the tribe. Furthermore, the violence of the Bondo men is not applied to Bondo women.

If the male mode of flirtation is robust, the females will not be intimidated, even though they must be tired after carrying the brass pots of wine for five hours across uneven terrain. A female neck and both arms are guarded with heavy brass-rings which may be used as weapons against any frivolous approach. The Bondo women, in other words, do know how to handle male molestation, just as they have learnt the art of haggling with strangers on the market and will not sell their goods under value.

ON BEING ETHNOGRAPHIC OBJECTS

On Thursday, 24 February, I had just arrived from Germany by 12 o'clock to meet Peter Berger and others at the *hat* and to have a drink or two while standing in the crowded open marketplace along with friends of former years belonging to all sorts of socio-religious categories. A British couple casually joined us for a round, avoiding a lengthy introduction. They smelled of anthropology. Without much success, the two were eager to make friends with any Bondo they could meet. Drinking at high noon seemed to offer such opportunities, as social distinctions had been overcome along with the gradual rise of spirits towards the climax of the market day.

Later we learnt that the couple had left Chalanput within 24 hours. On their own, they had moved up into the hills to return two days later, enriched by the characteristic experience. Their ethnographic rapport had been of the limited kind. Bondo men had thoroughly searched the British rucksacks to take all money and anything else of use. On top of it, the tribesmen had threatened the couple physically and, by the help of obvious gesticulations, instructed them to leave the hills for good. The visitors did remove themselves from the area without reporting to the police station some 20 km away from Chalanput, since the officer in charge, being unable to guarantee the foreigners' safety, had earlier explicitly prohibited any tour into the hills.

This was not my first experience of that kind. Having come to the Chalanput area since 1980, I had witnessed some European ethnographic expedition or the other that had almost every year failed in attempts to contact the Bondo, while year after year the hillmen's response to the intrusions was marked by increased aggression. My own failures to make Bondo friends had usually been topped by more dramatic experiences of colleagues who had moved into Bondoland on their own. To my knowledge, no ethnographer had lost his life and no injuries had been suffered, but over the years I had seen German, French, and Dutch anthropologists being eased of their material possessions and, thereafter, being recommended to stay away.

In January 1981, I had been able to have several meetings with two sober Bondo who were on their return from a five-year term in jail. With the help of their Dombo clients, they were purchasing gifts and liquor for the party they were expected to throw in their village. In jail the Bondo men had not been altogether unhappy, with food and tobacco in daily supply and relatively little workload to shoulder. They had become socially polluted, however. Anywhere in tribal middle India, regular contact with outsiders is considered to be polluting for a tribesman who must then be purified by a feast for the home community. Similar caste customs may indeed have arisen due to the tribal influence. Anyhow, my Bondo contacts at that time were eager to get home and happy to describe to me the conditions they had been missing for such a long time.

Later I had gone to the hills with a Muslim who had elaborate ties of 'bond-brotherhood'[4] among the tribesmen of the Bondo Hills. He was a craftsman at the bazaar of Chalanput and his family regularly hosted Bondo women and men, if these visitors could not avoid spending the night at a strange place. Contrary to the usual attitude, my guide had no inhibitions in treating his guests from the hills with ordinary hospitality. The Bondo in turn had come to trust him and seek his help when in difficulties, while he, being a man of very limited means, would regularly tour the hills to enjoy free rounds of liquor. When I arrived there in his company, we were treated decently, but nobody asked us to stay.

The religion of my guide is worth mentioning, since Muslims, originating from several south Indian states, had little hesitation in eating and communicating with the local tribesmen, whereas Hindus stood aloof. Some Muslims, generally, if mistakenly, called 'Pathan', had married and converted Gadaba women before settling down for good at marketplaces. Others, undoubtedly to their own advantage, were the major buyers of tribal products. I met just one Hindu living with a Gadaba mistress[5] while others occasionally employed tribal workers in their gardens, but generally the distance they kept was obvious.

In later years my Muslim friend, for good reasons, refused to take along any outsiders, since the hill men had openly declined to communicate with strangers. During the last week of my 1996 visit, however, he introduced me to a young Bondo at the *hat* who was willing to spend many hours with me at Chalanput, communicating freely. I invited him for meals and provided him with a much-coveted shirt, whereas he in turn elaborated the details of the relationship terminology and similar ethnographic stuff.[6] Both he and his comrade were polite and communicative, looking forward to my visit advertised for the following year. At that time, however, he was no longer available, because he was serving a long-term prison sentence. Having quarrelled with another Bondo on a market morning, he had to suffer an unknown immigrant's effort to make peace. In an instantaneous reaction, my informant had stabbed to death the self-appointed arbitrator. This kind of aggression may be seen as typical in relation to outsiders, since a Bondo would never try to mediate in a conflict. Furthermore, as Elwin (1950) has shown in many passages of his book, premeditated murder is quite uncommon.

After this episode, I have never again had the opportunity to befriend Bondo informants, nor have I made any efforts. Social anthropologists were and are the first to go for these tribal people, but the latter—both male and female—do not want to be anthropologized and throw out would-be-Elwins, relieving them of their cash in the course of the proceedings. Nobody would be robbed under ordinary conditions. The loss of a filled wallet is seen as the price for earlier inquisitiveness. Perhaps the Bondo sense anthropologists to be the first to analyse and publicize the specific way of life in the Hills. The principals are not at all keen on any such publicity, and it is time that we research enthusiasts took note of this intention.

We should also realize that ethnographic publications have indeed been the reason for existential changes among the subjects of the tribal monographs. Perhaps the most annoying case has been the stream of Western visitors to the Muria Gond in Bastar, eager to peep into the youth dormitories of Elwin's 'Kingdom of the Young' (1947).[7] Geographically not quite as exposed when compared to the Muria, the Bondo, exceptional by their baldness, their dress, their violence and their female seniority in marriage, have experienced similar reactions due to their ethnographic fame.

THE ETHNOGRAPHERS

Christoph von Fürer-Haimendorf (1943) had been their first professional guest. During his only visit in April/May of 1941 he had investigated into their memorial feasts for the dead and examined the megalithic constructions connected with these rituals, both being the standard subjects of the central European, particularly the Viennese, blend of 'Voelkerkunde' and prehistory. It should be mentioned that this pioneer, in not much more than a week, but before roads and bazaars had been constructed in the region, was the only ethnographer to find out anything about these Bondo rituals.

Von Fürer-Haimendorf being Elwin's friend, his short paper may have encouraged the latter's series of excursions from December 1943 onwards until 1945. This former Anglican pastor had given up his service and eventually his Christian faith, joined the Congress movement and taken up the tribal cause in many monographs and pamphlets against the British.[8] During the 1940s, he had been appointed 'Honorary Anthropologist to the Government of Orissa' and moved into the hills along with his Gond wife, his infant son, a number of friends and fellow amateur-explorers, as well as a police escort. In the course of these tours, his family was occasionally threatened. Ethnographic sailing was far from smooth. Since the fieldwork material was perhaps not quite satisfactory, Elwin, in later years, concentrated upon the life-histories of long-term inmates of the Koraput jail (see 1945). The prisoners must have been more becoming and sober informants. Given these conditions, the monograph on the *Bondo Highlander* (1950) was full of crucial observations. However, Elwin deliberately shunned academic anthropology. He ignored the standard functionalist publications of his time and had probably even declined to read them. The book on the Bondo offers fascinating stories and observations as well as the amateur psychology of a well-read Oxford don.[9] Unanswered was the omnipresent question: 'Why all that violence?' Later publications on the Bondo are not worth mentioning, but reference to Bikram Narayan Nanda's work cannot be avoided. It was accepted for a Ph.D. dissertation by Keele University in the U.K. and published by Sage in 1994. The thesis, filled with Marxist jargon, reproduces some of the known ethnographic details supplemented by juicy passages on sexuality. Such stuff is the very opposite of Elwin's ethnography or the observations of anyone else who has ever done serious fieldwork in tribal middle India.

Nanda's fantasies make him invent an 'Austro-Asiatic culture' of what he chooses to call 'early tribal and peasant producers' somehow linked to the 'well-known erotic sculptures . . . at Khajurao and Konarak' (1994: 25), i.e. medieval temples at a geographical distance of many hundred kilometres. In the course of his book he takes any opportunity to add statements like: 'the normal restraints that check gender relationships are largely forgotten; members of the same clan and relatives of forbidden degree are free to flirt, excite themselves with unrestricted interaction and, occasionally, even retire together in the woods' (ibid. 1994: 30).

All of this is nonsense. Even apart from the lewd passages, readers familiar with tribal India would be bound to notice numerous fantastic statements in Nanda's monograph. A general review would come to the following judgement: Whatever is credible in it, is not original, and whatever is original, is not credible. The inventions do, however, contain a certain unintended realism.

Immigrants from the plains[10] are baffled to see the women and men of the Koraput tribes dressed differently, communicating freely, and dancing together openly, when meeting during certain festivals or markets. The gossip among the immigrants from the plains is, of course, much concerned about an alleged 'primitive promiscuity'. One hears of elopements and the like and interprets these customs by the socio-cultural logic of the dominant plains people. The prudish caste ideology would induce wild and mistaken assumptions among immigrant young men who are usually taller and more outspoken than their tribal counterparts. Such misjudgements would furthermore lead these youngsters to molest and rape tribal women or commit open aggression under the guise of the annual Holi celebrations and similar pretences. Such a version of male violence is unknown to the 'savage' Bondo men, but these little fighters have been known to defend their women. Contrary to the fate of other indigenous females, Bondo women are not molested, if we ignore Nanda's dissertation.

IMMIGRANTS AND TRIBES

Who are the immigrant settlers, and who are the different tribes of the old Koraput district? The plainsmen are workers of several industrial plants located in the tribal region, such as the paper mills close to those eucalyptus plantations that have long since substituted the indigenous species of trees. Far away in the remote area of the province, connected by three or four roads in a vast area and beyond the control of the normal administration, such mills may pollute the environment, particularly the drinking water of the villagers, to an unlimited extent.

The particular site of Chalanput will, for obvious reasons, not be described in detail, but the immigrants witness rather similar conditions in all of these industrial projects. The officers managing such establishments, along with their families, move into company-houses graded by status, whereas the workers, mostly single men of all age categories, live in shabby tin-quarters. These labourers spend their money in bazaars like those of Chalanput where shopkeepers of all Indian regions and religions offer the small amenities of life, including liquor and women, on an open or a fairly open market.

Once such a colony of plainsmen has been established in the wilderness, schools and offices must follow. Since the early 1980s tribal land-ownership has been individualized and numerous scribes of the registration offices must see to it that the new owners pay revenue and extra-legal commissions. Cash crop plantations for coffee and cashew-nuts are run by officials and leased out to competent salesmen who are able to misappropriate the land, the government subsidies, and whatever other benefits are spilt into the 'backward' area.

Various kinds of development agencies also show up. In a village of the Bondo Hills, the major Gandhian organization has stationed an *opa* (i.e. paternal aunt), an impressive elderly lady leaning towards moral and material cleanliness, who is supposed to educate the Bondo by displaying the joys of a vegetarian diet and a celibate life. Her wards seem to have noticed the genuine conviction of the lady and hold her in great respect, even if they do not follow the lifestyle she is advocating.

Furthermore, a Special Officer of the Orissa Administrative Service has been appointed to head the Bondo Development Agency since the 1970s. The latter has a considerable budget to remove Bondo 'backwardness', so the officer's post in the malaria-infested hills is a prized position. Twelve tribes of Orissa, among them the Bondo, have been declared 'Primitive Tribes' by the government with the intention to support tribal 'uplift' in every conceivable manner, but I was unable to discover any kind of stocktaking exercise after the well-financed programme had been at work for more than a quarter of a century. Fortunately, at least in my eyes, the Bondo world has hardly changed, so the net result of the administrative activities may just have consisted in watching these potentially problematic citizens of India and enriching a few government servants.

The old Koraput district, comprising a territory of the size of Kerala state, was partitioned into four such administrative units in 1995, so that the major part of the Bondo Hills is now under the Collectorate of Malkangiri, a small town and one of the hottest of India, consisting of make-shift wooden huts in the few streets around the colonial buildings that house the present Collector and her staff. Until 1997, the then chief administrator of Malkangiri had been a merciless developer. One of his measures was to order all Bondo healers, or *dissari*, to headquarters where they were declared to be 'barefoot doctors' and provided with a short khaki uniform as well as Rs. 100 each. They appreciated this recognition, just as later they liked watching the video-recordings at the Collectorate, when they could admire the moving pictures that showed their formal institution during that public gathering.

The Collector's other innovation was even more radical, because it touched Bondo identity. The tribe is conspicuous because Bondo women shave their skulls and wear nothing but a miniskirt of some 30 cm length. They therefore do not look like other tribal women. I have tried to interpret Bondo baldness by a structural analysis of their myths and by a reference to the 'Magical Hair'-debate (Pfeffer 1997a). The then Collector, however, considered the female dress and tonsure to be a sign of their underdevelopment, just as he was annoyed by the regular marriages between junior men and senior women. Being an enlightened and academically trained progressive, he offered Rs. 200 in cash to every woman who was willing to let her hair grow, cover her body with textiles provided by the Collectorate, and marry a senior husband. While the latter decision could not really be verified, some women of some villages did indeed take up the offer and changed their outward appearance. At Chalanput and elsewhere, they can now be admired as individually representing the intermediary type of a culture by the half-long hair, resembling a European pony-tail, and the sheet of cloth, thrown over their shoulders, while the *ringa*, or miniskirt, still dangles around their hips.

Tribal males and females cover the same workload in the fields and forests of middle India. In the Bondo Hills women do much of the shifting cultivation and they collect the minor produce in the woods to sell it to the traders in Chalanput. The *ringa*, and nothing but the *ringa*, appears to be the proper dress for such a life, but beyond all utilitarian assumptions, a taboo has kept women from wearing saris and letting their hair grow, as Elwin has discussed at length (1950: 60-70) and as I have substantiated and elaborated in the paper on Bondo cosmology (Pfeffer 1997a). Thus the official intervention is an assault upon Bondo religion. Many women until today keep the old appearance in traditional style, and some of the 'reformed' group have relapsed into baldness after the transfer of the former Collector, even though, when coming to places like Chalanput, all female Bondo cover their backs with towels and their breasts with elaborate self-made jewellery. Government interventions in tribal affairs are, of course, a regular feature and need not be elaborated in detail. Powerful outsiders everywhere manipulate the indigenous inhabitants of the middle Indian hills. Thus on a number of occasions, I have witnessed how government agencies gave long-term employment to tribesmen, but officers failed to pay the wages due. The cheated individuals were all the same able to survive 'in the jungle', as they said, i.e. on their own socio-economic basis.

The Bondo and their many different tribal neighbours can do without the state and the market economy, even if they accept some of these outside forces. The term 'Bondo' is, in fact, the designation of outsiders meaning 'people of the *ban*', i.e. the jungle. Their own designation *remo* must be translated as 'human'.

LAW AND ORDER

Apart from the benevolent, if annoying, governmental interventions, the state's claim of 'law and order' has been a serious issue in the twentieth century. The colonial government took note of the fact that Bondo men were known to kill other men, be they brothers, or clan mates, or complete strangers. At present, I have found Bondo men to hold long-term grudges against other Bondo men, even against fellow villagers, whom they will attack one day, just as lethal action can arise from one moment to the next among Bondo who had cooperated over years. Members of neighbouring tribes may be among the victims, just as any non-tribal outsider who dares to interfere.

Bondo violence has nothing to do with clan feuds or forms of organized combat known in other tribal communities such as the Dongria Kondh in the Niamgiri Hills further north[11] (Nayak 1989). I would avoid any statement on the 'causes' of Bondo violence. Their immediate neighbours, the Didaye or *Gtaré*, i.e. humans, speak a very similar Munda language and follow the same economic calling and metaphysical concepts within the very same natural environment. Their population is of the same size, and they classify themselves in the very same clans and local descent groups applied by the Bondo, and yet the Didaye, or other neighbours, are not known for their acts of violence. Elwin has described at length, how a Bondo may for years care for the company of another but, while consuming the palm wine of the day, stab his drinking-mate without major or indeed, any provocation. The killers are also known for their honesty. After the deed, they make no bones about their action and readily follow policemen into court and conviction.

During the last few decades, a 'Model Police Station' has been operating some 20 km away from Chalanput and about 30 km away from the Bondo Hills. Perhaps because of Elwin's former visits, the personnel is said to have undergone some special training in view of the tribal population of the region, with particular reference to the Bondo. The practical consequences of the relationship were exemplified in autumn 1998. Two Bondo men were quarrelling on a Chalanput market day. Thereupon outsiders called the *sarpanch*, or elder, of the place who, having arrived on the scene and uttered only a few words, was instantly stabbed by one of the Bondo. Suffering from a grave injury, he was driven to Vishakhapatnam on the Andhra coast in an eight-hour car journey, where he expired in a hospital a few days later.

The culprit fled to his village, but since he, like every Bondo visitor, was known to the Chalanput home-guard, three constables marched up the Hills and persuaded the killer to accompany them to the 'Model Police Station'. On the way, they explicitly assured the apprehensive Bondo crowd that nothing would happen to their prisoner. They took him to a private home at Chalanput, shared their meal with him, and spent the night at his side before moving on to the Police Station on the next day.

Reliable sources have informed me that the Bondo killer, while being arrested in the police cell, insulted the officer-in-charge and repeated a promise, not uncommon for a man of his tribe, that he would kill the policeman on the next possible occasion. Thereupon the officer became angry and throttled the prisoner to death.

On the next day, the news was issued that the Bondo inmate had hanged himself in shame. It is, however, not the custom for the Bondo to commit suicide in police custody. About 100 tribesmen gathered around the station threatening the staff, particularly those constables who had been promising a safe passage. The press of coastal Andhra Pradesh did cover this unrest. The journalists, however, did not report another 'suicide' nine days later. The wife of the police officer was found hanging in her quarters being throttled by a rope. People believe her 'hanging' was manipulated by the Bondo, in the very same manner in which the police had faked the 'hanging' of their Bondo prisoner. After this incident, the site of the death, i.e. the police quarters, has remained empty. Nobody wants to live there any longer.

The agencies of the state are the major external force encroaching upon the Bondo Hills, but the enemies of the state have similar ambitions. For more than thirty years, the so-called Naxalites have moved through the hills at the border of Orissa and Andhra Pradesh, evading police and simultaneously attempting to set-up some kind of a counter order. In the last decade, a number of villages were occupied by young male and female members of the 'People's War Group' who were armed with machine guns. Like the special police forces on their heals, these self-declared liberators supplied themselves with village poultry and offered stern warnings. In deliberate attempts to improve tribal morality, the communists furthermore condemned the consumption of liquor and destroyed whatever liquids they could find. By contrast, their persecutors would regularly demand country brandy from the Bondo who were eager to avoid either of the two categories.

TOURISTS

The above-mentioned administrative efforts to bring the Bondo into 'the mainstream of Indian culture', to use the general formula for attempts to turn tribesmen into Hindus, is not without intra-governmental contradictions. One department is concerned with suppressing insurgency, another with fighting individual crime, yet another with benevolent efforts to 'civilize' the 'savages', and then there is the department for the promotion of tourism, a major source of foreign exchange in India.

The latter is eager to cultivate the attraction of the savage image. Thus the national Tourism Ministry publishes the magazine *Discover India* in bright glossy paper, distributing it all over the world free to attract well-to-do travellers. In one issue (Nath 1995: 34), an excellent photographer presents visions of traditional Bondo women, i.e. those without hair and dress. The bestseller of all Tourist Offices in coastal Orissa is a fine volume of colour photographs—made in China—by the French photographer Jean-Louis Nou, depicting a traditional young Bondo woman all over the fifth page.[12]

In fact, 'tribal tours' are part of an expanding industry. I have so far found travel agencies in Italy, Belgium, Germany and the United States offering tours to Chalanput. Nowadays they operate via Internet. Efficient managers meet the Western and Japanese visitors at the airports of Madras or Bhubaneswar to take them on the temple round and then fly them to Vishakhapatnam, the last halt before the drive to Jeypore. In this rather ugly capital of the former zamindar, some 60 km away from Chalanput, the foreign tourists can find one or two hotels with water-closets, digestible food and shower baths for the nights of Wednesday and Thursday. So the *hat* has become theirs. Air-conditioned jeeps take them into the wilderness to the naked Bondo. From October to March, elderly couples from Japan, Europe or the US are moved up the narrow track to Chalanput to spend an hour or two taking photographs and then return in time to make it to the water-closets in the Jeypore Hotel.

'Dad and I are on a world tour. We have just come from Bangkok/Thailand', a very gentle old lady explained to me once at Chalanput. An 80-year old Englishman who, judging from his looks, must have spent some time in the armed forces, was delighted to find a 'completely different race' at the weekly market. Each load of tourists, usually 10 to 20 individuals,[13] is driven to the big Banyan tree next to the site of the liquor vendors, refreshed with cool cola provided by the organizers, and then encouraged to take photographs with the help of most sophisticated equipment. Only traditionally-clad Bondo women, not the other tribal women in tribal saris, are worth this effort, and the former are well aware of this foreign preference. After initial refusals some years ago, they have now agreed to act as models, provided they receive a handsome honorarium. I have taken photographs of tourists who held a bunch full of ten-rupee bills in one hand, shooting photos with the other. Each snap was initiated by a tenner, or something like 20 cents in US currency. A Bondo woman would, as model, earn much more on a single Thursday morning than for all of her other work during the rest of the year.

ON BEING OUTSIDERS

The Bondo who see themselves as the humans in their own language are aware of being and always having been outsiders. The tribes of their neighbourhood fear and dislike the aggressive men who have so often disturbed their peace and killed or wounded many of their non-aggressive brothers. Moreover, neighbours such as the Didaye are nowadays jealous of the Bondos' spectacular income. The Gadaba are a much bigger tribe and yet, in the neighbourhood of the Bondo Hills, they have stopped their grand secondary funerals for fear of disturbances created by these neighbours. In short, peaceful communication with other traditional inhabitants of the region has been rare for the tribe.

In what I have called 'the Koraput complex' (Pfeffer 1997b: 16f) I associate the Bondo with other people of the administrative 'Backward' category in the region because of obvious cultural commonalities. Much of the province of Orissa is covered by several of such tribal complexes, though all share many cultural traits in contrast to caste society. The Koraput complex includes certain tribes known as *porja* or 'subjects'. Thus Bondo, Gadaba, Didaye, Joria, Matia, and Parenga form a common Desia society, i.e. 'the people of the land', that follows a broadly unified socio-cultural logic. In the region as a whole just as in numerous individual villages, they live interspersed with one another as well as with their landless clients (Scheduled Castes) and tribes of higher status and different administrative designation (Other Backward Classes) such as the Rona, the Bhatra, the Bhumia, or the *boro* (i.e. senior) *porja*. The status of the many Kond in Koraput is not quite clear and that of Gauda, Kumbhar and Mali, i.e. those specializing in cattle, pottery and kitchen-gardening, is ambivalent (see Berger 2002). Several intermediary categories, e.g. Dora, are unclear, because at times they combine their designation with others, at times not, yet all of these units belong to the Desia or local culture.

All the tribal categories of Koraput named so far share some, or all, of the same eight-clan categories (fish, cobra, cow, bear, leopard, monkey, vulture, sun) and all communicate with each other in Desia, the regional version of the Indo-European Oriya language, while some of them have retained Munda and Dravidian tongues. The Remo language of the Bondo, for example, is close to the Munda Gutob of the 'senior' Gadaba and unintelligible to the Dravidian Ollari of the 'junior' Gadaba. The Bondo tribe as a whole is made up of the two exogamous moieties[14] (cobra and tiger) known as *bonso* in Desia and, like that of their fraternal Gadaba, of four omnipresent local descent groups[15] (*kuda*) which I have sometimes called local lines, i.e. *boronaik*, *munduli* (or *chalan*), *sisa* and *kirsani*. These local descent groups include all Bondo but operate (and sometimes split) at the village level only, in the sense of opposing two secular and two sacred status groups in each settlement. The *kuda* rule of exogamy does not hold beyond the village level while *bonso* exogamy is universal. A Bondo must never take a wife of his mother's village, he would prefer to take one from his paternal grandmother's home.

With respect to the ritual relations, it may well be possible that the grand *gotr*, an extravagant give-away celebration, or 'total social fact', of the Gadaba (see Pfeffer 2001), is ideologically related to the *nandi* of the Joria[16] and the *bali* of the Mali.[17] Since the Bondo, like their Koraput neighbours on such occasions, have erected menhirs[18] and dolmens,[19] they are also likely to experience such 'total social facts' during rare and important celebrations, but we know nothing of them.

In short, the Bondo are a part of the greater tribal society of Koraput and Orissa respectively, with boundaries that are hardly visible. In the neighbourhood, like the tract of the Didaye in the Hills, tribal people mostly practice swidden cultivation, whereas all of the other Koraput groups mentioned have lost the forest and operate as if they were ordinary peasants, hardly distinguishable from other Indians, if it were not for their many socio-religious particularities that stand in marked contrast to the concepts of the plains. The Bondo operate within the same socio-cultural logic as these tribal people. However, contrary to the others, the Bondo equally disregard the lives of insiders and outsiders of their tribe or their tribal complex or of any human association. When the mythological origins of sun and moon are recalled, the Bondo associate themselves with the violent (and male) sun against the rest (see Pfeffer 1997a).

The immigrant settlers from lowland Orissa and Andhra Pradesh have always been ignored by the Bondo. After these little fighters have proved their militancy, even the most overbearing youths among the plains-people have left the Bondo alone. If decades ago, Frantz Fanon (1967) decried the settlers' exploitation of the natives in Algeria, South Africa and what was known as Rhodesia then, we cannot discover a parallel relationship in Bondoland, whatever individually overzealous administrators and policemen have tried to achieve. The general corruption of the administration is likely to save these mountain-dwellers from being modernized. Bondo violence has cautioned the immigrant settlers not to treat this tribe like others.

But tourism, undoubtedly initiated by anthropologists, may have a long-term adaptive effect. Both armed Bondo men and bare-breasted Bondo women adapt to their roles as models for colour photographs and video-recordings. If prophecies were a legitimate anthropological exercise, I would predict the construction of new roads right into the Bondo villages followed up by some well organized air-conditioned hotel nearby, so that the 'takes' will become more comfortable.

So far the men of the tribe have always closed their villages, whenever important ceremonies would take place. Outsiders were not welcome. We know very little of the Bondo world-view, and we should remain content with our ignorance. After an anthropological onslaught, the Westerners would be likely to 'buy' Bondo religion in the tourist style. The predictable result would be a definite confusion among the tribesmen. They might not remember what was tribal and what had become the commodity on sale, unless, of course, they retain their present policy by contacting tourists at the market only while keeping them out of their homes and villages.

NOTES

1. Aidan Southall took this stand in a conversation with me in 1983.
2. Such concepts of 'progress' would either associate the violence with 'backwardness' to justify external repression or with the overthrow of a 'reactionary' regime for the sake of some vague idea of 'liberation'.
3. Numerous Indian colleagues have written on this topic. I shall only refer to the classic of G.S. Ghurye, first published under the title *The Aborigines so-called and their Future* in 1943 and reprinted as *The Scheduled Tribes* in 1959 and subsequent editions. Ghurye, as may be seen in the following quotation, opposes any distinction of religion or a tribal status: '. . . large sections of the Hindu populace which, in comparison with the uppermost sections, appeared to belong to a different culture altogether, when the British appeared on the scene. . . . The old process of assimilation was upset' (1959: xiii).
4. This is an important quasi-agnatic bond and major inter-ethnic long-term contact known in all tribal areas of Orissa.
5. She, of course, thought he had abducted her as his wife in the legitimate Gadaba manner and was disappointed when he left her after a few years to return to the plains.
6. The outcome is published in Pfeffer (1999).
7. This is a book on one type of youth dormitory found among the Muria Gond in Bastar, a district neighbouring Koraput. Among unmarried youths, Elwin described a system involving regular changes of sexual partnerships. In a recent study among the Muria, Simeran Gell (1992) has, however, described the institution altogether differently.
8. The paperback version (Elwin 2001) of reprinted sections of his autobiography and ethnographic contributions has just come out.
9. For details see Guha (1999).

10. Nanda is a title of the highest, the Vedic Brahmins, of coastal Orissa.
11. After 15 months of fieldwork, Roland Hardenberg (2006) has just written up a comprehensive monograph on this Kond tribe whose members display major similarities and differences compared to the Bondo.
12. Jivan, Pani, and Jean-Louis Nou, 1994.
13. By 2003 each caravan of tourists included the passengers of 10 to 12 jeeps.
14. On the ground, the rule of exogamy can never be fully maintained because of demographic differences between the two units. Elwin's (1950) naturalistic approach and his general lack of anthropological knowledge caused his confusion over these issues.
15. Since even the most seminal essays of Leach are no longer standard knowledge, I must explicitly define the local descent group as 'the corporate group of . . . co-resident males representing, as a rule, three genealogical generations, namely: the old men or grandfathers, the normal adults or fathers, and the young adults or sons. In practice, membership of such groups is defined by descent as well as residence' (Leach 1961: 56). In the case of middle India, the local descent group must not be confused with a 'lineage' because two different local descent groups of two different villages—but named equally as, e.g. *Sisa*—may very well intermarry.
16. Peter Berger observed and filmed it but any reliable analysis must be based upon several experiences of this grand celebration.
17. Tina Otten hopes to study this equally great fertility rite that should not be confused with other rituals of the same name.
18. Among the Bondo, these vertically erected stone-slabs may reach the height of 1.5 m.
19. These table-like constructions contain a horizontal stone-slab on the top of three vertically erected stones of about 50 cm height.

REFERENCES

Berger, Peter (2002), 'The Gadaba and the "non-ST" Desia of Koraput, Orissa: Some Observations on their Interrelations', in G. Pfeffer and D.K. Behera (eds.), *Contemporary Society: Tribal Studies,* vol. 5, Delhi: Concept, pp. 57-90.

Elwin, Verrier (1945), 'Two Bondo Murderers', *Man in India,* vol. 25, no. 1.

———(1947), *The Muria and their Ghotul*, Bombay: Oxford University Press.

———(1950), *Bondo Highlander*, London: Oxford University Press.

———(2001), *Verrier Elwin: Philanthropologist. Selected Writings*, ed. Nari Rustomji, Delhi: Oxford University Press.

Fanon, Frantz (1967), *The Wretched of the Earth*, Harmondsworth: Penguin.

Fried, Morton H. (1965/6), 'On the Concept of "Tribe" and "Tribal Society"', *Transactions of the New York Academy of Science*, series 2, vol. 28, pp. 527-40.

Fürer-Haimendorf, Christoph von (1943), 'Megalithic Ritual among the Gadabas and Bondos of Orissa', *Journal and Proceedings of the Royal Asiatic Society of Bengal*, third Series, vol. IX, pp. 149-210.

Gell, S.M.S. (1992), *The Ghotul in Muria Society*, Chur: Harwood Academic Publishers.

Ghurye, G.S. (1959), *The Scheduled Tribes*, Bombay: Popular Prakashan.

Gutkind, Peter C.W. (ed.) (1970), *The Passing of Tribal Man in Africa*, Leiden: E.J. Brill.

Guha, Ramachandra (1999), *Savaging the Civilized: Verrier Elwinë—His Tribals, and India*, Delhi: Oxford University Press.

Hardenberg, Roland (2006), *Children of the Earth Goddess: Society, Marriage and Sacrifice in Highland Orissa (India)*. Münster : Habilitation Thesis: Wilhelms Universität Münster.

Helm, June (ed.) (1968), *Essays on the Problem of the Tribe: Proceedings of the 1967 Annual Spring Meeting of the American Ethnological Society*, Seattle: University of Washington Press.

Keesing, Roger M. (1992), *Custom and Confrontation: The Kwaio Struggle for Cultural Autonomy*, Chicago: University of Chicago Press.

Leach, E.R. (1961), 'The Structural Implications of Matrilateral Cross-Cousin Marriage', in E.R. Leach, *Rethinking Anthropology*, London: Athlone, pp. 54-104.

Nanda, Bikram Narayan (1994), *Contours of Continuity and Change: The Story of the Bondo Highlanders*, Delhi: Sage.

Nayak, P.K. (1989), *Blood, Women and Territory: An Analysis of Clan Feuds of Dongra Konds*, Delhi: Reliance.

Nath, Prathiba (1995), 'Die Volksstämme Orissas', *Discover India* (in German), February 1995, pp. 34-9.

Pani, Jivan and Jean-Louis Nou (1994), *Our World in Colour: Orissa*, Hongkong: Twin Age Ltd.

Pels, Peter and Oscar Salemink (eds.) (1999), *Colonial Subjects: Essays on the Practical History of Anthropology*, Ann Arbor: The University of Michigan Press.

Pfeffer, Georg (1997a), 'Die Haardebatte: Gender, Glatzen und Gewalt der Bondo'. *Zeitschrift für Ethnologie*, 122, pp. 183-208.

———(1997b), 'The Scheduled Tribes of Middle India as a Unit: Problems of Internal and External Comparison', in G. Pfeffer and D.K. Behera (eds.), *Contemporary Society: Tribal Studies*, vol. I, Delhi: Concept, pp. 1-27.

———(1999), 'Gadaba and Bondo Kinship Vocabularies versus Marriage, Descent, and Production', in Deepak Kumar Behera and Georg Pfeffer (eds.), *Contemporary Society: Tribal Studies*, vol. IV, Delhi: Concept, pp. 17-46.

———(2001), 'A Ritual of Revival among the Gadaba of Koraput', in Hermann Kulke and Burkhard Schnepel (eds.), *Jagannath Revisited: Studying Society, Religion and the State in Orissa*, Delhi: Manohar, pp. 123-48.

Sahlins, Marshall D. (1968), *Tribesmen*, Englewood Cliffs: Prentice Hall.

3

People of the Hills: How the Rona Deal with Social Change

TINA OTTEN

In Orissa there is a traditional division between the society of the plains which is called 'Hindu', and that of the hills, which is often called 'Tribal' (Fischer, Mahapatra and Pathy 1980; Kulke 1978; Pfeffer 1997). Even nowadays, it is obvious that many plains people believe that the people of the hills are 'primitive' and many use the word 'tribal' in a derogatory manner. As an anthropologist one has to criticize the use of the word in such a racist way. However, in India the word 'tribal' denotes a social category used by the administration, and in the Anthropology and Sociology of India the term 'tribe' is used or rejected as a *terminus technicus*, as anthropologists debate whether it is politically correct or not.[1]

In the present context the term does not refer to 'primitive society', but to social systems traditionally called 'tribes' in India, as a translation of the indigenous term 'adivasi'. For this historical reason the term is used as an analytical and structural category, which in this specific sense occurs only in the anthropology of India. I use the word 'tribal' throughout the paper, because alternative terms like acephalous society, indigenous people, etc., are also problematic. I am writing about people who have a clear sense of social hierarchy

*I take the opportunity to thank Sunita, Susmita and Sunny Suna very much of their collaboration and friendship. I also thank Professor Georg Pfeffer of the Freie Universität Berlin and the Deutsche Forschungsgemeinschaft, Bonn, for advice and funds without which my research would not have been possible.

and whose historical memory includes migrations and dealings with kings of long ago.

The inhabitants of the Koraput Hills refer to themselves as Desya.[2] A subgroup of them, classified as a 'Scheduled Tribe', call themselves Adivasi,[3] while the others (Scheduled Caste and Other Backward Classes) refer to themselves as Desya proper as a distinctive category opposed to Adivasi. Thus the word 'desya' denotes both an inclusive and an exclusive category in relation to the people of the hills.

This paper examines how one community among the complex society living in the hills of Koraput district deals with changes in their social and environmental circumstances. They are the Rona, living on the southern fringes of the predominantly tribal Koraput district, concentrated in the areas around the former royal capitals of Nandapur and Jeypore. The title 'Rona' is derived from the Rajput royal title of 'Rana' applied to the noblemen of western India (Pfeffer 2000a: 162). Most probably the people adopted the name Rona at the time when the ideas usually referred to as Rajputization reached Orissa in the eighteenth century.[4] The Ronas consider themselves as the leading members of the former *paik* militia[5] of the king of Nandapur, who has been residing in Jeypore for more than 200 years. He is the head of one of the oldest Hindu royal houses of Orissa.

G. Ramadas has established the date of the foundation of Jeypore from archival records. According to him, 'the royal family was "forced" in AD 1753 to take shelter to the west of the Eastern Ghats and to build the present town of Jeypore'(Ramadas 1931: 9). Previously, the ghat area was under the command of subsidiary fort commanders, while the Maharaja himself resided in the plains area around Bobbili and Narayanapatnam and to the north towards the upper Vamsadhara valley. The Oriya Paikas, of which the Rona were one group, served both in the plains and in the hills and some of them were *muthadars* (commanders of local militia and tax collectors). The Ronas claim to have settled in this area 'seven generations ago'. The number seven should be regarded as mythical.[6] Nobody knows if the Ronas were already present in the Nandapur area before that time, but it is likely, since Oriya influence in general, the reign of

Oriya kings under the supremacy of the Orissan empire, and the impact of pan-Indian culture can be traced several centuries back. Nandapur was the capital of a kingdom from at least the fourteenth century (Berkemer 1993: 191) but as its large temples date back into the twelfth century, it might even be older. The oldest evidence of pan-Indian influence are the Jain ruins around Nandapur which can be dated to the ninth century (Donaldson 2001: 8).

The Rona community is divided into a senior section, called *boro* Rona and a junior section called *sano* Rona or *kuttia* Rona.[7] This division has characteristics which places it conceptually close to moieties, with the main difference that intermarriage rarely occurs and there is no division of political or ritual tasks between the two groups. The only difference between the *boro* and the *sano* Rona is that the senior section inherits a higher status than the junior section. The *boro* Rona are classified by the administration as an 'Other Backward Classes' (OBC) since 1950,[8] while the *sano* or *kuttia* Rona have always been classified as a Scheduled Tribe (ST). Both sections are considered as tribals in Andhra Pradesh, where the *boro* Rona are known both as Rena and Rona and *kuttia* Rona as *sano* Rona.

The Ronas speak Desya[9] as their mother tongue. They observe exogamous patrilineal and patrilocal kinship rules and use clan categories to differentiate between agnates and affines. Ronas recognize eight different clans: sun (*kora*), cobra (*bantal*), tiger (*killo*), monkey (*golori*), fish (*macho*), bear (*kimidi*), vulture or hawk (*pangi* or *gidh*) and cow (*goru*).[10] In contrast to other Desya communities, they don't carry their clan designations as names, but use titles like Pujari, Kotelel, Mahji, Patro, Tiltang, Alang or Pardani. They can intermarry with any clan from their community except their own. The marriage pattern follows symmetric exchange, and marriage with the *menaboini:* mother's brother's daughter (MBD) or father's sister's daughter (FSD) are the preferred spouses, and such marriage is accorded highest status.

Most of the Desya earn their income by cultivating their fields, some by slash and burn cultivation (*podu*), while others, who are better off, own or rent permanent fields (*bera* or *poda*). Due to their former affiliation to the king, most of the Ronas own some permanent (*beda* or *poda*) fields. Here they cultivate rice (*dhan*) millet (*mandia*), cash crops like oilseed (*alsi*) and Ayurvedic drugs like *pippali*.

By the year 2000, the Rona were only slightly affected by the changes of modern life. However, the rate of change has increased these last years. A major change may appear, now that alphabetization compaigns among adults have started.[11] In local and boarding schools the children are educated by Hindu teachers who do not speak the regional dialect of Oriya, but the Oriya of the plains. The teachers want to teach them 'proper' Oriya alongside with 'proper' conduct which for the teachers is the Hindu way of life. Government agencies and non-governmental organizations both try to organize village life according to their way of thinking, which differs from Desya values. From time to time they visit the villages, and tell the people to observe the ban on alcohol. Most of them have no understanding of the value of country liquor in the symbolic universe of the people.

Among the Desya in the district live newcomers, who have settled since the late 1940s to work in the newly-established hydroelectric projects. The Desya must cope with these foreigners, who treat them as inferiors and remain outsiders to them. These projects have affected the environment. Some Desya have had to leave their villages when their homes were submerged by the rising waters. I have not come across any stories of resistance among the Ronas against this exercise of governmental power. The effect of NALCO, the National Aluminium Corporation, on the environment is seen in several areas. But the most visible damage to the environment is the almost complete deforestation of the area by logging companies. Among other calamities, this has led to the loss of species of plants for food and medical treatment.

In the last decade, religious reform movements like the Mahima Dharma movement have become very popular among the Desya, and in nearly every village, one or two houses follow their teachings. Many households have taken initiation (*dikhya*) into the Mahima Dharma because of illness, misfortune and poverty in the local line. This implies an expectation that the prime deity of Mahima

Dharma, Alekh, will prove more powerful than their former house god (Guzy 2001). Whereas followers of Mahima Dharma are mostly found among Ronas and Malis (gardeners), both labelled as 'OBC' by the government, Christianity is found mostly among the member of the Scheduled Castes. Missionaries of the Pentacostal churches and the Lutheran church (Breklum Mission) have been active in this district since the end of the nineteenth century (Waack 1997).

Tourism, too, is now beginning to have an impact on the region, though the number of tourists is still very small. Most visitors come only for the day to see the weekly markets or the hydroelectric power plants.

Then there is the impact of biomedical concepts. Since the middle of the twentieth century, dispensaries and governmental health stations have been inaugurated in the area. About a decade ago, a non-governmental Christian organization established a comparatively well-run hospital in the area, training village women as primary health workers.

How do the Ronas cope with these social changes? Do they affect their system of values, and will they cause a crisis of identity? We shall see that the Ronas adapt many foreign ideas into *their* categories and modes of organization. I shall discuss this against the background of the Rona world-view, social organization and system of knowledge. The main point here is their categorization of illness and health. I describe the traditional healing specialists and how the Ronas categorize illness, to show how the general concepts and ideas of the larger society have their impact on a specific system of knowledge, the traditional healing system.

'TRIBAL IDEAS': A THEORETICAL INTERLUDE

In the Koraput district, the indigenous communities speak languages which have their roots in the Dravidian, in the Indo-European and in the Munda language families. Despite these language differences all the inhabitants call themselves Desya. They share the same values and structure their communities in a similar way. Pfeffer (1997) calls the Desya society the 'Koraput Complex'. This complex should not be identified with the geographical area of the old Koraput district.

There are other areas with other social characteristics, somewhat distinct from the Koraput Complex.

The Desya of Koraput have developed a system of values distinct from that of the Hindu society of the plains. The Desya world-view is made up of what Pfeffer calls 'tribal ideas' which I summarize below (2000a, 2000b). The word 'tribe' as used here for the Desya communities, denotes a form of social organization with the following characteristics:

- The principle of seniority is the most important structuring idea among the Desyas. This principle indicates status difference and hiearchy—or unequal rank of interrelated parts with reference to the common whole.
- A tribe is not a single united community. Customs and major rituals seem to change gradually, so that they look different every 30-50 km (Pfeffer 2000b: 162), recalling the variations shown by Leach (1954) for the Kachin and of Eichinger Ferro-Luzzi (1987, 1989) for Saivite temples in the Hindu context.
- Tribal society lacks the kind of political organizations which imply formal administration (Sahlins 1968). In other words, tribes in general have not developed a centralized political organization. Tribal societies in India are often subject to forms of political organization in which they have only a marginal role.
- Tribes lack centralized political power. 'No "chiefs" or "headmen" find obedience . . . among neighbours, even though all of them have "elders" or individual positions called "big men" and "petty chiefs" in Sahlins' terminology (1968)' (Pfeffer 2000b: 163). This indicates political forms like segmentary organization in Durkheim's (1968) sense. Tribal society has limited economic specialization and is characterized by a general decentralization.[12] It shows a lack of group or tribe identity beyond the villages with whom the local lines of a village have relationships.
- Tribal people live in a set of relationships that is not limited to the human species, but includes relationships to the spiritual beings of their whole environment. The material basis of this set of relationships is the land. The land issue is therefore central for

the tribal groups. And with the increasing danger of losing their land, their whole social existence is in jeopardy.

One of the most influential ideas which structures tribal society is the principle of seniority, in indigenous terms the categories of *boro* (senior) and *sano* (junior) (Fig. 1). Members of the senior groups are considered superior in status to those of the junior groups. This does not mean that the senior group holds more power than the juniors. Senior status just indicates that seniors are seen to have a '. . . greater proximity to the world beyond as well as greater wisdom as the result of an existence that encompasses the life of juniors. Nothing more' (Pfeffer 2000a: 342).

In Desya society, rank is attributed according to seniority. Hierarchy is here defined in terms of seniority, while in Dumont's analysis of Hindu society from the perspective of Brahmans, hierarchy is defined by degrees of purity (Dumont 1980). Seniority and purity are structural equivalents, alternative indicators of hierarchy in accordance with their specific social context.

boro	*sano*
senior	junior
big	small
old	young
status high	status low
sacred	secular

Fig 1: The Semantic Fields of *Boro* and *Sano.*

Hierarchy is most strongly emphasized at the upper and lower ends of the ranking system. In Hindu society, both Brahmins and ex-Untouchables form categories quite distinct from the rest, while in the middle, issues of power are more important than questions of purity. In the tribal society of Koraput the Hindu values of purity and the resulting social stratification are absent.

There are structural similarities, however. In the ranking of Desya society, the Rona have the highest status, and everybody agrees that the Dombos, the clients of the other groups, who are musicians and weavers, are among the lowest.[13] In the middle, the distinction of rank among Mali (gardener), Sundi (distillers of country liquor), Gouda (herdsmen), and tribals such as the Gadaba are less clear.

Thus even if social stratification may be absent, Desya society is based on complex systems of hierarchy expressed in the idiom of seniority (Pfeffer 1997).

The categories of senior and junior are used to subdivide every middle Indian tribe into a senior and a junior section.[14] Even though the Ronas do not consider themselves as tribals, we find the same structural principle among them. The *boro* Ronas are seniors to the *kuttia* Ronas. This basic distinction can also be observed at the village level, where the categories of senior and junior are used to indicate status groups. Here again, the opposition does not signify older or younger in terms of biological age, but works as a structural principle of hierarchy.

A member of a tribal society can be senior in one social context and junior in another—quite independent of biological age. The permanent opposition of senior and junior is also found in the form of kinship categories, such as moieties, clans and lineages in which barriers of commensality and intermarriage are a general issue.

During more than 18 months of fieldwork in Koraput district, I did not observe much difference between the Ronas and the people who are called adivasi in terms of their way of life, ideas, and social activities. One main distinction is that the communities labelled as OBC wear the sacred thread and abstain from consuming beef. In this context, I do not discuss whether the Rona are 'actually' a tribe or a Hindu caste which has become tribalized. For the present analysis it is more important to stress that the Ronas share a set of tribal ideas such as the principle of seniority, the antagonism between adjacent generations, and the equation between alternate generations, with their neighbours. They share the same exogamous totemic clans, they celebrate the annual tribal festivals, and their rituals are similar to those of other Desyas.[15]

THE IMPACT OF SOCIAL CHANGE: GENERAL FEATURES

At the beginning of the twenty-first century, the people of the Koraput district experience many kinds of development, limited in themselves, but which are indicators of a general process of accelerated social change. The most obvious are the better quality of roads and the improved system of buses. People have gained greater mobility and tourists who want to have a glimpse of the hydroelectric projects are now brought into the area for short trips. New bus lines connect the small towns, which are virtually and geographically at the end of the road. The little towns in the area, which often consisted of just one street with a few shops, now grow rapidly. In the place from which the bus departs for Vishakhapatnam, for example, there seems to be a new shop every month. These changes affect mainly the small market towns of the district, though. Only since 2000 have phone facilities become available in these small towns. Most of the Desyas, however, live in their villages, still without electricity and motorable roads, but they are nonetheless indirectly involved in, and affected by, social change.

There are several factors which influence the Desya, resulting from their contact with people they see as foreigners. Changes occur in fields such as education, religion, economy and medicine. But while such elements of influence and social change are manifold in the district, I would argue that the resulting adaptations have not changed the fundamental values of Desya society, and thus remain mostly superficial. Moreover, wherever the Desyas can choose, adaptations only occur when they fit their system of values. My experience among the Ronas indicates that these new adaptations are considered 'junior' and therefore inferior to traditional institutions.

I shall illustrate this by showing how the Ronas reject or incorporate stimuli for change into their system of values. These adaptations are selective processes that do not affect the structure of their society or their thought. My contention is that either the junior parts of the society try out most of the changes, or that the adaptations themselves are considered as junior in relation to more stable social values, and therefore, not taken too seriously.

The Ronas still remember the mistrust against foreigners in colonial times. In the village where we lived, the people who are now 40 to 50 years old told me they themselves as children were greatly afraid when foreigners came to the village, since they believed they would be taken away from their home and never brought back. The contact with foreigners (Indian and non-Indian) and their connection with strange ideas and values is a decisive issue.

Nowadays, there are various kinds of foreigners in Koraput district: the teacher who comes from the plains and lives in the village to teach the children; the social worker who lives for a limited time among the Desya to carry out a social programme; governmental officials during election compaigns; doctors from governmental and non-governmental health institutions; Rashtriya Swayamsevak Sangh (RSS) activists,[16] ethnographers from Indian and foreign universities; and an increasing number of tourists.

The tourists are taken by car or bus into the hills for a day. Indians usually visit the hydroelectric plants, foreign travellers come to see the weekly markets and pay a fortune—in the eyes of the tribal people—to see the parody of a tribal dance or to buy a broken bow and arrow or some pearls. The Desyas wonder about the behaviour of these people, but also learn how to make money from them. The Bondos, for instance, nowadays come to the weekly market not only to sell liquor, but also to offer their beads for a relatively high price.[17]

But these contacts remain largely superficial. People do not have a real idea of the life of foreigners. Repeatedly the villagers asked me, whether white people also die. They also asked several times, whether a Desya would be beaten up, if he travelled to the white men's place. These attitudes show that a latent fear or at least uneasiness about the doings of foreigners is still present in Koraput district.

Governmental and non-governmental organizations with Christian or Hindu backgrounds carry out social education programmes. Especially members of government organizations with a Hindu religious background and Hindu activists try to 'educate' the tribal communities. They want 'the naked'[18] to become more 'civilized'.

The education towards a life of Hindu values begins in school. Schoolchildren are educated in coastal Oriya and not in their Desya dialect. Most of the teachers come from coastal towns and make no effort to learn the local language. They incite the children to abandon beef, and to refrain from alcohol. The children are often beaten in these schools, and the pupils are kept on a meagre diet.

Complaints that the teachers embezzle money given to feed the children are commonplace. There are also complaints that the teachers force their pupils to work for them. Often the pupils and their parents are not even aware that this exploitation is not the normal practice at schools.[19]

There are also government programmes for the adults. In this area hardly any Desyas know how to read and write, and government programmes try to spread literacy. The idea is that adults should study at night after finishing their work. But the men openly refuse to learn reading and writing. The women who are structurally and hierarchically junior, and among them especially the younger ones, meet from time to time when the officials come, to give the impression that they study. Here again we observe that new elements are taken up by members of junior status in society.

In 2000, the government prohibited the consumption of alcohol. Regularly, government officials visit the villages to check if the tribal people drink. This prohibition ignores the fact that the ritual drinking of liquor is an integral part of tribal culture.[20] The drinking ritual is important to honour guests, to mark masculinity, to fix contracts and agreements, and to enjoy festivals. It is also an important part of the village rituals, in which the deities are often offered alcohol. Many ritual specialists drink alcohol to achieve the required spiritual state. This state of altered consciousness is also reached through other practices like fasting, chanting and breathing exercises. It is important to stress that the contact with the other world forms a structural element in tribal culture and that it is an important goal. Because of this I do not expect the anti-liquor campaigns of the government to be successful, as long as the Desyas themselves do not consider teetotalism as an achievement.

What government regulations from far-off Bhubaneswar do not achieve, religious reform movements do. In the whole Koraput district, religious reform movements like Mahima Dharma are growing rapidly. The members of these sects abstain from liquor and meat. This can be seen as an indigenous critique of the consumption of alcohol and it may lead to more voluntary changes from the side of the tribal population. Interestingly, the conversion to Mahima

Dharma follows the traditional divide in tribal society: the younger members of the local lines (*kuda*) convert most often to Mahima Dharma (Guzy 2001).[21] Thus potential adaptations are often tried out by the junior parts of society. Such a mode of adaptation fits into the general structure of thinking and reasoning. The senior members of Desya society hold on to their old values and the junior ones try to evade the pressures from above and venture into new modes of life.

It also happens that in a village the junior and therefore lower status part of a community converts to Christianity. The Ronas rarely do this, but their clients, the Dombos, often become Christians. However, there are villages where the younger part of a Rona community has converted to Christianity. Many converts regard the membership of a new religious community as a test period in which they see whether the deities of that creed are more powerful than the old ones. They will not hesitate to change their religion back again, if the conversion does not work. Some people have long conversion histories. They turn from the worship of tribal gods to the worship of Hindu gods, next they convert to a religious reform movement like Mahima Dharma, or they take a trial run of the Lutheran or Pentacostal churches.[22]

Koraput was and still is a remote area. Changes have been slow and the impact of foreign ideas was for a long time confined to the vicinity of a few roads, the Vizianagaram-Jeypore railway line and a few military establishments. But after Independence the rate of change has increased considerably. New infrastructure, the big hydroelectric projects, the exploitation of mineral resources and new military facilities brought a large number of plains people to the hills. Living conditions have changed gradually and new prospects of life have begun to influence the population in the towns. In a recent paper by Strümpell (2001), the author describes how the Desya people reflected upon the hydroelectric projects of the area, which were built in the 1940s. The tribal people heard about and observed workers die while building the dam. It was believed that such a huge construction demanded a lot of human sacrifice for the gods of the site, and thus many Desyas refused to work there.

Similarly, the indigenous population held that there was a high risk of death for contract workers in the tea gardens of Assam. These observations add up to a general impression: that the Ronas believe changes in the mode of life to be connected with violent and ritual death. At several occasions, I was asked by the Rona whether the white people still perform human sacrifice, a custom which was believed to be necessary to deal with the radical changes caused by white people everywhere.

The reinterpretation of industrial accidents as human sacrifice shows how the Ronas and all other Desyas incorporate social changes within their world-view. For them, the social actions of the foreigners, formerly the British and now the Indians from the plains, are taken to be governed by the same social structure as their own. Since the sacrifice of human beings (Boal 1982, Carrin-Bouez 1978) is an important factor in the life of all middle Indian tribes, they naturally fit their observations into the pattern of their social experience, which leads them to assume that the 'accidents' in the life of the foreigners are sacrifices in disguise.

THE SYSTEM OF ILLNESS UNDER THE IMPACT OF SOCIAL CHANGE

I shall now illustrate in more detail how the Ronas deal with social change in the medical sector. First, I discuss the roles of ritual specialists in the Desya system of health and medicine. Then follows a short description of the other medical facilities available in the district. Then I show how the Ronas adapt their concept of illness, using malaria as an example.[23]

Among the Ronas, ritual specialists diagnose illness and perform rituals of healing. There are different kinds of specialists: astrologers, ritual sacrificers, sorcerers, mediums of deities and traditional birth attendants. Because there is no direct translation into English of the terms that denote their tasks and duties, I prefer to describe them in terms of their indigenous names.

The *disari* (astrologer) and the *pujari* (ritual sacrificer) are responsible for the well-being of the whole community. These posts are hereditary. Besides the secular leader, the *naik*, the *disari* plays an important role as spiritual leader in village politics. The *disari* knows how to interpret the movement of the celestial bodies announcing the beginning of the seasons and is able to specify the good or bad qualities of months and days. With this knowledge he determines the season, the day of the week and the hour which is favourable for rituals, seasonal feasts, marriages, house building, sowing and harvesting. All major activities in the villages are carried out according to his advice, in order to satisfy the gods who would otherwise become malevolent and bring misfortune and disease. Among the duties of a *disari* we may also include the collecting and processing of medical plants in the area around the village, and the preparation of herbal medicine. Banishing malevolent influences and performing healing rituals are also part of his activities.

The *pujari* is the one who sacrifices animals, vegetables and fruits to the village goddess Hundi. According to their status, the *pujaris* from the different communities offer the animals that they can themselves consume. Thus the *pujari* from 'Other Backward Classes' offers sheep, goats and fowl. The *pujari* from adivasi communities also sacrifices pigs and buffaloes. Here again we find the distinction between beef-eaters and non-beef-eaters. However, both categories of *pujari* worship the deities of the village and its environment in the name of the whole community, and in this way prevent calamities.

Other healing specialists do not inherit any role in the leadership of the village and do not interfere in village activities. One of them is the *gunia* (sorcerer), who heals by extracting foreign material like glass, wood or malevolent water from the body. He or she knows how to cast spells and is also familiar with ways of controlling evil forces to cast illness or death on a person.

Gurumai are mediums who are able to get possessed by deities and spirits. They can communicate directly with all gods and spirits that live in the world of the Desya. As mediums they do not only heal but can also accept worship.

Lastly, there are the *bandki-dokeri*, who are midwives and herbal specialists. They also practise massage to alleviate pain. They are always female and are the ones among all the healers who are most body-oriented in their treatment of illness.

The Rona ritual specialists are among the most popular with the Desyas. They perform the same tasks as the ritual specialists of the other communities, but where the *boro* Rona live, they have the seniormost status. The specialists are categorized according to the same principle as all other groups in the area, the division of senior and junior, *boro* and *sano*. We find junior and senior specialists at the village level; we also find this division between the villages.

Every ritual position is split into two posts. At the village level there is a senior astrologer (*boro disari*) and a junior (*sano disari*), a senior medium (*boro gurumai*) and a junior (*sano gurumai*), a senior sacrificer (*boro pujari*) and a junior one (*sano pujari*). The senior *disari* is mainly important for issues of the whole village such as festivals while the junior ritual specialist is called for minor affairs.

The diagnostic methods of the ritual specialists show a synthesis of Hindu and tribal concepts. Rona *disari* use the Hindu astrological almanacs, the Oriya calander, palm leaf manuscripts of local variations of the Puranas, and the night sky to determine the time for auspicious activities. However, they also apply the tribal method of 'reading rice' (*arkot*) in order to diagnose an illness. A *gurumai* asks tribal and Hindu deities alike to identify the agent that makes the patient suffer and the nature of the illness it has inflicted. The deities invoked for healing rituals offer a clear example of social change. They include, besides traditional ones, modern figures such as Indira Gandhi and God Nalco. Nalco is the 'god' of the NALCO, a company that has left its marks not only in the natural, but also in the spiritual world of the people of Koraput.

Apart from the traditional system, there are few options for cure in the area. From time to time a Bengali Ayurvedic practitioner, a *vaid*, sells Ayurvedic drugs. People also have the opportunity to go to the few biomedical doctors and hospitals.

Three different kinds of institutions are presently practising biomedicine in Koraput. There are a small number of private doctors, two government hospitals, and a missionary hospital was established five years ago. The practice of the private doctors and the two government hospitals fall short by far of Western standards. One hospital is being run without a doctor, and the staff are practically unaware of Western hygienic standards.[24]

The three hospitals carry out primary health programmes. The government health care workers mainly conduct vaccination programmes. The non-governmental approach involves village people more actively. The plan here is to train one woman per village as a primary health worker. The villagers can choose the person from among themselves. Normally they select women from among those who are most highly esteemed among the traditional midwives. These primary health care programmes, dealing with illnesses like leprosy, malaria, tuberculosis, polio and scabies, the programmes of sterilization, and of mother and childcare, may very well have a future influence on the way health and body are seen.[25] This is the more likely since investigations on medical pluralism in other regions have shown a similar tendency (Beals 1976; Leslie 1980; Nichter 1980, 1983). Some indigenous and biomedical illness explanations fit each other well, as Marglin (1990) has shown in her investigation on smallpox, and as I shall demonstrate for the concept of malaria.

The Ronas distinguish different causes of illness. I have classified these causes in eight groups. The groups are not explicitly named by the Ronas as eight causes of illness. They are valued differently and may be ranked by the observer in an order which is reminiscent of the hierarchical pattern of seniority described above.

I will concentrate here on the causes of those illnesses which are ranked highest and lowest, or senior (*boro*) and junior (*sano*).[26] Senior causes of illness are always found in a person's destiny. The highest category of illness is accordingly called 'just as it was written in one's destiny'. The juniormost cause of illness is named 'it comes in its own way' and has no causal link to the destiny of a person. Here we find a clear distinction between the idea of the person and his or her role and agency in the community on the one hand, and the concept of the physical body on the other. The person as a social entity is ranked senior to the mere physical body.

A person's destiny depends on two things: The Ronas say that deeds in the former life determine fate in the present existence; but fate also depends on luck: it depends on the deities a person meets before birth on the way back to earth. If these deities like the person, the burden of life will be less strenuous. Whether the individual has more or less luck with the deities is a matter closely connected with the social person, i.e. it follows from the role he or she plays in society, which depends on the social position one was born into but also by the way he or she establishes himself or herself in society.

The causes of illness seen to be related entirely to the physical, 'natural' body are considered lower in status, and they cause smaller (*sano*) disease. Such illnesses are by no means less serious and may also cause suffering and death, as is obvious in the case of malaria. In this case, however, the cause is of little significance socially.

It was a surprise to me, that where I lived the villagers had got to know the Western name of malarial fever only in recent years. The Western concept of the illness was explained to them by the doctors of the Christian NGO hospital who created an awareness of this new concept of the illness among the Ronas. What I want to show is that the Ronas did not have a concept of illness for malaria that could be translated into our biomedical concept. Of course, malaria has long been rampant in the district, but malarial fever had many different names and was attributed to many different causes. Malaria has been one of the illnesses most obviously influenced by social change. However, only one fever, which the traditional healing specialists diagnose as malaria, is considered as such. In other cases the fevers are put into other causal categories of illness, regardless of their biomedical cause.

The Ronas take modern medication now and go to the hospital in order to cure malarial fever, but they interpret the biomedical concepts in their own way. Doctors from the hospitals complain that even though they provide an effective treatment of malaria and give medicine free in case of emergency, many villagers still fail to bring their patients to the hospital in time, and malaria still claims a lot of lives. What could be the reason?

Malaria is incorporated in the classification system of illness under the 'smallest', the junior category. Malaria is caused neither by angry gods, nor by hungry souls of dead relatives, by anti-social behaviour of the sick person nor by the sorcery of a greedy relative. The Ronas say, 'malaria just comes by its own will' (*tar monke heba rog*). People are aware of the fact that it is transmitted by mosquitoes and that the hospital will provide medicine against it.

If the ritual specialist diagnoses a fever which belongs to a higher cause of illness, no medicine taken internally can stop the disease. Only an offering, most often a fowl as a substitute for the ill person, can satisfy the angry deity or the deceased relative and appease its hunger, in order to get rid of the fever.

But in many cases Ronas just wait for a few days to see which way the illness develops. Treatment will only be given if a person is still alive at the end of his 'dangerous' day, which occurs once a week and which is the third day of the week after the day of his birth. If it is clear that the person will surely die, the ritual specialists will not attend to the person any more. The healer will offer treatment only if he sees a chance to interfere with the causes of the illne

In the hospital, however, the doctors treat any person regardless of how close they are to dying. For the Desyas, the hospital is therefore an ambiguous place. On the one hand, people hope that the doctors may be able to save their relatives who otherwise would surely die. On the other hand, dying in the hospital is very inauspicious. According to my observations, people go to hospitals for family planning and malaria treatment. Injuries are also frequently attended to in the hospital, and men seem to frequent hospitals more often than women. The hospital is a place outside the village, and dying outside the village means that the soul might not find its way back. In such cases of death away from home one must perform elaborate rituals. A person who dies in the hospital cannot be brought into his house after death, which is necessary in order to perform the funerary rites. This is because people of foreign origin and lower status, even 'untouchable' persons, may have touched his body after death, and thus left the corpse too impure for the 'sacred' sphere of the house.

The traditional medical system is closely connected with other aspects of the world-view of the Desyas, like deities and souls of the deceased (*duma*). The person and the body are vulnerable to attacks from deities, *duma* and humans. Following Iteanu (1990) one may establish a ranked order of values in which non-human beings are incorporated into society. The illnesses they bring are closely connected with the status of the aggressor. Humans must honour the deities, the souls of the deceased as well as their fellow humans and must act according to the norms of the society. Those who do not honour social norms are likely to suffer from attacks which bring illness and against which rituals have to be performed.

In conclusion I make two points. In many societies, adaptation to modernity is a selective process. Desya society is a good example here, since the agency of this process remains with the indigenous people. I have shown how biomedicine has been adapted into the Desya medical system.

Adaptation of biomedicine into the traditional medical system as a structurally junior (*sano*) category, is but one aspect of a wider framework of crisis and adaptation in the Koraput Hills. As long as the impact of foreign ideas remains comparatively weak, there is a chance that the Desyas remain the masters of their future.

There are, however, many examples from neighbouring districts in which the inhabitants are subject to dramatic and dangerous changes. While on the coast the global warming demands its victims, other man-made disasters cause havoc in Kalahandi District. Deforestation, poisoning of rivers, and overpopulation produce changes which are beyond the control of the inhabitants. Similar negative effects may be expected on the environment of the Desyas of Koraput. We can only hope that the positive aspects of change will act fast enough to offer the indigenous population a chance to remain in control of their way of life.

NOTES

1. See for instance Bailey 1960, 1961, Dumont 1957, Guha 1999, Pfeffer 1982, 1997, Prasad 2003, Sinha 1980, Skoda 2005.
2. From the Sanskrit word *deśa* (land), *deśya* means those of the land, indigenous people.
3. In India we find the distinction between the first inhabitants of a place and the people who live there now. *Adi-* means 'first', *vaasin* means 'one who dwells'.

4. See the critical analysis of the concept of Rajputization in Orissa by Banerjee (1928), and the discussion, in a wider context, by Sinha (1962). There seems to be a diffusion of Rajputization from Rajasthan towards the east. The idea had probably not reached Orissa before the eighteenth century (Berkemer 1993: 212f). On the Rajput problem see also Schnepel and Berkemer (2004: 15-16).
5. Ronas stress that they should not be lumped together with other *paik* communities (Choudhury 1964-5).
6. The king is still present in the myths and legends of the Ronas. This king of the legends is the king of Nandapur. This town is still seen as the true seat of power, as the focus of their identity, and the final destination in their migration to the Koraput region. Both the king of Jeypore and the modern government of Orissa are called 'shadow governments' by the Ronas. The 'real' king is expected to return in a better future.
7. The word *kuttia* in general refers to houses made from mud and straw and denotes a 'hut'. It leads to the impression of remoteness (Niggemeyer 1964: 11).
8. Ronas were in the list of hill tribes under the A.T.I.L.T. Act from 1931 up to 1950 (Behuria 1964). After the division of the Vishakhapatnam agency 1936 the Ronas in Andhra Pradesh retained their status as tribals and are still considered as such.
9. Desya is spoken within an area comprising the subdivisions of Koraput city, Jeypore, Nawarangpur and Malkangiri in the district of Koraput. It differs from the standard Oriya of coastal Orissa to the extent of being almost unintelligible to a newcomer.
10. In one village my informants told me that there is one more clan name. It is dog (*kukur*) and the people of this clan carry the name *kichei*. However, nobody knew where they might be found.
11. Most of the Ronas are illiterate, but a lot of the ritual specialists know how to read and write as one of the skills of their profession. Some do not know more than a few ideograms, however, which they use to recall oral texts.
12. In the middle Indian model the Orissa structure classifies both exogamous (like the African ones) and non-exogamous descent categories within a hierarchical framework of seniority (Pfeffer 2001 a, 2001 b: 337ff). There are some factors that distinguish both tribal structures: 'African and biblical clans depend on pedigree and generational inclusion. The middle Indian model is lacking these two

crucial features. Oppositions at higher organisational level fail to influence those at lower levels. (. . .) The idea of seniority is the common denominator, but the social organisation remains uncoordinated.' (Pfeffer 2001 a, 2001 b: 343).

13. The Ghasias (cleaners of the streets) and Goruas (collectors of leftovers from cremations grounds) are considered junior to the Dombos, but they are very few in number (Berger 2001 a, 2001 b: 23).
14. Desya groups are divided in two, sometimes three sections. Gadaba: Gadaba and Ollar Gadaba; Rona: (*boro*) Rona and *kuttia* Rona; Mali: *boro* Mali, *Modhya* Mali and *sano* Mali.
15. The present discussion is based on research conducted by Peter Berger (2001a, b) among the Gadabas and the author (2000) among the Ronas as well as publications on tribals (Boal 1982; Carrin 1999; Pfeffer 1982, 1996, 2000 a, 2000 b; Pati 1993; Vitebsky 1993) and on tribal healing systems (Behura 1997; Nichter 1992; S.C.&S.T.R.&T.I. 1997a, 1997b).
16. National self-help society, a cultural organization of the Hindu right, which, among other activities, propagates a fundamentalist Hindu way of life among tribal communities.
17. The internet is one of the agents which bring more tourists to this region. Under the headings 'Orissa' and 'tribals' the internet page of 'Tribal Tours' from Bhubaneshwar is indicated as the most popular internet page.
18. The Bondos, who call themselves Remos; are the proverbial 'naked savages'. Their garment for women is a little skirt around the hips and a bunch of beads round the chest. Since this outfit provokes their 'civilized' neighbours, they are not allowed to wear such dress in public. Government authorities threaten them with arrest if they do not cover their bodies with a piece of cloth when going to the market. Their nakedness, however, makes them one of the most popular attractions for tourists in the district (Pfeffer, this volume).
19. This fact seems to be commonplace in schools were tribals are educated. These practices can also be observed in the vicinity of Sambalpur (Behera 2001).
20. There is not much literature available about the use and misuse of alcohol in India. For an anthropological view see Hardiman (1985).
21. Lidia Guzy has conducted fieldwork on the various features of Mahima Dharma (2001).
22. Missionaries from the North Elbian Mission Centre settled in the

Jeypore area from 1882 and established the J.E.L. Church. Others, like the pentacostal churches, followed. For Christian Mission in the Koraput district the most exhaustive source is the work of Otto Waack (1997).

23. Issues of health and systems of medicine were already contested fields in colonial India. This has been demonstrated by authors such as David Arnold, David Hardiman, Mark Harrison and Biswamoy Pati (Arnold 1993, Hardiman 2000, Harrison 1994, Pati 1998).
24. There is no money to buy the necessary equipment, and the ten old injection needles in the possession of one clinic are being 'sterilized' again and again in the same pot of lukewarm water. The hospitals are the institutions in the hills in which Indian bureaucracy makes itself felt most distinctly. Hence the non-government Christian hospital is the only one whose basic medical care is tolerably efficient.
25. We may hope, too, that this process will work the other way round: there are now doctors from the hospital who take an interest in the Desya methods of midwifery.
26. Due to limited space, not all the categories of illness have been discussed here. I have described some others elsewhere (Otten 2000, 2004a, 2004b).

REFERENCES

Arnold, David (1993), *Colonizing the Body: State, Medicine, and Epidemic Disease in Nineteenth-Century India,* Berkeley: University of California Press.

Bailey, F.G. (1960), *Tribe, Caste and Nation: A Study of Political Activity and Political Change in Highland Orissa,* Manchester: Manchester University Press.

———(1961), 'Tribe and Caste in India', *Contributions to Indian Sociology,* 5, pp. 7-19.

Banerjee, R.D. (1928), 'Rajput Origins in Orissa', *Modern Review,* vol. 43 (March), pp. 285ff.

Beals, Alan R. (1976), 'Strategies of Resort to Curers in South India', in Charles Leslie (ed.), *Asian Medical Systems: A Comparative Study,* Berkeley: University of California Press, pp. 184-200.

Behera, Deepak Kumar (2001), 'In Between Two Cultures: The Process of Educational Institutionalization of Tribal Children in Orissa', paper presented at the Annual Meeting of the Orissa Research Project, Salzau, Germany.

Behura, N.K. (1997), 'Cultural Dimensions of Diseases and Their Treatment: Case Studies from Tribal Societies of Orissa', in *Adivasi*, vol. 37, pp. 1-20.

Behuria, N.C. (1964), 'Final Report on the Major Settlements Operations in Koraput District 1938-1964' (unpublished manuscript, courtesy Bidiyut Takri).

Berger, Peter (2001a), 'The Gadaba and the 'non-ST' Desia of Koraput: Some Observations on their Interrelations', in Georg Pfeffer and Deepak Kumar Behera (eds.), *Contemporary Society: Tribal Studies,* vol. 5, Delhi: Concept.

———(2001b), 'Feeding the Dead: Rituals of Transformation Among the Gadaba of Koraput', *Adivasi,* vols. 40/41, nos. 1/2, pp. 35-50.

Berkemer, Georg (1993), *Little kingdoms in Kalinga: Ideologie, Legitimation und Politik regionaler Eliten,* Beiträge zur Südasienforschung, Südasien-Institut Universität Heidelberg, Nr. 156, Stuttgart: Franz Steiner Verlag.

Boal, Barbara M. (1982), *The Khonds: Human Sacrifice and Religious Change*, Warminster: Aris and Phillips.

Carrin-Bouez, Marine (1978), 'Acculturation and/or Dialectics: The Relevance of the Hinduization Model for the Understanding of Santal Society', in Rupert R. Moser and Mohan K. Gautam (eds.), *Aspects of Tribal Life in South Asia I: Strategy and Survival.* Proceedings of an International Seminar held at Bern 1977, Bern: The University of Bern, Institute of Ethnology, pp. 83-92.

———(1991), *Inner Frontiers: Santal Responses to Acculturation*, Bergen: Christian Michelsen Institute.

Carrin, Marine (ed.) (1999), *Managing Distress: Possession and Therapeutic Cults in South Asia*, Delhi: Manohar.

Choudhury, B. (1964-5), 'Notes on the Ranas of Koraput', in *Adivasi*, vol. 4/5, no. 2, pp. 51-6.

Donaldson, Thomas E. (2001), 'Jaina Art in Orissa', in *Ravenshaw Historical Journal*, 2, pp. 7-10.

Dumont, Louis (1980), *Homo Hierarchicus: The Caste System and Its Implications*, Chicago and London: University of Chicago Press.

Dumont, L. and D.F. Pocock (1957), 'For a Sociology of India', *Contributions to Indian Sociology*, 1, pp. 7-22.

Durkheim, Émile (1968), *The Elementary Forms of Religious Life*, New York: Free Press.

Eichinger Ferro-Luzzi, Gabriella (1987), *The Self-milking Cow and the Bleeding Lingam: Criss-cross of Motifs in Indian Temple Legends*, Wiesbaden: Harrassowitz.

———(1989), 'The Polythetic-Prototype Approach to Hinduism', in Günther-D. Sontheimer and Hermann Kulke (eds.), *Hinduism Reconsidered*, Delhi: Manohar, pp. 187-95.

Fischer, E., S. Mahapatra and D. Pathy (eds.) (1980), *Orissa: Kunst und Kultur in Nordost-Indien*, Zürich: Museum Rietberg.

Guha, Sumit (1999), *Environment and Ethnicity in India 1200-1900*, Cambridge: Cambridge University Press.

Guzy, Lidia (2001), 'Voices of Gods: Ecstatic Alekhs and Local Configurations of Mahima Dharma', in *Adivasi*, vol. 41, no. 1/2, pp. 61-70.

Hardiman, David (1985) 'From Custom to Crime: The Politics of Drinking in Colonial South Gujarat', in Ranajit Guha (ed.), *Subaltern Studies IV*, Delhi: Oxford University Press, pp. 165-228.

———(2000), 'Healing and Civilising: Missionaries and Nationalists in Western India, 1880-1998', paper presented at 16th European Modern South Asian Studies Conference, Edinburgh.

Harrison, Mark (1994), *Public Health in British India: Anglo-Indian Preventive Medicine 1859-1914*, Cambridge: Cambridge University Press.

Iteanu, André (1990), 'The Concept of the Person and the Ritual System: An Orokaiva View', *Man*, N.S., vol. 25, pp. 35-53.

Kulke, Hermann (1978), 'Early State Formation and Royal Legitimation in Tribal Areas of Eastern India', in Rupert R. Moser and Mohan K. Gautam (eds.), *Aspects of Tribal Life in South Asia: Strategy and Survival.* Proceeding of an International Seminar held at Bern 1977, Bern: The University of Bern, pp. 29-38.

Leach, E.R. (1954), *Political Systems of Highland Burma*, London: Athlone.

Leslie, Charles (1980), 'Medical Pluralism in World Perspective', in Charles Leslie (ed.), *Medical Pluralism*, Special issue of *Social Science and Medicine*, 14 B (4), pp. 190-6.

Marglin, Frédérique Apffel (1990), 'Smallpox in Two Systems of Knowledge', in F.A. Marglin and S.A. Marglin (eds.), *Dominating Knowledge: Development, Culture, and Resistance*, Oxford: Clarendon Press.

Nichter, Mark (1980), 'The Layperson's Perception of Medicine as a Perspective into the Utilisation of Multiple Therapy Systems in the Indian Context', in *Social Science and Medicine*, 156, pp. 225-33.

———(1983), 'Paying for What Ails You: Socio-cultural Issues Influencing the Ways and Means of Therapy Payment in South India', in *Social Science and Medicine,* 17 (14), pp. 957-65.

———(1992), 'Of Ticks, Kings, Spirits, and the Promise of Vaccines', in Charles Leslie and Allan Young (eds.), *Paths to Asian Medical*

Knowledge, Berkeley, Los Angeles, Oxford: University of California Press, pp. 224-53.

Niggemeyer, Hermann (1964), *Kuttia Kond: Dschungel Bauern in Orissa*, Munich: Renner.

Otten, Tina (2000), 'In a Remote Area: Categories of the Person and Illness Among the Desya of Koraput, Orissa', *Journal of Social Sciences*, vol. 4, pp. 347-56.

———(2007), 'Given by God' and 'Come by Itself': Concepts of Illness Among the Rona, in Georg Pfeffer (ed.), *Periphery and Centre*, Delhi: Manohar.

———(2006), *Heilung duroh Rituale. Von Umgang mit Krankheit bei den Rona im Hoohland Orissa.* Berlin: LIT, Verlag.

Pati, Biswamoy (1993), *Resisting Domination: Peasants, Tribals and the National Movement in Orissa 1920-50*, Delhi: Manohar.

———(1998), 'Siting the Body: Perspectives on Health and Medicine in Colonial Orissa', in *Social Scientist*, vol. 28, pp. 3-26.

Pfeffer, Georg (1982), *Status and Affinity in Middle India*, Wiesbaden: Steiner.

———(1996), 'The Young and the Junior set in Tribal Middle India: On the Category of Age', in Georg Pfeffer and Deepak Kumar Behera (eds.), *Contemporary Society: Childhood and Complex Order*, Prof. Satya Narayana Ratha Festschrift, Delhi: Manak Publications, pp. 98-109.

———(1997), 'The Scheduled Tribes of Middle India as a Unit: Problems of Internal and External Comparison', in Deepak Kumar Behera and Georg Pfeffer (eds.), *Contemporary Society: Tribal Studies I: Structure and Process*, Delhi: Concept, pp. 3-27.

———(2000a), 'Tribal Ideas', *Journal of Social Sciences*, 4(4), pp. 331-46.

———(2000b), 'The Structure of Middle Indian Tribal Society Compared', in Georg Pfeffer (ed.), *Im entlegenen Gebiet: Gesellschaftsentwürfe und interethnische Beziehungen in den Distrikten von Koraput und Sambalpur, der regionalen und sozialen Peripherie Orissas*, Orissa Project Research Papers, pp. 156-76.

Prasad, Archana (2003), *Against Ecological Romanticism: Verrier Elwin and the Making of an Anti-Modern Tribal Identity*, Delhi: Pauls Press.

Ramadas, G. (1931), 'Vedullavalasa Copper-plate Grant of Vira Sri Viswambaradeva Maharaja', *Journal of the Andhra Historical Research Society*, vol. 6, pp. 8-15.

Sahlins, Marshall D. (1968), *Tribesmen*, Englewood Cliffs: Prentice Hall.

Scheduled Castes and Scheduled Tribes Research and Training Institute Bhubaneswar (1997a), 'Tribal Medicine and Medicinemen: An

Exploratory Study of the Bondo of Orissa', *Adivasi*, vol. 37, no. 2, pp. 33-71.

———(1997b), Bhubaneswar: 'Tribal Medicine and Medicinemen: An Exploratory Study of the Didayi of Orissa', *Adivasi*, vol. 37, no. 2, pp. 72-3.

Schnepel, B. and G. Berkemer (2004), 'History of the Model', in G. Berkemer and M. Frenz (eds.), *Sharing Sovereignty: The Little Kingdom in South Asia*, Berlin: Klaus Schwarz, pp. 11-20.

Sinha, Surajit (1962), 'State Formation and Rajput Myth in Tribal Central India', *Man in India*, vol. 42, no. 1, pp. 36-80.

———(1980), 'Tribes and Indian Civilization: A Perspective', *Man in India*, vol. 60, nos. 3-4, pp. 1-15.

Skoda, Uwe (2005), *The Aghria: A Peasant Caste on the Tribal Frontier*, Delhi: Manohar.

Strümpell, Christian (2001), 'Industrialisation in a 'Tribal Zone': The Desya of Koraput and a Hydro-Electric Power Plant', in *Adivasi*, vol. 41, nos. 1-2, pp. 71-81.

Vitebsky, Piers (1993), *Dialogues with the Dead: The Discussion of Mortality Among the Sora of Eastern India*, Cambridge: Cambridge University Press.

Waack, Otto (1997), *Church and Mission in India: The History of the Jeypore Church and the Breklum Mission (1876-1914); with Contribution by Alfred Bruhn, Anton Asha, and S.C. Sekhoro Mohoriya*, Delhi: Indian Society for Promoting Christian Knowledge.

4

Impact of Mega-Dam Project on the Social Life of the Pengs of Orissa

DEEPAK KUMAR BEHERA
SRIKANT PATEL

INTRODUCTION

'Jungle' is often opposed to forest in that it grows on its own and is only marginally influenced by human activity. But the people living in the jungle traditionally adapted themselves to live in harmony with their immediate environment without damaging it. They ensured the reproduction of the jungle through a symbiotic relationship. These adaptations had survival value and protected the forest communities from extinction (Gadgil and Guha 1995, Arnold and Guha 1995). Keeping in view the prevailing conditions people gradually adopted new techniques or abandoned old ones according to their efficacy. The different adaptations were institutionalized through various cultural practices and those who failed to observe them were punished or ostracized. However the ongoing process of modernization has adversely influenced such arrangements. The once meaningful adaptation now fails to bring the desired results in the changing conditions. Many development projects among tribal populations are not sustainable as they are mostly designed without taking the interest of the indigenous population into account. Moreover, tribal people seldom understand the long-term implications of development projects, hence fail in their effort to devise measures to counter them.

The traditional way of life of indigenous peoples is threatened by the ongoing process of globalization. Here, indigenous knowledge is regarded as the unique, traditional, local knowledge existing within and developed around the specific conditions of indigenous people in a particular geographical area. It is the sum total of knowledge and skills which people in a particular geographical area possess, and which enables them to get the most out of their natural environment. Much of this knowledge and skill has been passed down from earlier generations, but individuals in each new generation adapt and add to this body of knowledge in a constant adjustment to changing circumstances and environmental conditions. They in turn pass it on to the next generation, to provide them with survival strategies. Though indigenous knowledge has seldom been systematically documented, it should be seen as dynamic and based on innovation, adaptation and experimentation. It covers critical issues such as primary production, human and animal life and natural resource management. The practical implications of the interconnections between the social and the environmental can be very important, and it is often the case that subsistence practices triggered by cultural beliefs appear to regulate resources (Behera 2000: i).

OBJECTIVES AND METHODOLOGY

The present paper deals with the impact of a mega-dam project on the long-standing cultural adaptations of the Peng, a tribal community of Orissa. Their traditional adaptation is shifting cultivation, which demands pooling of work at the time of clearing and burning the forest. Conversely, during the three lean months of the year there is a need to redistribute the results of the dispersed productive activities that are possible (fishing, gathering of forest products) in order to ensure survival for all. This production cycle was regulated by the ritual year, which helped to ensure that resources were not used prematurely and were thus maximally distributed. The necessary cooperation and flexibility of personnel was ensured by kinship networks. The impact of the dam has been to destroy or separate common territory, making cooperation difficult, as also to separate kin groups from each other, disturbing patterns of marriage and cooperation among kin. Thus the paper critically examines various changes that have occurred in the traditional adaptation processes of the Pengs due to their exposure to external forces. Finally it analyses the efficacy of new adaptive strategies in the light of the changing conditions.

Data was collected from three resettled villages of the upper Indravati river valley. The sample villages, namely, Sanchhatrang, Dudungchuan and Bagbeda are inhabited mostly by Pengs. Some additional information was collected from village Podaauding to supplement our analysis. Observation, interviews and case studies were used for data collection. An attempt was made to reconstruct the traditional adaptation processes of the Pengs in the old villages to facilitate comparison.

THE PROJECT AND ITS CONTEXT

Dam building in India after Independence became a major symbol of modernization. Even today, the mega-dam continues to be seen as a symbol of progress, of man's supremacy over nature, of prosperity and pride. In the 1970s, however, some notice was taken of the widespread damage caused to the landscape by dams, and in the 1980s the socio-economic costs of large dams began to be recorded across the world. But it was only in the 1990s that the social impact of the dams brought ecological and economic arguments to the fore, as marginalized and displaced communities gained a voice in the political arena.

We may note that the livelihood of the displaced people has not been restored; in fact, the vast majority have become impoverished (Mohapatra 1990). The millions of people forcibly dislocated from their lands are usually from among the poorest and most vulnerable sections of the population. Upon dislocation, these communities are pushed into further poverty. This in itself constitutes grave violations of human rights. In spite of tall claims of welfare for the indigenous people as a goal in the planning era, the indigenous people remain victims of exploitation by the so-called civilized people from the plain areas. Land alienation, de-peasantization and indebtedness continue unabated (Pattnaik 1972; Pathy 1982; Fürer-Haimendorf 1982; Mohanty 1997; Agnihotri 1996).

Most of the mega-dams, mines, wild life sanctuaries and heavy industries were set-up in remote areas, displacing indigenous people on a massive scale (Areeparampil 1996; Fernandes 1991, 1997; Mohapatra 1990; Mishra 1996). Among them, the cumulative effect of these experiences has gradually forged animosity and hatred towards the people of the plain areas. They consider the larger society as exploitative and oppressive, as a category to be opposed and fought. Thus it could never become a standard of evaluation, emulation and aspiration (Xaxa 2001: 2770).

In this context developmental measures planned and implemented under the tutelage of representatives of the larger society are not easily accepted or appreciated by the indigenous people (Mohanty 2003: 92). To quote Fürer-Haimendorf (1982: 128): 'as long as they operate within their familiar atmosphere tribals evince as much perspicacity, skill and even true wisdom as any other population, but as soon as they are faced by social attitude rooted in a different system they become unsure and often behave in a manner detrimental to their own interests'.

The indigenous people remained victims of exploitation by outsiders. Forests, the mainstay of the indigenous economy, were reserved in the interest of the nation, with indigenous people at the mercy of officials from the plains. Forest resources were taken away from the remote areas for the development of the more advanced communities (Vyasulu 1985; Mohanty, 1997).

Most development projects in Orissa are located inland in the hills, basically inhabited by ethnic communities belonging to Scheduled Tribes (ST), Scheduled Castes (SC) and Other Backward Classes (OBC) (Swain and Panigrahi 1999: 164-5). Needless to say, big dams and irrigation projects are the most important causes of displacement. It has been calculated that during the last forty years about 56.377 families comprising a population of some 270,000 have been displaced due to irrigation projects in Orissa. In other words, on an average 5,000 persons have been displaced per year

(Daula 1993: 25). The case of the Hirakud Dam may be cited as an example. It has a dyke of 13 miles, the main dam is about 3 miles long and the maximum height is 195 ft. It has affected 249 villages, 22,144 families, 18,432 houses and 112,039 acres of cultivated land submerged by the Hirakud reservoir (Baboo 1992: 31).

Scattered in the *Dongerla* region are numerous small hamlets of the indigenous people. Apart from the Peng, other ethnic groups affected are the Jhadia (ST), Kondh (ST), Dom (SC), Päik (OBC), Sundhi (OBC) and Gouda (OBC). The mountains have sustained them both materially and spiritually for centuries. They worship forests, hills and water, believing they are controlled by their presiding gods and goddesses, and that unless they satisfy these spirits they will cause misfortune.

The plan to construct a multipurpose hydroelectric project on the river Indravati was conceived in the year 1959 and in the same year investigation of its feasibility commenced. However, its approval by the Union Planning Commission was delayed until 1977 because of problems concerning the equitable distribution of water resources. The construction began only after obtaining financial assistance from the World Bank in 1985. According to official sources, about 17,000 people from 97 villages—44 villages from undivided Koraput and 53 from Kalahandi districts—were affected by the construction of the dam (RRU 1997: 3). The Krushak Mahasangha and the Indravati Gana Sangharsha—local NGOs—even put the figure at 30,000. Evacuation started in 1989 and continued till 1993, being carried out in four phases. To begin with the Resettlement and Rehabilitation Unit constructed two rehabilitation colonies, Sashahandi and Talejaring, to relocate the displaced. These sites, however, were found unsuitable by the evictees. As a result, they were given a free hand to relocate in their place of choice. Most of them preferred to settle near the shores of the reservoir, with minimal displacement from their ancestral land and social network. The majority of them are tribals, who lived in the fertile Indravati river valley. Among the various tribal populations, the Peng are the largest group seriously affected by the project. The impact of the dam was felt by them from the very conception of its construction.

THE PENG: AN OVERVIEW

The Peng are one of the various indigenous populations in the district of Kalahandi, which borders on Koraput district (Pfeffer; Otten, both this volume). They consider themselves as Parja—the ruled or the commoners—and also identify themselves as Desia—the indigenous. While the word 'parja' has a political sense, Desia connotes the people living within the territory. The Pengs can hardly conceive of living in any territory outside their social boundary. It is interesting to note that the other tribal groups such as Jhodia, Parenga, Gadaba, Kondha, etc., living in this region also consider themselves as Parja or Desia, which tends to confuse outsiders. Hence, the latter sometimes treat the Jhodia, Pareng and Kondha as subsections of Parja. However, to lump them together under the generic term 'parja' misses the point since we are dealing with separate entities, even if they have much in common within a broad cultural mosaic. Though interdependent in many walks of life, each group has its own distinct socio-cultural system. Hence we treat the Peng of Kalahandi district as a distinct tribal group. Inter-tribal communication in this region is carried out within a common *lingua franca* known as Desia bhasha. The Pengs also communicate with other non-ST Desia groups in the region through the *lingua franca*. They may be broadly classified into two categories, highlanders and plains dwellers. The highlanders (locally known as Dongerla Pengs) are less exposed to the outside world than their brethren in the plains. The present study is confined to the Dongerla Pengs living in a mountain pass which forms part of the Eastern Ghats. They call the pass *dharam-dooar* (the gate of truth), and they have been living there since 'times immemorial'. Scattered in the dongerla region are numerous small hamlets of the Peng tribe. The Pengs' world must be seen through their eyes, as they live in an intangible as well as a tangible world. The intangible world, very significant to a Peng, can hardly be perceived by an outsider. They worship the mountains, the growth and the under-growth as gods and goddesses and hold them in high esteem. They believe that the village deity and other demi-gods protect them; hence they feel more confident and secure in their ancestral land. They are hardworking people, subsisting on a simple technology. Their economy has multiple loci, centering on cultivation by slash-and-burn, collection of forest produce, hunting wild game, and wage earning as agricultural labourers.

The Pengs are aware that the natural resources have survival value and that their depletion by improper utilization may prove fatal to the community. Management of these resources, such as forest, land, water, etc., needs collective action and there is no ambiguity whatsoever among the Pengs regarding resource management through cultural practices.

A traditional Peng village has various functionaries such as the *dhangda majhi* (headman), the *jani* (priest and medicine man), the *disari* (astrologer), the *gunia* (shaman), the *gurmai* (lesser shaman) and the *barik* (messenger). The *barik* is often from the Dom community. He collects contributions for any festival or ritual from each household. The money is used to buy animals and other goods for sacrifice at the market. This is the *barik*'s duty, as he is adept at striking a good bargain.

MODE OF PRODUCTION, RESOURCE COLLECTION AND UTILIZATION

The Pengs produce for subsistence, so surplus or hoarding do not make any sense to them. Their calendar year starts with *Poos* (mid-December to mid-January)[1] to end with *Pond.* Their economy centres round *khadi* (food) and they organize themselves to be assured of it all round the year. Their economy is seasonal and they pursue different kinds of economic activities in accordance with the availability of natural resources (see Fig. 1).

Most of the Pengs are landless and those having land are marginal landholders.[2] They practice shifting cultivation on the slope of the hills, and the amount of land used for crop production barely exceeds two acres per household. The Pengs are not nomadic by nature, but those living in the Dongerla region and practising shifting cultivation change the site of settlement along with their clearings. These movements are restricted to pre-selected sites, following a cyclic order. Their mode of cultivation is primarily a multiple-

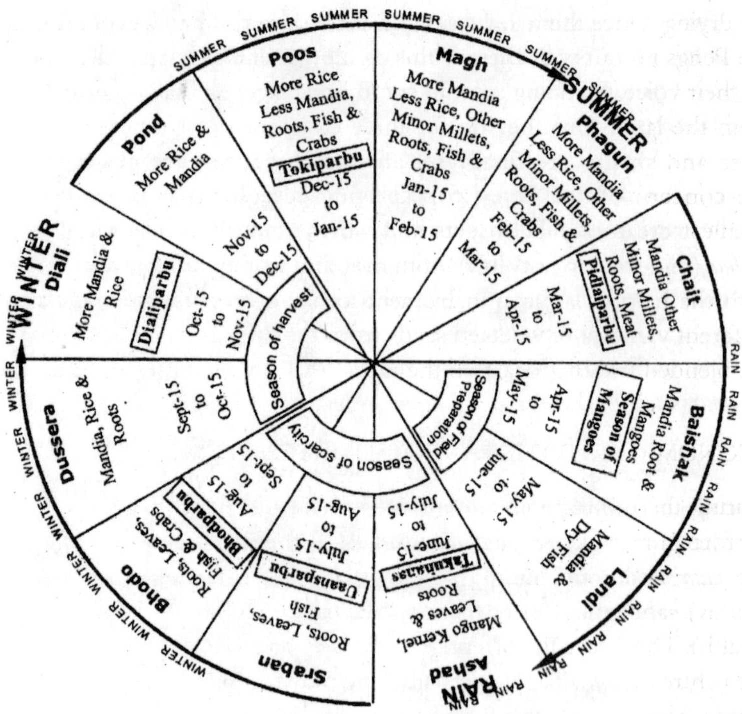

Fig. 1: The calendar year of the Pengs showing different seasons, months, food habits and ritual (adopted from Elizabeth F. Andrews, 1996).

cropping pattern. They grow a variety of crops in the same field and at the same time, ranging from different minor millets to coarse cereals and pulses; rice is also grown in the *dongar* as well as in the plain. On an average, the land requirement for the Pengs' shifting cultivation is much less than that of non-tribal peasants practising settled cultivation. Still, environmentalists and others concerned with such issues condemn the tribal communities for this mode of production. It is a strange paradox that while non-tribal intruders misappropriate forest wealth by their greed and graft, the tribals are blamed for their creed and craft.

Cultivation activities start from the month of *Landi* (mid-May to mid-June). Having selected a patch of land the Pengs slash the growth and undergrowth and leave the plants exposed to the sun for drying. Once the felled trees and shrubs are ready to be set afire, the Pengs go out with their drums to the site and shout at the peak of their voice. By doing so, they try to drive away all living creatures from the land. This they do for three consecutive days before the trees and shrubs are finally set afire. This procedure speaks for the concern of the Pengs for all living beings, may they be the smallest creatures like insects and worms. During the month of *Ashad* (mid-June to mid-July), both men and women furrow the land with the help of an iron instrument locally known as *kodki*. Then different varieties of selected seeds from the previous year's harvest are blended and broadcast on the fields.

ECONOMIC ACTIVITIES AND ASSOCIATED RITUALS

During the month of *Saraban* (mid-July to mid-August) the Pengs perform a ritual known as *Uaansparbu*. On the day before the ritual, the *jaani* and *disari* bring a *dera* (bottle brush millet) and a *kuling* (paddy) sapling and offer them to Sitakania (goddess of crops and wealth). They leave the offerings in the *gudighar* (abode of the deity at the centre of the village) overnight, and pray for the growth of these plants. Similarly, all the Pengs bring *dera* and *kuling* saplings from their respective fields and place them before Sitakania, requesting her to protect the crops from external dangers. These *dera* and *kuling* saplings are considered to be sacred. The next day they celebrate *Uaansparbu* and the sacred saplings are transplanted in the field.

Saraban is the month of surveillance of the crops. They watch the standing crops in the field and worship Sitakania for their protection and proper growth. During the month of *Bhodo* (mid-August to mid-September) the crops are ready for harvesting, and the *Bhodparbu* ritual is performed, in order to get permission from Sitakania to bring the crops home from the field. Until the *Bhodparbu*, nobody is allowed to harvest the new crops. It is believed that if someone eats the new rice without performing the *Bhodparbu*, tigers from the forest would attack the village and destroy both cattle and humans. For the same reason, the early cob of *jahna* (maize) from the field cannot be plucked without the performance of the *Jahnamara* ritual.

It is interesting to note that most activities related to cultivation start with one ritual and end with another. We agree with Lee who points out, 'there exists a core culture in the primitive society that is intimately linked to mode of production. It is much longer lived, has a much deeper time depth . . .' (1988: 255).

Most of the Pengs' requirements are met by their own production, and their dependence on the market is minimal. The produce from the field is rarely sold in the market, but may be bartered when needs arise. Their main crops are *kuling* and *dera*. They, as well as *kohoda* (a kind of minor millet), *arku* (minor millet), and *kating* (a kind of pulses), are mainly produced for home consumption. The Pengs have elaborate rituals concerning the cultivation of these crops, which are harvested and brought to the *katar* where it is threshed and after *Katar puja* (a ritual performed during harvesting and threshing) the crop is divided among the claimants and taken to their respective homes.

The months of *Dussera*, *Diali* and *Pond*—named after these festivals—are times of rejoicing. Then the home of the Pengs is full with *pachee* (harvest), and they celebrate with merry-making, fun and frolic. Old debts are repaid and new investments are made in buying clothes, fowl or cattle.

The Pengs experience a lean period during the months of *Ashad, Saraban* and *Bhodo*. During these crucial months, they rely heavily on natural resources like forests, rivers, and ponds, for mere survival. Their needs are met partly by gathering from the forest, by fishing in rivers and ponds, and also by wage earning both within and outside the village. This is the time when they fall back upon their social networks to survive. Distribution during the lean season therefore emerges as a pragmatic adaptation, which has endured the ravages of time and sustained the Pengs through the vagaries of life.

The Pengs' resource utilization, then, is characterized by aggregation during part of the year and distribution and utilization at other times. The entire cycle from resource collection to utilization is guided and monitored by cultural sanctions and institutions. During the month of *Chait* (15 March to 15 April) the Pengs perform two rituals, namely, *Chaitparbu* and *Pidlaiparbu*. *Chaitparbu* heralds the beginning of the hunting expedition. During *Chaitparbu* all able-bodied men go hunting in the forest. When the kill is made, all members of the community share it equally. The practice of going to the forest for game is known as *bentaboola*. For eight days the male members go hunting and once they make a kill they return home. Not until the eighth day are other economic activities resumed. Thereafter *bentaboola* ceases to be a regular activity and eventually stalls during the month of *Landi*. *Bentaboola* is not confined to the Peng, other tribal and non-tribal Desia also participate.

It is forbidden to pluck mangoes before the *Pidlaiparbu* ritual. If someone does so without performing the ritual it is believed to bring bad luck for the whole village. It is interesting to note that the Pengs may have to perform more than one ritual for using different parts of the same product. For example, they can eat only the pulp of the mango by performing the *Pidlaiparbu*; another ritual known as *Takuhanas* must be performed if the mango kernel is to be eaten. It is dried and stored for use during the lean period, when a kind of gruel is made from mango kernel. Both the *Pidlaiparbu* and *Takuhanas* rituals are performed at a fixed time of the year and there can be no deviation whatsoever. The *Takuhanas* ritual is performed in the month of *Ashad* (mid-June to mid-August), at the beginning of the lean period. Several other rituals are performed during the collection of other forest produce like roots, tubers, leaves, honey, resin, etc. The mode of collection of these resources shows their efforts at managing them.

A careful analysis of various rituals and their timing reveals that these cultural practices help the Pengs to space the utilization of resources in accordance with their need, minimizing risk and uncertainty. These mechanisms act as a cultural safety-catch and regulate the over-exploitation or over-utilization of resources. Viegas and Menon are right in stressing that 'the tribals built cultural and religious myths, rituals and social control mechanisms which were geared to maintaining a balance between human and ecological needs' (1989: 59).

During the hunt, game is carefully selected. Pregnant animals are seldom hunted and the very young ones are released when trapped.

The Pengs not only protect their respective totems like *langlabehing* (tiger), *zabeing* (snake), *kotchim* (turtle), etc., they also take an interest in their regeneration and growth. All this shows an endeavour to space the available resources and restrain the users from over-exploiting them, saving them for when they are highly needed, and checking depletion of natural resources. Hence it can be argued that the economy of the Peng is embedded within the cultural matrix and each component of the economy is culturally ordained and patterned. The economy of the Peng is so designed that it not only provides livelihood in the present but also assures the basic needs of future generations. Polanyi is quite clear on this point, saying that 'man's economy, as a rule is enmeshed in his social relationships' (1957: 46).

The cultural practices of the Pengs are, in fact, adaptive structures which maintain a balance between the population and natural as well as social resources within their immediate environment. However, such arrangements get eroded by the intrusion of various external forces under the aegis of development. As a result, the age-old adaptation fails and institutions once benign become deleterious.

IMPACT OF FORCED DISPLACEMENT

For all indigenous people, access to land is fundamental, not only in an economic sense, for the importance of land is usually reflected in almost all parts of indigenous culture. Their kinship system is instrumental in distributing rights to land, and religion is commonly related both to land and kinship system. If sudden and extensive changes occur, they have consequences for the entire culture. Loss of land and of the traditional resource base, then, is not merely economic. Displacement as a consequence of the Indravati project has led to physical exclusion from a geographic territory but also to economic and social exclusion from a set of functioning social networks. The consequences of displacement also include desecration of ancestral sacred zones, scattering of kinship groups and families, with the disorganization of informal social networks.

The project has altered land use patterns that traditionally supported farming, grazing and fishing. Thus indigenous populations have lost substantial parts of their traditional income base, and were marginalized when they had to move from fertile valley-bottom lands uphill to inferior soils. Marginalization also occurred through the loss of other sources of income. Economic marginalization was accompanied by social and psychological marginalization.

Asked by the investigators from a Catholic Management Institute, 'What does the dam construction on the Indravati mean to you?', villagers from the project area answered:

> We are people in the woods. We need the woods because we manage our livelihood from them. To our belief, the land belongs to Gods, not to the Government. If it belongs to the Gods, how can the Government take it away from us? We shall neither abandon this land nor our houses. If the wood disappears under water, the people will go down too. (XIM 1994)

The institute also reports some other findings. The baseline survey failed to determine the exact number of people displaced, and there was no meaningful participation of the affected people in the planning, implementation and monitoring of the project. They did not receive complete and authentic information on the project, on the extent of displacement or on the Rehabilitation and Resettlement (R&R) provisions. The delay between the decision to build the dam and its construction, meant that indigenous people lived for decades starved of development and welfare investments. The government did not want to spend money for development in a region which was going to be submerged. The affected people experienced a series of problems related to infrastructure, occupation and social support mechanisms in the resettlement sites. The submergence of vast areas of land brought a major setback to the economy of the indigenous people, yet they did not receive water or electricity services or any social or economic benefits. Large inequalities were found in the compensation packages given by the project authorities to the evacuees, leading to marginalization of some already weak sections of the population like women, children and widows. The construction of the dam has transformed the landscape of the region, creating risks to the ecosystem (XIM 1994).

RESISTANCE TO THE PROJECT

A local leader from the district of Nawarangpur was instrumental in motivating the displaced persons of Nawarangpur to fight for their rights. The Budi Anchal Paraja Dabi Committee (BAPDC) was formed on his initiative, as was another such committee formed by the displaced persons of Kalahandi. The first meeting of the BAPDC was held in Kalahandi in 1977. Now BAPDCs have been formed in all the affected areas—Kalahandi, Nawarangpur, Rayagada and Koraput.

At the time of displacement many facts related to rehabilitation and compensation were not made public. The BAPDC played an important role in bringing to light facts which were deliberately suppressed by the project authorities. The movement also tried to make the evacuees aware of the long-term consequences of the project. The BAPDC organized a rally on 31 December 1997, attended by around 15,000 people affected by the project. Their main slogan was 'do not keep quiet, disclose your identity while fighting for your rights'. Another major rally was organized in 1999 when a charter of demands was sent to the Governor of Orissa, followed by a hunger strike in 2001. But the demands have not been fulfilled, leading to a lot of frustration. One assurance made by the project authorities was the inclusion of all sons more than eighteen years old in the list of Project Affected People. Though there was an advertisement inviting applications from all eligible sons, the officials have yet to take any action on the applications received.

The indigenous people have very little economic support to fall back upon if they begin an agitation; illiteracy is high and they do not have the confidence needed to deal with project officials and the state machinery. Though some of the Committee's demands have been fulfilled, many others have been sidelined by the project authorities.

In the initial phase people participated enthusiastically in the Committee's activities. But they slowly lost interest finding it somewhat ineffective. The Committee could not acquire the required momentum due to financial hardship, co-ordination problems and lack of effective leadership. As an alternative some of the displaced people started fighting for their rights through a local lawyer.

DISRUPTION OF SOCIAL NETWORK

Sukuli is a partially submerged village of Maligaon Gram Panchayat under the Thuamul Rampur Block. Here the villagers, with the support from some indigenous people, have launched a protest movement challenging some of the rehabilitation measures adopted by the project officials. In Sukuli, people have lost almost all their lands in the plain and are left with only a little *donger* land. The reservoir, which surrounds their village on three sides, acts as a geographical barrier against collecting and selling firewood, to which evacuees of other settlement clusters have taken for maintaining their livelihood. There are few wage-earning opportunities in both the agricultural and non-agricultural sectors. The people of Sukuli made a representation to the 'Jana Samparka Shibira' held in October 1996. While many government officials listened to their grievances, no significant action address these issues so far. The protest movement therefore continues with the support of the BAPDC.

Most of the Peng evictees preferred to stay as close to as possible to their ancestral land and the social network because they did not like to start life afresh in a new environment about which they felt uncertain. Baboo (1991: 288-303) made a similar observation in his study on the evictees of the Hirakud Dam Project. He noted that people did not like to be cut-off from their kinship, caste and village networks especially when they were not the direct beneficiaries of the irrigation scheme.

But the Pengs' idea of using the social network did not work when the project officials came up with an innovative idea for their resettlement. They made it mandatory for the evictees to utilize at least 50 per cent of the cash compensation to buy land. This policy led to forced buying of land, which generated individual landholdings and gave property rights to the new landholders. The solidarity within the family and kin group was adversely influenced by this, and cooperation and collective action diminished, giving rise to animosity and mutual bickering. Generally, the Pengs do not divide their land among the claimants. Most often, they cultivate the field jointly and share the produce equally. This arrangement has proved economically more sustainable than individual holdings and it also augments intra-familial co-operation. Labour is pooled from within the family, or exchanged with other members of the village, without hiring in from outside. Whenever labour is hired from within the village, all those who work are equally paid in kind, irrespective of age or sex.

The Pengs, accordingly, used one half of their compensation money to buy agricultural land. But land was not available in or near the resettled villages. All the land available there was highly priced by the proprietors. Therefore, they bought new patches of land in different villages, far away from the place of resettlement, in order to qualify for the other half of the compensation money. Initially, they could manage economically, as the water was not impounded immediately in the reservoir, and so the condemned land was still available for cultivation. The Pengs continued to cultivate their old lands for almost five years, and did not concern themselves with the newly bought land. The new lands became a point of concern for them only after the impoundment of the reservoir and inundation of their *jhola* land. The *jhola* lands are the most fertile in the region and are suitable for paddy cultivation. Once the *jhola* lands were lost to the reservoir, the Pengs were left with a little *dongar* land on the hills to cultivate minor millets, by the slash-and-burn method locally known as *podu.* Only then, did they start to take an interest in the new lands they had purchased in different villages. Since the people of one village had bought land at different places, far from the place of resettlement, they found it difficult to pool labour from the same village or the same *tonden* for cultivation. A larger unit would have been economically more viable than a nuclear domestic group, but exchange of labour among them has become a thing of the past, as it cannot be applied where they have bought their new land. It is not argued, here, that the kinship ties have ceased to exist. The relationships still exist at the normative and ideal level, but they have lost much of their meaning and purpose in the new resettlements. Both the inter-village and intra-village relationships have undergone drastic change after displacement (Patel and Behera 1999: 98).

Hiring labour has increased the cost of production. As a result some of them have leased out their land in *adhi* to the landlords from whom they bought it, and now receive half of the produce as their share. A few have sold their land back to the same landlords. Some of their lands have also been encroached upon by unscrupulous landlords and local people, as the evictees are not there to look after them. These developments have adversely affected their economy, and led many of the male villagers to migrate for wage work to various urban centres, such as Nawarangpur and Bhawanipatna in the state and Raipur and Hyderabad outside Orissa, thus leaving many female-headed households behind.

The large reservoir created by the dam has alienated and disrupted the social networking of the Pengs. Previously, they had a wider range of choice from which to find a spouse from their traditional affines, but now the barrier created by the reservoir has curtailed this practice. Traditionally, the young prospective males of one village visit another, where the girls welcome them. The girls and boys identify and assess the feasibility of marriage between them through the *laga geet* (songs). All through the night they sing around a fire. They propose to each other by revealing the *mannahai*, their place of residence, and so on. After impoundment of water, the communication with a good number of potential affines' villages have been cut-off, and the prospective grooms are left with less choice in the selection of a spouse. The marriages are now governed by the access to resources in the form of forest and *donger* land for sustenance in the affines' village. Today, uxorilocal residence has become very common among the Pengs of the Indravati river valley, as the girls from traditional villages will not accept the reduced standard of living of the resettled groups.

CHANGING RELATIONSHIP UNDER THE *MULKA-THAKADA* INSTITUTION

Traditionally the Pengs maintain a ceremonial relationship with the Doms, who are one of the scheduled castes in Orissa and are considered as Untouchables. The Pengs do not accept food from them. Yet the Doms are well versed in the language of the caste people who represent the great tradition (Redfield 1955) in the region. Due to their better communicative ability and exposure to the wider society, the Doms shuttle between the *dongerla* (hills) and the plains, mostly inhabited by the caste people.

A Dom enters into a ceremonial relationship with a Peng by investing in a *gamchha* (towel), some country liquor, and a chicken which he gives to a male member of a Peng family, normally the head of the household. The Dom promises the Peng to be his trusted friend, lead him safely through difficult circumstances, and protect him from the evil designs of the non-Desia communities. He becomes the *mulka*—the leader and the Pengs the *thakada*—the tail. The Pengs, having limited contact with the outer world and remaining distant from the system of power and administration which is exogenous to their concerns, then seek the help of the Doms in matters pertaining to tenurial, judicial, and market affairs.

The Doms are part and parcel of the Pengs' social life and play a significant role in their village organization. After the advent of the Indravati dam project the *mulka-thakada* institution has changed into an exploitative one. Because of their exposure to the wider society, Doms were better informed about the project than their Peng counterparts. This asymmetry created a large information lag between them. The Pengs relied on the Doms on matters related to enumeration, disbursement of compensation, and purchase of agricultural land. The Pengs were paid in currency notes of higher denominations; and they sought the help of their respective *mulkas* for counting them. This gave scope for the Doms to swindle and misappropriate a major chunk of the compensation awarded to the Pengs.

Though the Pengs sometimes felt cheated, they stuck to their *mulka* for matters related to compensation and rehabilitation, as they thought it better to be with a known enemy than an unknown friend. Scudder and Colson, on the basis of their study on rehabilitation and resettlement, observe that the situation of rural communities under 'relocation theory' is one of 'extreme stress'. These communities tend to see socio-cultural systems as closed. After moving they cling to familiar people and institutions during the initial years. As the stress mounts close to a critical threshold, radical changes from within (revitalization) and intervention from outside to change the social organization are both rejected (Scudder et al. 1975:

264). In the case of the Pengs, however, the relation to the Doms, though maintained, is strained today. There is lot of discontent and disaffection between the two.

Apart from buying land, the cash compensation paid to the evicted families in lieu of the condemned house and land was not used by the Pengs for asset-building, nor were they able to keep it for long. It was mostly spent on alcohol and merry-making during festivals. The Pengs are used to make merry and spend lavishly after the harvest and the cash compensation was no more than what the *pachee* brought in a good year. Moreover, there was no cultural safety-catch to prevent over-utilization of cash. Hence the cash compensation fizzled out in no time.

CONCLUSION

The construction of the upper Indravati hydro-electricity project has had a deep impact on the social life of the Pengs. It has devastated the social networking system—the life line of the community—and depleted the natural resources and the life sustaining support system. It has eroded the values and the ethos—the guy wire of their social system—and created an atmosphere of uncertainty and fear among the people affected. The project's effort to rehabilitate the evicted population has in fact done more harm than good, as it was designed half-heartedly without any imaginative anticipation.

Under the changing scenario the economy of the Pengs has undergone drastic changes. Their dependency on the forest has multiplied manifold. They now harvest forest produce, not only for their own consumption but also for the daily market in the nearest town at Khatiguda. Many Pengs are today selling firewood to officials and other outsiders in Khatiguda. It is a pity to see the constructive dependence changing into an exploitative one. Since the *donger* land is not adequate for their sustenance, the fallow period has diminished significantly from six to three years. The younger generation is no longer concerned about their totems and some do not hesitate to kill them for their benefit.

Before displacement by the dam, castes like the Paik, Sundhi and Gaud lived near the Pengs' hamlet. The Pengs choose to stay close to the forest but the caste people have migrated to distant places owing to their wider social network. They once played an important role as moneylenders: Whenever required, the Pengs used to borrow money from the caste *sahukar* but they now find it hard to borrow money as the Sundhi and Paik *sahukars* have left. This arrangement has now been snapped off, ending the long-standing patron-client relationship between the communities and leaving the Pengs poorer in terms of social resources.

The large reservoir provides an opportunity for fishing, but though the Pengs used to fish in the Indravati river and small water bodies, their traditional technology is not suitable to fish in large lakes. Moreover, this region has drawn many able fishermen from the Chakma refugee community. The Pengs find themselves no match for these fishermen. While the Chakmas have boats the Pengs fish from the banks with fishing hooks and small nets, and their catch is small compared to that of the Chakma. Still, they are trying to develop new adaptive strategies to survive. They now use many fishing hooks and poles at one time to make a better catch in a relatively short time. They install these fishing poles on the banks of the reservoir. Knitting of fishing nets has now become a popular pastime and a means of livelihood among the Pengs, and young and old men are found engaged in this work.

Sustainable practices are important for tribal people since it was traditionally the only guarantee for their survival (Behera and Erasmus 1999: 28). The value of indigenous knowledge is increasingly recognized, especially in the context of management of resources. Local communities have a number of socio-cultural practices for resource management, which contribute significantly towards long-term sustainability of resources. However, the recent rapid technological advancement, unrivalled economic and political strength of world capitalism, and the rising power of neo-colonialism have created conditions for the invasion and extraction of natural resources from the ecologically fragile territories of indigenous peoples. These factors have irretrievably mutilated their distinctive socio-cultural organization and cognitive framework. When state and other agencies interfere to introduce 'rational' measures to conserve resources, ignorant of local cultural representations, their purpose is often incomprehensible to locals. Similarly, even with the best of intentions, government may interfere with cultural regulators (purposeful or inadvertent) which are often, in the long run, more effective than the government measures.

NOTES

1. The intermediate months are *Magh, Phagun, Chait, Baishak, Landi, Ashad, Saraban, Bhodo, Dussera,* and *Diali.*
2. Their average landholdings are less than two acres.

REFERENCES

Agnihotri, A. (1996), 'The Orissa Resettlement and Rehabilitation of Project-Affected Persons Policy, 1994—An Analysis of its Robustness with Reference to Impoverishment Risk Model', in A.B. Ota and A. Agnihotri (eds.), *Involuntary Displacement in Dam Projects*, Delhi: Prachi Prakashan, pp. 19-42.

Areeparampil, Mathew (1996), 'Displacement Due to Mining in Jharkhand', *Economic and Political Weekly*, vol. 31, no. 24, pp. 1524-8.

Arnold, D. and Ramachandra Guha (eds.) (1995), *Nature, Culture, Imperialism*, Delhi: Oxford University Press.

Baboo, B. (1991), 'Big Dams and the Tribals: The Case of the Hirakud Dam Oustees in Orissa', *Social Action*, vol. 41, no. 3, pp. 288-303.

———(1992), *Technology and Social Transformation*, Delhi: Concept.

Behera, D.K. (2000), 'Editorial Note', *Journal of Social Sciences*, vol. 4, no. 1, p. i.

Behera, D.K. and P. Erasmus (1999), 'Environment, Tribal People and Development: Some Reflection from the Third World', in D.K. Behera and G. Pfeffer (eds.), *Contemporary Society: Tribal Studies*, vol. 3: *Social Concern*, Delhi: Concept, pp. 21-35.

Daula, A.K. (1993), *Environmental Impact of Large Reservoir Projects on Human Settlement*, Delhi: Ashish.

Fernandes, Walter (1991), 'Power and Powerlessness: Development Projects and Displacement of Tribals', *Social Action*, vol. 41, no. 3, pp. 243-70.

———(1997), 'Displacement of Tribals: Struggles and Implications for Resettlement', in George Pfeffer and D.K. Behera (eds.), *Contemporary Society: Tribal Studies*, vol. 2, Delhi: Concept, pp. 71-91.

Fürer-Haimendrof, C. Von (1982), *The Tribes of India: Struggle for Survival*, Delhi: Oxford University Press.

Gadgil, M. and R. Guha (1995), *Ecology and Equity: The Use and Abuse of Nature in Contemporary India*, London: Routledge.

Lee, R.B. (1988), 'Reflection on Primitive Communism', in T. Ingold et al. (eds.), *Hunters and Gatherers: History, Evolution and Social Change*, vol. I, Oxford: Berg, pp. 252-8.

Mishra, Nita (1996), 'Tribal Resistance in the Chhechhari Valley: A Report', *Economic and Political Weekly*, vol. 31, no. 24, pp. 1539-40.

Mohanty, B.B. (1997), 'State and Tribal Relationship in Orissa', *Indian Anthropologist*, vol. 27, no. 1, pp. 1-17.

———(2001), 'Land Distribution among Scheduled Castes and Tribes', *Economic and Political Weekly*, vol. 36, no. 40, pp. 3857-67.

———(2003), 'Educational Progress of Scheduled Tribes: A Discursive Review', *Man and Development*, vol. XXV, no. 2, pp. 91-106.

Mohapatra, L.K. (1990), 'Rehabilitation of Tribals Affected by Major Dams and Other Projects in Orissa', in A.P. Fernandes (ed.), *A Report on the Workshop on Rehabilitation of Persons Displaced by Development Projects*, Myrada (Bangalore): Institute for Social and Economic Change, pp. 85-99.

Patel, S. and D.K. Behera (1999), 'Doomed by a Dam', in D.K. Behera and G. Pfeffer (eds.), *Contemporary Society: Tribal Studies*, vol. 3: *Social Concern*, Delhi: Concept, pp. 85-100.

Pathy, J. (1982), 'Politics of Tribal Welfare: Some Reflection', *The Eastern Anthropologist*, vol. 35, 4, pp. 285-300.

Patnaik, N. (1972), *Tribes and their Development: A Study of Two Tribal Development Blocks in Orissa*, Hyderabad: National Institute of Tribal Development.

Patnaik, S.M. (1996), *Displacement Rehabilitation and Social Change: The Case of the Paraja Highlanders*, Delhi: Inter-India Publications.

———'The Structure of Middle Indian Tribal Society Compared', in Georg Pfeffer (ed.), *Im entlegenen Gebiet: Gesellschaftsentwürfe und interethnische Beziehungen in den Distrikten von Koraput und Sambalpur, der regionalen und sozialen Peripherie Orissas*, Orissa Project Research Papers, pp. 156-76.

Polanyi, K. (1957), *The Great Transformation*, Boston: Beacon Press.

Redfield, R. (1955), *The Little Community: Viewpoints for the Study of a Human Whole*, Chicago: University of Chicago Press.

RRU (1997), Brochure on Resettlement and Rehabilitation Activities of UIP, Khatiguda.

Scudder, Thayer, et al. (1975), *Man-made Lakes and Human Health,* London: Academic Press.

Swain, M. and N. Panigrahi (1999), 'Development, Displacement and Rehabilitation in Orissa', *Man and Life*, vol. 25, nos. 3-4, pp. 163-75.

Viegas, P. and G. Menon (1989), *The Impact of Environmental Degradation on People,* Delhi: Indian Social Institute.

Vyasulu, V. (1985), 'Under Developing Koraput', *South Asian Anthropologist,* vol. 6, no. 1, pp. 63-71.

Xavier Institute of Management (XIM) (1994), *Socio-Economic Study on the Displaced Persons of the UIHEP,* Report submitted by XIM to R&R Unit, UIHEP, Khatiguda.

Xaxa, Virginius (2001), 'Protective Discrimination: Why Scheduled Tribes Lag Behind Scheduled Castes', *Economic and Political Weekly*, vol. 36, no. 29, pp. 2765-71.

5

Santal Autonomy as a Social Ecology

MARINE CARRIN

INTRODUCTION

Historians associated with the subaltern project have published oral testimonies of social conflict, but they have also sought to restitute the muted voices behind the tropes of silence which punctuate contesting narratives (Dube 1998). In Dube's study of an untouchable sweeper community in Chhattisgarh, contesting voices rise from the bottom of the social hierarchy to denounce the arrogance of the landlords. In Santal narratives, paradigms of space and time are entwined to forge an understanding of the landscape capable of inspiring symbolic autonomy in a context where Santals were economically dependent on dominant communities. This way of identifying with the landscape is often seen as typical of indigenous peoples, or 'tribals'.

The category tribe, salient in colonial ethnography, is problematic to historians today (Bates 1995) who tend to see it as a legacy of colonial discourse. Certainly, the publication of various compendia of tribes and castes encouraged a consolidation of ethnic ascriptions which was used for manipulation by colonial administrators. The political controversy over tribal identity emerged with the process of designating tribes which began during British rule, as part of a strategy of taming the wilderness. The colonial administration realized its inability to deal with the cultural domain of such peripheral peoples, which seemed to defeat rationalist reduction. Zones of anomaly were 'defined by the unique combination of tribal people and forest landscape. For the purpose of governance it was also a space less legible than other surrounding it' (Sivaramakrishnan 1999: 165). Thus the colonial state tried to control the economy of tribal regions but also to protect the specificity of tribal institutions.

British anthropologists and administrators argued that tribes were different from castes, while nationalist anthropologists 'argued that tribes were just a poorly integrated part of the Hindu society' (Baviskar 1995: 86). The latter was Ghurye's position (1943), when he called the tribes 'backward Hindus' and held that they could not be proved to be India's aborigines. Recently, too, Indian sociologists have questioned the applicability of the concept of tribe to India (Béteille 1998). To the nationalist mind, stressing the indigenous status of parts of the population was politically dubious. Thus while some scholars acknowledge the existence of tribal features and construct an ideal type defined by self-sufficiency, isolation, and partial autonomy, most Indian social scientists talk of 'tribes in transition', presupposing an evolution from hunters and gatherers to peasants. This may lead to denying any particular indigenous status to Indian tribes. With the common use of terms like Sanskritization (Srinivas 1952, 1962), the cultural dominance of Hinduism implies economic and political subordination of tribes.

Yet it is sometimes difficult to identify particular groups as tribes or castes, using 'objective' criteria. The problem is at least partly resolved if we turn to the groups' identification of themselves, which means that we have to consider it in terms of ethnicity.

An ethnic group may be defined as a 'collective wihin a larger society that claims common ancestry, a shared past and shared subjective identifications' (Nevitte and Kennedy 1986: 2). This claim is often part of a process of legitimation and implies a subjective dimension as a group having indigenous institutions is not necessarily acknowledged as culturally specific by its neighbours. Such ethnic identities may be unstable or may be used to organize people for political purposes. Thus as A. Prakash (2001: 3) puts it the 'term ethnic group is a sociological category whereas ethnic identity refers to a politically relevant identity'. This apparent contradiction is resolved if we accept, as Barth (1969) does, that ethnic identities are constructed through interaction and expressed in a logic of contrasts.

I shall argue that the Santals, who number some five million, have an ethnic consciousness, considering themselves as a tribal people speaking a different language (Austro-Asiatic) and as sharing a way of life implying values different from those of the Hindus. My argument is based on a consideration of emic categories which emerge through fieldwork and translation of Santal texts.[1] Identities are always multiple and reinvented and Santal traditions reflect this process. My position here is close to that of B.P. Karlsson (2000) whose discussion of Rabha identity stresses ethnicity as a political phenomenon, which evolves from fuzzy identities in the pre-colonial setting to ethnic boundary-making in the modern period. In India we are used to think of civilizations as long-term continuities but as Robb (1997: 245-6) puts it, concerning the construction of the North-East Frontier during the colonial period: 'There is no analytical contradiction . . . between long-term civilizational continuities and emerging forms of "constructed" identity'. This paper deals with the way Santals have been constructing their identity, taking into account pre-existing and competing identities, social and economic as well as political forces and other indigenous processes.

A broader theoretical issue concerns the development of the awareness of the other, producing rivalry and conflict. Thus, Santal identity may have resulted from a competitive process where minor Munda-speaking groups such as the Birhor, or even the Kharia, were unsuccessful, for demographic reasons, in forging similar strong identities. Their lack of success may also be due to their location beyond the boundary, as defined by British administrators, to demarcate those who were to be treated as British subjects. The turning point here was the use, by the East India Company, of Santal labour to clear the wild tracts of the Damin-i-Koh, which later became the Santal Parganas. As the Santals were seen as hard workers they were allowed to participate in the establishment of colonial modes of production and, in return, receive 'protection'. Their turbulent neighbours the Paharias, who lived in the hills, refused, on the other hand, to work for the British. But with settlement, the Santals had to face the intrusion of British middlemen such as merchants and moneylenders, as well as dominant castes such as Hindu landlords. They experienced State intrusion and integration in the market economy, as well as increased ideological dominance through Hinduization and modernization.

I thus prefer to view Santal tribal identity as construed in opposition to dominant castes and hegemonic ideologies such as colonialism and Hinduism. Ranajit Guha, in his analysis of rebellions and resistance movements (1982), asserts that tribals possess symbolic autonomy. Sumit Guha (1999) answers that the dominated tribal lands were not isolated from the turbulent politics of the peninsula, but participated largely in state formation. Though his argument is convincing if we consider the Bhils or the Gonds, it is less evident for the Munda-speaking tribes who were engaged as labour but not as soldiers and who did not identify with the Raj.

Since the nineteenth century, the Santals have produced symbolic answers to dominance in order to resist oppression. I shall analyse paradigms of Santal identity, to show how it is rooted in the consciousness of a distinctive past, linked to particular places, such as the old forts (*mare ghar*) of their mythical kingdom Champa[2] in Hazaribagh. This mythical past contrasts with the labels of tribe or adivasi with their evolutionist implications. Thus resistance inscribes adivasi consciousness in a divided world, the fragments of which reflect both the nostalgia of a golden age, when theirs was a 'high' culture, and the will to inscribe adivasi experience and action, with its associations of underdevelopment and neglect, in a political agenda. Their historical experience is reflected in the way Santals act in different social and political contexts, as members of a scheduled tribe, as adivasis or as Jharkhandis. Yet tribal experience has generated a consciousness of resistance, and political activists among the Munda and Oraon have used the term 'adivasi' since around 1908 to express their identity and to oppose caste ideology. Adivasis have used their cultural traditions, selecting from them and transforming them to cope with changing conditions of exploitation. This process of 'reinventing tradition' characterizes the adivasi experience.

THE SANTALS ON THE MOVE

Under the Mughals, large tracts of jungle inhabited by tribals extended through the entire Chotanagpur area, including Birbhum and western Burdwan. These Jungle Mahals were nominally under Mughal control, but little attempt was made to extract revenues or exert political authority due to their inaccessibility (Poffenberger 1995: 337). Much of the area was wild and remote, offering an ideal refuge for tribal and other groups fleeing from oppression (Mukherji 1975). Chotanagpur was primilarly populated by Mundas, Oraons, Hos, Santals, Birhors, Kharias as well as low-caste Hindus and also by Bhumij in Birbhum and western Burdwan. The Santal and Bhumij practised shifting cultivation as well as hunting, and gathered minor forest products. They traded in firewood, silk, resin, deer and buffalo horns, wax, honey, bark fabric, lac, herbal remedies and charcoal (O'Malley 1911). They resisted the imposition of taxation through a series of armed revolts. Though the Chuar rebellions which lasted from 1767 to around 1830 were essentially agrarian in character, other revolts used symbolic language to express tribal grievances (Carrin 1996). In 1833, the British organized the Jungle Mahals into a special administrative region, the South-West Frontier Agency (SWFA).

The people of Chotanagpur had seen a steady flow of outsiders even in the pre-Mughal period. But from the Mughal period the indigenous peoples, apart from losing their ancestral lands, gradually became minorities in their own territory (Ghosh 1999: 104). Hard pressed, the Santals moved in search of lands to practice slash and burn cultivation. But they still associate migration with a golden age when ancestors were searching tubers and forest products, as the nomadic Uthlu Birhors[3] still do. The latter speak a language very close to Santali and share several clan and god (*bonga*) names with them.

The Santals who came to occupy fringe areas were recent settlers in the early nineteenth century. The displacement of the Santals in the early colonial period produced a split in their clanic system as they spread out to work on land, and in indigo factories, or build railways from 1850 onwards.

Santal resistance has found expression in various ways since the nineteenth century, the best known being the Santal rebellion of 1855. After the rebellion, part of the Jungle Mahals became non-regulation provinces. From 1874 a special tenancy law sought to prevent land alienation to non-tribals (Sivaramakrishnan 1999: 65). Baden-Powell notes, in 1892, that a chief (*ghatwal*) was entitled to the revenue of a hill or frontier tract on condition of maintaining a police force to keep the peace and prevent the attacks of robbers. He mentions the *pargana,* a council comprising 10 to 12 village *panchayats* and notes that 'final authority' rests with the *lo bir sendera*, the judgement of the burnt forest, which provided a unifying mechanism among the dispersed Santal communities across space and time (Duyker 1987: 169).

Messianic movements do not exist among the Munda groups today, as they did in the nineteenth century, but belief in restoration of the past is an important part of the outlook of many contemporary tribal movements. It is framed by the idea of an ecological revival of the country, associated with the idea of ethnic assertion.

It is significant that the *lo bir* was taking place while hunting (Carrin-Bouez 1986). It was from the forest that social conflicts were solved and that patterns of authority could emerge. Santal identify the forest with power and construct a politicized environmental history. The forest has provided the Santals with an arena of discourse which I shall evoke through narratives, to show how the definition of *colon* (Santali) or *niam* (Bengali)—both words meaning custom or rule—was essential to the assertion of identity. I shall show how they have been dealing with others, the neighbouring tribal groups and the Hindu castes, to negotiate autonomy and to engage in rivalry. It was through these encounters that they developed an autonomous consciousness in opposition to the hegemony of outsiders.

Tribal societies have developed an attachment to the environment couched in terms of knowledge[4] which also means that social identities are constructed around images of the landscape. This remains so, even if the degradation of the forest have altered their ecological adaptation. The Santals are now aiming at building a new ecological consciousness able to cope with the effects of exploitation and dominance.

This link between landscape and identity has been noted by scholars (Gold 1999; Vitebsky 1993).[5] Skaria (1999) shows us how, through narratives, the people of the Dangs of south Gujarat imagine their indigenousness as rooted in the landscape's wilderness, implying that they see themselves as peripheral people. This peripheral situation contrasts with the centre, identified with the state.[6]

I shall explore how images of ancestral land and forest have allowed Santals to reinvent tradition (Ranger 1993) and construct their cultural and political resistance. To what extent are they able to articulate this social ecology into a coherent model of survival, to construe the idea that they are the best custodians of their land? Their special relationship with the land has helped the Santals to forge a historical consciousness even as they were on the move. Far from creating a social amnesia, the constraint of migration in search of new lands invests them with the position of mediators, as those who articulate the passage between waste and cultivated land. I explore two Santal paradigms of space and time: the forest as an apt simile for survival, and the mythical landscape. I argue that these paradigms allow them to claim the Jharkhand territory as a space of legitimacy.[7]

FOREST AS AN APT SIMILE FOR SURVIVAL

The erosion of popular forestry rights in India can be traced to 1865, when a first Forest Act was passed, to be followed by the provisions of Act VII of 1878. But in 1894, the Forest Policy issued by the government aimed at defining the rights of the state and local groups in relation to the forest. The British divided forests into five classes: reserved forests, private forests, protected forests, village forests, and wastes. In the last three categories, tribal as well as non-tribal rights continued to be respected. In the village forests there was no ban on grazing and felling, while in private forests, zamindars imposed restrictions or transformed access to a right which could be exchanged against forced labour (*begari*). The main victims of these new regulations were the tribals of central India, and adivasis had to adjust to new codification of time and space, which curtailed their rights. By the Survey Settlement of 1873 more forests were reserved.

The administration aimed at maximizing the commercial value of timber. Straight line planting of foreign species replaced irregular jungles with their symbolic centres, the *sal* and *mahua* groves of the Santal myths. In 1910, 192 sq. miles of forest in the Santal Parganas came under government supervision, while the Bihar Private Forest Act of 1927 and the Private Protected Forest Act of 1949 gradually brought the entire forest area under State Control.[8]

New codification of privileges and offences followed the measurement policies. Soon the exploitation of minor forest products was leased to non-tribal contractors. Hunts were disrupted, deities offended, ancestral places profaned. Guha (1989) shows that there was an increase in offences against forest regulations during 1911-13 and 1938-9, corresponding to periods of drought when scarcity of food must be compensated at any cost. But by the 1930s, the colonial authorities seem to have realized that these policies wrought peasant and tribal resistance. As Swami Sahajanand (1998: 107) notes: 'Every outsider has to pay a tax of four *annas* annually, whether he cuts wood or not.' Though the National Forest Policy of 1952 aimed at increasing the wooded area, the Jharkhand region has in fact been more quickly deforested since Independence.

By virtue of the Land Acquisition Act of 1894, the state could secure for the mining companies an almost limitless access to tribal lands. The terms of these land transfers were far from equitable even when tribals were ready to accept monetary compensation. The iron and steel industry first made a mark on the tribal landscape in Singhbhum. Land was also lost to mica industries in Hazaribagh. With the opening up of the area to mining, tribals were further uprooted from their lands. They became low-paid and unskilled workers in the new industries, an important factor in capital formation. Industries and power projects established in the region needed skilled employees and the specialists came from outside. Immigrants came in large numbers, encouraged by the Government of Bihar (Ghosh 1999: 105). According to leaders of the Jharkhand movement, till 1971 only 24 per cent of the workers employed in the industries of the region were from the scheduled tribes or scheduled castes. While Chotanagpur, Santal Parganas and parts of south Bengal were flooded by immigrants, these areas became a source of cheap labour for the Assam tea gardens, and elsewhere.

The Santal discourse on landscape reveals how the Jharkhandis' identity is rooted in the idea of a restored landscape expressed symbolically as a cultural renaissance of the Munda groups and allied castes. The symbolism of the forest has been central to most events and processes by which tribal solidarities were affirmed. Thus the charismatic leaders of the Santal rebellion (*hul*) as well as the Birsa movement of 1895 emphasized the importance and meaning of the forest and ancestral places. The forest becomes an apt simile for survival: this is generally true in India where forests are associated with religious values and are 'the local landscapes of Indian magical realism' (Corbridge 1991). I argue that repeated themes of memory and environmental history are interwoven in such a way that memory is embodied in the landscape. This is what Gold and Gujar means by memory 'as a social fact', belonging to collective mentalities but individually experienced: 'Memory has a "thick autonomy"; its thickness reveals modes of embodiment, sensuousness, places, materiality, the everyday and vanished landscapes' (2002: 80).

PARADIGMS OF THE SANTAL MYTHICAL LANDSCAPE

The Santal creation myth takes us back to the time before these landscapes existed, telling us how a couple of wild geese nested on the surface of the ocean. They laid two eggs, giving birth to a pair of siblings who became the ancestors of humanity. From excess of water the myth proceeds to the excess of fire, in the form of a 'fire rain' that Thakur, a god of Hindu origin, showers on humanity. Thakur introduced boundaries, work and money in this world, and his name evokes *kaliyug*—as opposed to the mythical golden age, when Santal women gathered roots, leaves and tubers in the forest while the men were hunting. *Kaliyug*, then, becomes the time of deforestation and loss of Santal land.[9]

In Santal poetry the degradation of the forest symbolizes loss of memory and more specifically the decline of kinship ties. The loss of the forest alludes to colonial practice when forest officers saw the forest as a commercial resource and transformed hill tracts for cultivation. Encroachment by landlords was justified by economic rationality: Tribal communities were fined for fetching firewood and had to pay taxes on *mahua* flowers, the pulp of which was eaten during the rainy season. From 1860, the demand for timber accelerated the exploitation of the forest and raised the value of forest lands. The nationalization of forests tended to transform timber contractors into dealers in illegal timber, employing the Santals as well as other adivasis in their onslaught on the forests.

The tribals' use of the forest became limited. They had been used to hunt in the forest, as well as to pick dry branches for fuel, collect fodder and hew timber for building. Santals were using both herbal remedies and animal products in their pharmacopia, and they still eat a number of wild leaves, mushrooms and tubers (Carrin-Bouez 1991). But deforestation and the introduction of foreign trees such as eucalyptus have destroyed the traditional economy of Santals and other adivasis. Yet, though I have observed a loss of knowledge in terms of vegetal and animal taxonomies, animal and plant symbolism is still important in riddles, folk-tales and songs (Carrin-Bouez 1985, 1987).

FOREST, BODY AND PLEASURE

The importance of the forest is also reflected in the calandar: the new year begins with the flowering of the *sal* tree (*Shorea robusta*, L.). In traditional songs, wealth is associated with *sal*. The Santal use *sal* leaves to make leaf cups and plates which they sell in the market, and which are essential for offering rice-beer and ritual food to ancestors and deities. Whenever Santals migrated in search of new lands, the chief brandished a *sal* branch: lifting the branch conveyed the orders of the chief. The connotations of the *sal* branch are numerous: it may indicate a fixed appointment, the number of leaves showing the days outstanding before an event. If the leaves are upside down, an offence such as incest has been committed. The branch also stands metonymically for a kinship tie. Branches of other trees such as *karam* (*Adina cordifolia*, Hook.) evoke fictive kinship which implies economic and ritual solidarity. Trees are associated with Santal deities, especially in the sacred grove, where the villagers propitiate the bongas who look after the crops. Felling a tree is often seen as a transgression since trees are the abodes of deities. The Santals use a great variety of trees: *sal* as well as other trees no less valuable for their timber. Another jungle product is lac which zamindars used to monopolize, depriving the peasants of a valuable resource. During the rainy season, villagers feed on jungle products, such as *mahua* flowers (*Bassia latifolia*, L.) which can be stored and dried. During the Baha festival, three men considered as oracles go to collect *mahua* branches in the forest, which are distributed to the women of the village as a token of fertility (Carrin-Bouez 1986). In 1897, a bumper harvest of *mahua* and an abundant supply of jungle produce averted impending famine[10] (Damodaran 1998: 860).

Hunting was practised differently by the various Munda groups: while Mundas and Oraons hunted only big game, the itinerant Uthlu Birhors snared small monkeys which they still sell illicitly. They also collect the fibre of chop creeper (*Bauhinia wahili*, L.) to make ropes which they sell in the markets. The Santals hunt both big and small game. The availability of small game such as rodents and birds has been important for tribal communities, and may have decided them to settle even where the forest was degraded. A deep knowledge of the forest environment was of critical importance for all the Munda groups.

Santals associate the loss of indigenous tree cover with a perceived change in climate, but also with deterioration in social relations. Their clans, they say, started to fight with the beginning of *kaliyug* and this war 'between brothers' is described in Baha songs as the 'madness of epilepsy' (*mirgi*) or as a sudden 'hot wind' associated with malevolence. Significantly, the hillside burnt for planting is the theatre of clanic war and 'in the forest with a heavy sound the leopard's child is crying' (Carrin-Bouez 1979; Carrin forthcoming).

The symbolic meaning of the forest is still present in stories about hunting. Totemic names as well as sub-clan (*khunt*) stories emphasize the relationship between men and wild animals (Carrin-Bouez 1991). Fur animals are seen as vehicles of the bongas. Recollections of hunting celebrate the abundance and beauty of the game: stories about hunting evoke childhood memories. The following lines from an old story express the pleasure of going to the forest:

Formerly, when we were children, we went to the forest, and we loved to go hunting, we felt very happy.
And even now, when we hunt we are happy. Men are very eager to go, they do not stay behind,
When the hunt takes place in the forest, whatever the place, young people do not delay, they come.
When they grow older, they go hunting on the hill Kah Lutia and there it was decided (that): In Mihdi village, there was a man whose name was Camu Baһtar, he was a *dihuri* (hunting priest) to lead the hunt in that forest,
And they stayed five days hunting in that forest,
And in that forest, there were plenty of wild animals.
And at the time they talked about the animals which were to be found in the forest.
And near the river, on the top of the hill there were many peacocks and we found insects there. And the peacocks opened their tails and it was so beautiful to watch. It looks like paddy being tied up in sheaves and thrown on the ground.
There is so much to see, there are so many fowl, and deer, and boars, and so many cows, they look so sweet.
And tigers, and wild bears, they are plentiful and they eat grass,
And the hunters, they bring back the flesh of all kinds of animals
And it was possible to see and tell about all that. And this story is true . . . .[11]

The forest was where one learnt discipline, obeying the orders of the Dihuri baba,[12] organizing the hunters and preventing them from fighting each other. The hunt was where one learnt to use 'true' as against false speech. This was also where was expressed the Santal sense of justice, when the chief or *pargana* staged a court the night of the first day of the hunt.

The forest is a place of enchantment, where people make love illicitly—often evoked as 'resting under *mahua* trees'. It is where men or women encounter bongas who seduce them. The supernatural dimension of the forest is clear from the story of a woman who delivers her baby in the forest. As her mates leave her alone, she meets a bonga who aids in the delivery. When she returns to the village in the morning, carrying her son in her arms, the villagers see a bright halo radiating from her body.

To give birth in the forest links the sylvan landscape to the human body. Metaphorically, Santals say a tree is *jankadeae,* it has bones, and the pericarp of a seed is compared to human flesh (*jel*). Trees, bones, and grains are linked to evoke time, and a sapling means a 'generation'. Santal hunting songs (*sendera seren*) evoke human sexuality as necessary for the fertility of the forest soil, and this is ritually enacted when hunters urinate on Rongo ruji, the burnt vulva of the hunt's patroness (Carrin-Bouez 1986).

In *bir seren* (forest songs) the sexual act is sometimes likened to hunting: 'your elder brother has been hunting, he has killed a hare, and my vagina is heating'. Other songs describe desire, but also evoke the incest of the creation myth. The ferment for rice beer (*handi*) is associated with wild plants, said to have been eaten by a hare since fermentation is conceptualized as digestion. The forest songs allude to sexual taboos but also describe sensuality and intimacy, with emotions compared to the maturing of plants. The myth of the origin of tobacco tells of a beautiful girl secretly desired by her brothers. They decide to eat their sister's flesh instead of raping her. She becomes a tobacco plant, enjoyed by men.

The forest is where young men learn about taboos, pleasure and social justice, but also where they may provoke the forest deities by transgressing their rules. Thus a man who picks up certain fallen branches under a tree where bongas live is defying the deities.

The bongas themselves defy sexual norms, attacking women who collect firewood. When women return to the village loaded with branches, they must take care to avoid such attacks (more often from forest officers, these days) as the forest is the place for sexual assault. The emphasis on the forest has allowed the Santals (as well as other adivasi of the region) to express social cohesion in ecological terms and to think of deforestation as a cultural loss.

Here, Santals share with other Mundari-speaking groups a common history where conversion to Christianity and the access to writing have implied both a loss and a gain. Egalitarian ideas were strengthened by Christianity and writing provided the means to express them as a coherent ideology. The loss can be seen as a cultural amnesia, which has an ecological parallel in deforestation.

THE JHARKHAND MOVEMENT

Santal history reflects the pervasive effect of British colonialism, as well as the influence of missionaries who contributed to build tribal elites, but also divided Christians from non-Christians. The belief in restoration of a Santal *raj* had inspired the leaders of the Santal rebellion of 1855. Since then, the political revendications of the Santals long retained a religious overtone. The creation of the Jharkhand party in 1950 was an important step, and the role of the Santals in the movement has been crucial, while reflecting Santal specificity. Since the formation of the party, adivasis have claimed a separate Jharkhand state, which was finally created in 2000. From 1952 to 1957 the Jharkhand won many votes, especially in Chotanagpur and the Santal Parganas. But the party did not have an agrarian programme, as its urban leaders were out of touch with the village economy. From 1957, Santals participated in several Hindu reformist associations.

Meanwhile, the Bihar government pushed ahead with massive exploitation of forest and mineral wealth. The cities of Ranchi, Jamshedpur, Rourkela, and Dhanbad continued to grow by immigration of *dikus*.[13] The leftist and industrial pressure groups like the Birsa Seva Dal had already emerged as a strong component of the Jharkhand. Around 1961, the proportion of adivasis in the region's population had decreased, especially in Bihar and south-west Bengal. Struggles to stop these changes brought new political organizations such as the Birsa Seva Dal and the Jharkhand Mukti Morcha (JMM). The new political consciousness was expressed by the JMM whose aim was to form a separate state to end exploitation of tribals by non-tribals, more specifically by the higher castes. The JMM led some struggles of the 1960s, as the agrarian situation in Chotanagpur deteriorated, and the younger generation grew more radical. By 1963 the JMM joined the Congress but could not unite the different strains of opposition to the governments of various states, where tribals were a minority both in tems of population and of power politics. A coalition government was formed in Bihar in 1969 in which the Jharkhandi splinter groups participated as a unified Jharkhand legislative party to extract concessions in exchange for support to the coalition government. 'These concessions implied that a statutory board would be set for regions such as Chotanagpur and Santhal Parganas with complete powers to decide matters pertaining to development policies in the region' (Prakash 2001: 115). But they failed to extract any major concession. Meanwhile, the Kurmis[14] sought restoration of land and allied themselves with the Santals.

The year 1972 can be interpreted as a shift in the political dynamic of the Jharkhand from regional to national politics. A Marxist Left Wing was founded in 1973, but the 1980s brought a return to ethnic assertions with the formation of the All Jharkhand Union and the Jharkhand People Party. The Jharkhand movement was undermined during the period of the Emergency from 1975 to 1977. In Bengal, landless Santals participated in the Naxalite struggle in Birbhum, but later founded another movement of re-tribalization, the Sari Dharam. From the late 1970s, in Bihar and Orissa, the JMM forged a successful cultural revival known as Sarna Dhorom. In 1977-8 the demand for a separate state became more insistent, to include Chotanagpur, the Santal Parganas, the Santal country in the north of Orissa and the West of Bengal, the region of Siliguri and two districts of Madhya Pradesh. Between 1978 and 1980 Shibu Soren, the founder of the JMM, became a quasi-divine hero, compared by Santals to Chando bonga, one of their main deities. He finally allied himself to the Congress. By the early 1980s development problems had become acute in the region, sidelining the issue of autonomy (Prakash 2001: 117). Around 1980, an alliance of adivasis and non-adivasis was formed, but defeated in 1984.

From 1978, the Jharkhand movement grew in the wake of the ecological movement (Jangal Andolan) which burst out in Singhbhum. The cracks that had developed in the Jharkhand movement by the early 1980s were followed by further splits, the leftist factions argued that the JMM[15] had become a close ally of the Congress. The murder of the president of the JMM in 1984 activated the movement, now focusing on ethnicity. From 1987 to 1990, a series of important strikes united the two main factions of the movement, the JMM led by Shibu Soren and the All Jharkhand Union of Binod Bihari Mahato. The JMM launched a programme to recover tribal land from moneylenders and farmers in the north of Chotanagpur, and tried to obtain waste lands and irrigation for tribals. But during the 1990 elections the JMM joined the BJP—which is powerful in south Bihar—in order to get non-adivasi support, accepting the party's proposal to limit the creation of a Jharkhand state to Chotanagpur and the Santal Parganas. That year, the Central Government proposed an Autonomous Council for the thirteen districts of Bihar, which was founded in june 1995. The reason behind the BJP demand for a separate state was certainly the poor development profile of the region. The BJP, who had been able to generate a substantial following in the Jharkhand region among tribals and non-tribals, now asserted that the region had been under an economic blockade.

Thus, the BJP decided to propose a separate state Vananchal, 'the Forest country', to replace the projected Jharkhand. The name Vananchal alludes to Hindu representations of the forest as expressed in the *Mahabharata,* and in the classical tropes of renunciation. The tribal sections of the population preferred the term Jharkhand, however, and the Jharkhand state, consisting of the Bihar districts but without any reference to Marxist ideas, was finally formed in November of 2000. Yet the state has a non-tribal majority, and we may well ask whether tribal identity will be able to make its voice heard in Jharkhand.

SARNA DHOROM OR THE RETURN OF THE SACRED GROVE

While different political factions were demanding a separate state, other wings of the Jharkhand movement concentrated on social reforms and cultural revival. In 1971-3, when I was in Orissa, several associations endeavoured to revitalize Santal culture within a pan-tribal ideology, as well as creating cooperatives to improve living conditions. In Dhanbad, the Sonot Santal Samaj promoted education as well as religious and artistic revival, while traditional Santal institutions were revived. The old practice of tribal government *kulhi durup* (lit. sitting and talking in the village street) was renamed *atu baisi* while the *vichar baisi* was given jurisdiction over 10 to 20 villages. The JMM created a supreme council called 'Palma' entrusted with policy-making and coordination of the various associations. The movement was keen to raise the status of women and fight polygamy, wife-beating, and witchcraft accusations. They implemented marriage reforms to reduce the bride-price and tried to impose prohibition, as drinking was seen as a source of indebtedness. The JMM also worked to promote literacy among tribals by organizing evening schools (Carrin 2003).

Reading historical events as moments in a struggle, sustained over many years, tempts me to see various scenes of Santal resistance as part of the same canvas. The Santals themselves view their past in the present in a cyclic way. Though they consider the 1855 rebellion as their major political act, they often mention plundering, vengeance or disobedience as instances of political as well as daily resistance. They commemorate the birthday of the leaders of the Santal and Munda rebellions whenever they organize demonstrations. Similarly, the death or the arrest of a political leader is often compared to the arrest of past heroes. Situating events in the collective memory they cast their past in particular places to which they periodically return, associated with particular landscapes and natural motives such as forests, rivers and groves. Thus, to protest against the installation of a mine or a steel-plant, the Mundas and the Santals have organized processions and meetings around the Rokoe Hill near Ranchi, the very place where Birsa Munda was trying to resist the British in 1895.

Cultural associations were strong in the Santal Parganas, while in Mayurbhanj the Sarna Dhorom insisted on the propagation of a Santal script and conveyed its political message by renewing the village theatre. A similar strategy was found in Singhbhum in the movement of Lako Bodra who, like Ragunath Murmu of the Sarna Dhorom, invented a new script. Lako claimed to have found the

Ho script painted on rocks on top of a sacred hill (*buru*). Since the Jharkhand became a separate state, local action groups have concentrated on the environmental crisis and cultural claims. The green flag of the Jharkhand Party symbolizes the ecological concern of the tribals as well as the *Sadans*—low-caste Hindus—who are their allies. The traditional weapons of bow and arrow, clearly evoking the forest and the hunt, are symbols of tribal identity.

The careless attitude of the Bihar Government with regard to environmental issues has provoked a series of protests in Chotanagpur. These include resistance to teak planting around 1978. The Santals and the Mundas argued that nothing grows under teak and certainly not the grass, roots and tubers on which people subsist during difficult times. In 1976 the government took over the *sal* leaf trade and in 1978, the minor forest products were taken over. The phase of environmental vandalism that occurred in Jharkhand in the 1980s and 1990s led to reassessment of indigenous forests rights. Still, contractors and timber merchants have taken advantage of the Jungle Andolan to loot the forest. The Jungle Bachao Andolan (forest movement) in Singhbhum gained importance among the Hos during 1978-80. Stocks of *kendu* leaves were burnt and forest godowns looted in tribal protest. In some cases, local initiatives proved fruitful and led to collaboration between forest experts and local communities (Poffenberger 1995). The JMM tried to identify the problems faced by the people of Jharkhand and suggest measures to overcome them. One meeting in December 1990 in Bokaro resulted in launching an environment brigade to protect the deteriorating ecological balance of the region.

This process has helped the Santals develop an environmental knowledge which does not necessarily fit the rationale of certain ecologists, who view the adivasis as noble savages, having an ancestral wisdom preventing them from overexploiting the environment. Gadgil and Guha (1992) rewrite Indian history as an essay in social ecology, foregrounding indigenous caste-based knowledge to an extent which presents an idealized version of the past. It is less than obvious that people like the Santals were free to adapt prudently to the conditions of lasting settlement, since they have constantly been under pressure to move to new lands. Knowledge of nature does not necessarily translate into conservationist policy.

Tribal knowledge of nature is formulated and passed to the young generation in terms which differ from the way knowledge is taught and transmitted in literate societies (Padel 1998). This knowledge concerning plants, animals or techniques is constantly tested. Today, as the forest has deteriorated, the species of plants and animals which lived in the forest are sometimes forgotten. The villagers are conscious of this loss, and often associate the regeneration of the forest with a better future. Though they value nature and the forest, adivasis have often protested against the state by burning the forest as they felt it to be their unique possession. But they have also been planting trees in order to regenerate the forest. Though tribal knowledge of nature does not necessarily convey ecological wisdom, it is expressed in some religious movements such as the Sarna Dhorom—'return to the Sacred grove' (Carrin 2003).

The cultural renaissance implies the dream of a common pantheist religion centred on the bonga cult, as well as an ecological awareness. In Chotanagpur, the JMM emphasized the cultural revival of rituals related to the land. In 1992, Damodaran attended a *Sarhul puja,* the Oraon festival of the sacred grove, traditionally confined to the village but which has now become a grand political event in urban centres, accompanied by processions, drum beating and dancing (2000: 19). In the context of a despoiled landscape, the ritual evokes an idyllic environmental past to revive memories of better times, and to criticize the inequities of the current regime. The Sarna Dhorom has played a similar role in the Santal cultural revival.

THE SARNA DHOROM AND THE RITUALIZATION OF ETHNICITY

During a meeting of the Mayurbhanj association in 1978, Mundari was declared the common language of the Munda-speaking peoples. Resolutions were adopted declaring Sarna—which means the sacred grove in Munda—to be the common religion of these groups. The Santal association compared the rituals of the different Munda groups to see if they could be simplified, to express the founding of a tribal *raj*.

In 1981, a Santal Jharkhandi, called Gulia, was possessed by the deities of the sacred grove, and a few days later wrote a play where the deities call for a renewal of ritual tradition. In Gulia's new theology, the sacred grove was still the main cult place of the village, but Gulia's disciples, the gurus of the Sarna Dhorom, were to celebrate the most important rites, leaving the traditional village priest only the care of some rituals of the agricultural cycle. One month later, Gulia founded an ashram, recruiting disciples who shared both his ritual and theatrical inspiration, and his political involvement in the Jharkhand. Moreover, Gulia and his Munda and Ho counterparts (possession cults have adepts in neighbouring tribes too) allied themselves with local chiefs in order to reorganize the inter-tribal hunt on a Jharkhand basis.

In 1978 and 1981 I attended several sessions of the Sarna Dhorom. They took place on the top of a hill enclosed by streamers of white flags. The 'gurus' of the ritual—all engaged in Jharkhand activities—wanted to eradicate all Hindu gods from the tribal pantheon. Small shrines, dedicated to tribal deities, were built and pilgrims came to visit them.

But then, one of the gurus tried to introduce a Kali idol in memory of the Santal rebels of 1855 who beheaded Hindu moneylenders, dedicating them as a sacrifice to Kali. This ritual innovation shocked Gulia greatly: he did not, at any cost, want to emphasize violence through ritual. Gulia was neither naïve, nor reformist: he felt that at some point violence could not be avoided, but feared that pilgrims possessed by Kali might develop an agressively militant mood. Gulia decided to exclude Chotrae, the other guru, from the movement. Chotrae left the sacred hill, taking his clay idol of Kali away in a rickshaw, and leaving the pilgrims astonished. Excluding his adversary for bringing in a Kali idol, Gulia seemed to prove his exclusive attachment to the tribal deities. But he had also implicitly showed outsiders that the Sarna Dhorom movement was becoming a sect.

Later Gulia developed, through his theatre activities, the heroic role of the Santals, who, according to his point of view, ought to lead the Jharkhand. His cult of the charismatic leaders represent a translation into cultural tradition of what a Jharkhand leader should be. Despite his alliances with local chiefs, Gulia's strategy did not stress their authority. On the contrary, he wanted to avoid their influence in order to legitimize his own 'reformist' movement. Like Sidhu and Kanhu, the leaders of the Santal rebellion of 1855, Gulia claimed to be possessed by the jaher bonga, the deities of the sacred grove, so as to reject Hinduization and the power of the more Hinduized priests.

When Gulia was first possessed he staged the story of the possession in a village open-air theatre where large numbers of tribals flocked every night. The stage became a place to experiment with new symbolic elements. It also provided an opportunity for Gulia to develop a Santal ethnic myth—despite his conscious efforts to construct new pan-Munda rituals in collaboration with other local Jharkhand leaders. From a formal point of view, the stage could well mediate between the Jharkhand meeting—where factional interests were at stake—and the 'new rituals'. In the theatre, the actors work to produce new emotions by linking the past—the nostalgia of a tribal kingdom—with expectations for the future, the political claims of the Jharkhand. From a ritual point of view, the commemoration of martyrdom aimed at inspiring the Jharkhand struggle, but was still dominated by a Santal overtone.

The question of cow sacrifice was discussed among tribal leaders, who declared that the Mundari sacrifice *par excellence*, was the salei bonga, the ritual killing of a cow in memory of a prestigious deceased. Such a sacrifice had, in fact, been performed a few months earlier in the village of Ragunath Murmu, also an author of theatrical plays expressing a revival of the bonga cult. Here again a ritual innovation—the sacrifice of a cow as performed in the past—was used as an image to recreate an independent ritual universe in a context where it was difficult to re-establish the customary cow sacrifice.

Gulia's effort to put events on stage did not even spare the anthropologist who was asked to perform her role on the village scene, narrating her discovery, in Norway, of the archives written by Santals under the instigation of the Lutheran missionaries. This evocation of an unknown past, involving Santals of another region who had themselves written the account in roman script, seemed to fascinate the audience, creating a link which seemed to restore a loss explained to me in terms of fragmentation of space and time. My Santal friends in Mayurbhanj did not know about the roman script, just as they ignored the fact that Santals had been converted to Christianity in the Santal Parganas during the nineteenth century. Yet Santals of Orissa, Santal Parganas and Birbhum had much in common. They had all lost much of their ancestral lands, despite efforts at juridical protection, like the Chotanagpur Tenancy Act of 1908.

The Sarna Dhorom *pujas* became a highly elaborate way to restore harmony by staging a ritual on a sacred hill. Sarna religion teaches vigilance in ecological matters and aims to restore harmony between society and nature, the implication being that restoring nature also restores moral integrity.

It is part of the originality of the Jharkhand movement to be grounded in Mundari semantics and values. Santal discourse on identity has inspired the Jharkhand movement as a popular force, but can this symbolic struggle for survival stand up to Hindu prejudice? In my view this reinvention of tradition shows rich cultural potential, able to resist and transform the readymade ideologies which may be imposed on tribals.

CONCLUSION: SYMBOLIC AUTONOMY AS A PLEDGE AGAINST ALIENATION

In the Jharkhand territory migration has produced a multi-cultural society, and the culture of the region includes different streams—such as the Brahmanic culture of the dominant Hindu castes, which clash with the tribal ethos. The tribes remain a minority in the new state, and labour migration has not achieved feedback effects since the emigrants' earnings are meagre. Some elements of tribal culture have become stigmatic: the Santals, who were beef-eaters are reluctant to continue the practice, fearing conflicts with their Hindu neighbours. Thus Sarna Dhorom members in Mayurbhanj and Singhbhum have been trying to rid themselves of the stigma of beef-eating, even if it is associated with ancestor-worship in Mundari cultures.

The tribal society, traditionally seen as egalitarian is becoming divided on communal lines as notions of caste and class creep in. Agriculture has become subservient to business and industry but adivasis have not been able to take up these new opportunities and fail to compete with *diku* candidates for jobs. In spite of the efforts of cultural revivalist movements to promote literacy, attendance at school is still insufficient: as shown by the 1981 census, the literacy rate is still very low among the adivasis in south Bihar. Thus it is difficult for Santals in the Jharkhand region to take advantage of the reservations provided by the Constitution. Poverty and indebtedness favours child labour and sexual exploitation of women. Corruption makes labour regulations difficult to enact in a region where business is run by *dikus*.

Land and forest alienation, migration, cultural subjugation, and underdevelopment are the major issues around which the Jharkhand movement revolves. Santal autonomy has been forged in the history of the movement but is threatened by several factors. From the beginning we see divisions resulting from confessional, economic or cultural schisms between rural and urbanized Santals, as also between Santals and other Munda groups. Yet in spite of these threats, there seems to be no reason to doubt the survival of an autonomous Santal identity.

I wish to stress the strength of symbolic autonomy in opposing the stigma which might otherwise pervade the tribal consciousness of exploited workers. The anger of adivasis has embittered their relationship with the *dikus* but also drawn them closer to the Scheduled Castes. The environmental issues seem to me one of the best common platforms for demands shared by adivasis and low castes, representing as it does a domain of practical experience and tribal knowledge. If the relationship of the adivasis to the forest is highly symbolic, forest semantics organize the space and stand as a metaphor for withdrawal, even if the forest has become a theatre of power relationships and is no more a refuge. Yet, Santals in particular are still able to think their future embedded in a regenerated forest, even if the real forest gives way to hydraulic projects. Memoranda concerning the forest—like the one which emanated from six political factions of the Jharkhand in 1978—seem particularly important in this respect as they transcend factionalism. The memorandum included demands to end destruction of *sal* trees, while *segun* trees were to be planted in selected areas, and proper wages paid to those working for the Forest Development Corporation. Significantly, the memorandum also insisted on education in tribal languages, showing how environmental issues and cultural needs are intertwined. The semantics of space has inspired a Santal reinvention of tradition which is not to be neglected as it might produce a new social ecology, a way to tackle industrialization, urbanization and immigration.

We face a multitude of Santal retrospective interpretations, formulated by descendants of the protagonists of past events. Accounts of such events are framed by different experiences and entangled in webs of interest. These re-enactments are sometimes surprising, as all Santals do not share the same history. The differences appear in Santal writing when witnesses of the Hul of 1855 describe local events. Here emerges the individual as a protagonist who casts his own version of the plot. Though we may admit with Keesing (1992) that we, too, are situated, steeped, by our education, in imperialist discourses, as an anthropologist I have tried here to translate another, subaltern, consciousness.

NOTES

1. The Norwegian missionaries who came to Santal Parganas around 1867 to build a Santal 'National' Church, taught a roman script to transcribe Santali. The missionaries' collaborators collected a great number of texts in Santali which were deposited in Oslo University Library after the death of P.O. Bodding, the author of the *Santal Dictionary* which was later published from 1929 to 1936. For an index of the Santal archives, see S. Soren 1999.
2. The claim for this mythical kingdom inspired the leaders of the 1855 Santal insurrection (Carrin, 2006).
3. The Uthlu Birhors who number a couple of thousand live in temporary camps (*tanda*) in Palamau and Hazaribagh. They are hunters and gatherers.

4. Gadgil and Malhotra (1994) propose that, 'the caste system achieves prudence of management by resource partitioning by authoritatively allocating resources on the basis of castes'.
5. Most studies dealing with environmental history have concentrated on the arable. More recently, one has attempted to document the forest and the non-cultivated part of the environment, and its importance in sustaining the identity of indigenous peoples. (See Introduction to this volume).
6. Hindu kings could not afford to ignore these peripheries, whose tribal peoples paid him tribute and often defended his kingdom. S. Guha shows how royalty was defined by the capacity to tame the wilderness and its inhabitants. In Orissa, a tribal chief used to put the *tika* on the king's forehead (Kulke 1976).
7. The immigration to Chotanagpur and Santal Parganas has been growing steadily since 1891, reaching 1,429,805 in the 1971 census. Statistics for emigration are not available since 1921, when it reached 947,000 (Corbridge 1991: 142). Only 29.29 per cent of the population of Jharkhand are now tribals (Prakash 2001, p. 173).
8. In the Chotanagpur region 54,000 acres of forest area were taken over by the government in 1947. As Ghosh notes (1999: 103) it may be argued that the government's approach to social forestry 'though may have a bit of forestry in it, lacked any social content'. This policy led the government to grant leases to middlemen who were entitled to collect minor forest products. These agents hired tribal workers whom they exploited.
9. This ecological connotation of *kaliyug* is also found in Rajasthan (Gold

   1999: 22). She analyses popular stories of ecological loss, comparing them with the discourse of ecologists.
10. As Damodaran notes: 'Chotanagpur famine throws useful light on the very sharp correlation between ecological degradation, forest reservation and the onset of famine conditions' (Damodaran 1998: 885).
11. *Sendera reak' katha* (story of hunting), written in the 1890s by Sagram Murmu, and found in the archive of P.O. Bodding's collections of Santal folklore, Oslo University Library.
12. The *dihuri* or hunt priest is often an *ojha,* a priest and diviner who knows how to propitiate the forest deities. When a dozen of villages (*parha*) used to join a ceremonial hunt, each group of two or three villages was generally led by a *dihuri.*

13. Santals call all outsiders *diku,* but the term's pejorative implications are particularly attached to the higher castes.
14. A large caste of poor farmers and agricultural labourers who had lost much land to the Bihari dominant castes. The Kurmis are close, in social terms, to the Santals with whom they sometimes intermarry. Before 1970 they had shown little interest in Jharkhand.
15. The JMM continued to exist divided in two groups: the Marandi and Soren; they had marginal roles in the Parliament and the state legislature along with other, even smaller Jharkhandi parties (Prakash 2001: 126).

REFERENCES

Barth, F. (1969), 'Introduction', in *Ethnic Groups and Boundaries: The Social Organization of Cultural Difference,* Oslo: Universitetsforlaget, pp. 9-38.

Baden-Powell, B.H. (1892), *The Land System of British India,* 3 vols., Oxford: Clarendon Press.

Bates, C. (1995), 'Lost Innocents and the Loss of Innocence: Interpreting Adivasi Movements in South Asia', in R.H. Barnes, A. Gray and B. Kingsbury, *Indigenous Peoples of Asia,* Ann Arbor, Michigan: American Association for Asian Studies, pp. 103-19.

Baviskar, A. (1995), *In the Belly of the River : Tribal Conflicts over Development in the Narmada Valley,* Delhi: Oxford University Press.

Béteille, A. (1998), 'The Idea of Indigenous People', *Current Anthropology,* vol. 39, 2, pp. 187-91.

Bodding, P.O. (1925), *Studies in Santal Medicine and Connected Folklore,* Part 1: *The Santals and Disease,* Calcutta: Memoirs of the Asiatic Society of Bengal, vol. 10, no. 2.

Carrin, M. (1996), 'Les tribus de l'Inde: repli identitaire et mouvements insurrectionnels', in C. Jaffrelot (ed.), *L'Inde Contemporaine de 1950 à Nos Jours,* Paris: Fayard, pp. 421-40.

———(2003), 'Retour au bosquet sacré: réflexion sur la réinvention d'une culture adivasi' in M. Carrin, and C. Jaffrelot (eds.), *Tribus et Basses Castes: Résistance et Autonomie Dans la Société Indienne,* Purusartha, 23: Paris, EHESS, pp. 233-64.

———(2006), 'Héros et identité régionale au Chotanagpur', in V. Bouillier and C. Le Blane (eds.), *L'usage des héros.* Paris: Champion, pp. 121-51.

———(forthcoming), *Le Parler des Dieux: genres et argumentation du discours rituel santal,* Paris.

Carrin-Bouez, M. (1978), 'Acculturation and/or Dialectics: the Relevance of the Hindu Model for the Understanding of Santal Society', in R. Moser and M. Gautam (eds.), *Aspects of Tribal Life in South Asia*, Bern: Institute of Ethnology, Studia Ethnologica Bernensia, 1, pp. 83-92.

———(1979), 'Le Retour de L'Origine: mythe, chant et rite dans une fête santal', *ASEMI*, vol. 20 (2, 3, 4), pp. 87-117.

———(1985), 'La Proie du Vautour: devinettes et pensée symbolique chez les Santal', *L'Homme*, 95, vol. XXV, no. 3, pp. 71-96.

———(1986), *La Fleur et l'Os: symbolisme et rituel chez les Santal*, Paris: EHESS.

———(1987), 'Le Talon d'Achille de la Tortue: espèces animales et genres littéraires chez les Santal', *Cahiers de Littérature Orale*, 22, pp. 611-32.

———(1991), *Inner Frontiers: Santal Responses to Acculturation*, Bergen: Chr. Michelsen Institute.

Corbridge, S. (1991), 'Ousting Singbonga: the Struggle for India's Jharkhand', in C. Dixon and M. J. Hefferman (eds.), *Colonialism and Development in the Contemporary World*, London: Mansell, pp. 153-82.

Damodaran, V. (1998), *Nature and the Orient: The Environmental History of South and South-East Asia*, Delhi: Oxford University Press.

———(2000), 'History, Landscape and Indigeniety in Chotanagpur, 1850-1980', paper presented at the Conference on Indigenous Peoples, Uppsala.

Dube, S. (1998), *Untouchable Pasts: Religion, Identity and Power among a Central Indian Community*, Albany: State University of New York Press.

Duyker, E. (1987), *Tribal Guerillas: The Santals of West Bengal and the Naxalite Movement,* Delhi: Oxford University Press.

Gadgil, M. and K.C. Malhotra (1994), 'Adaptive Significance of the Indian Caste System: An Ecological Perspective' in R. Guha (ed.), *Social Ecology*, Delhi: Oxford University Press, pp. 27-41. Originally published in *Annals of Human Biology*, IOV (1983), pp. 465-78.

Gadgil, M. and R. Guha (1992), *The Fissured Land: An Ecological History of India*, Berkeley: University of California Press.

Ghosh, A. (1999), *Jharkhand Movement: A Study in the Politics of Regionalism,* Calcutta: Minerva Publications.

Ghurye, G.S. (1943), *The Aboriginals so-called and their Future,* Bombay: Popular Book Depot; reedited and revised 1959 as *The Scheduled Tribes,* Bombay: Popular Book Depot.

Gold, A. Grodzins (1999), 'From Wild Pigs to Foreign Trees', in S. Toft

Madsen (ed.), *Ecology, Environment and Crisis in South Asia,* London: Curzon Press, pp. 20-58.

Gold, A. Grodzins and B.R. Gujar (2002), *In the Time of Trees and Sorrows: Nature, Power, and Memory in Rajasthan,* Durham and London: Duke University Press.

Guha, Ranajit (1982), 'On Some Aspects of the Historiography of Colonial India', in *Subaltern Studies,* I, Delhi: Oxford University Press, pp. VII-VIII.

Guha, Ramachandra (1989), *The Unquiet Woods: Ecological Change and Peasant Resistance in the Himalaya,* Delhi: Oxford University Press.

Guha, S. (1999), *Environment and Ethnicity in India, 1200-1991,* Cambridge: Cambridge University Press.

Karlsson, B.G. (2000), *Contested Belonging: An Indigenous People's Struggle for Forest and Identity in Sub-Himalayan Bengal,* London: Curzon.

Keesing, M. (1992), *Custom and Confrontation: The Kwais Struggle for Cultural Autonomy,* Chicago: University of Chicago Press.

Kulke, H. (1976), 'Ksatriyaization and Social Change in Post-Medieval Orissa', in S.D. Pillai (ed.), *Changing India: Studies in Honour of Professor G.S. Ghurye,* Bombay: Popular Prakashan, pp. 398-409.

Mukherji, S. (1975), 'A Chapter on the Tribal Sources of Bengal History in the Muslim Period', *Bulletin of the Cultural Research Institute,* vol. 11, nos. 1-2, pp. 20-4.

Nevitte, N. and C.H. Kennedy (eds.) (1986), *Ethnic Preference and Public Policy in Developing States,* Boulder, Colorado: Lynne Rienner.

O'Malley, L.S.S. (1911), *Bengal District Gazetteers: Santal Parganas,* Calcutta: Bengal Secretariat Book Depot.

Padel, F. (1995), *The Sacrifice of Human Being: British Rule and the Kondhs of Orissa,* Delhi: Oxford University Press.

Poffenberger, M. (1995), 'The Resurgence of Community Forest Management in the Jungle Mahals of West Bengal', in D. Arnold and R. Guha (eds.), *Nature, Culture and Imperialism,* Delhi: Oxford University Press, pp. 337-69.

Prakash, A. (2001), *Jharkhand: Politics of Development and Identity,* Delhi: Orient Longmans.

Ranger, T. (1993), 'The Invention of Tradition Revisited: The Case of Colonial Africa', in P. Kaarsholm and J. Hultin (eds.), *Inventions and Boundaries: Historical and Anthropological Approaches to the Study of Ethniciiy and Nationalism,* Roskilde: Roskilde University, International Development Studies, pp. 9-50.

Robb, P. (1997), 'The Colonial State and Constructions of Indian Identity: An Example on the North-East Frontier in the 1880s', *Modern Asian Studies,* vol. 31, no. 2, pp. 245-83.

Sivaramakrishnan, K. (1999), *Modern Forests: Statemaking and Environmental Change in Colonial Eastern India*, Delhi: Oxford University Press.

Skaria, A. (1999), *Hybrid Histories: Forests, Frontiers and Wildness in Western India,* Delhi: Oxford University Press.

Soren, S. (1999), *Santalia: Catalogue of Santali Manuscripts in Oslo.* Compiled by Santosh K. Soren, Copenhagen: NIAS.

Srinivas, M.N. (1952), *Religion and Society Among the Coorgs,* Oxford: Oxford University Press.

———(1962), *Caste in Modern India and Other Essays,* Bombay: Asia Publishing House.

Swami Sahajanand (1998), *The Teaching of Swami Sahajanand*, ed. Walter Hauser, Delhi: Manohar.

Vitebsky, P. (1993), *Dialogues With the Dead: The Discussion of Mortality Among the Sora of Eastern India,* Cambridge: Cambridge University Press.

6

Literacy and the Legitimation of the Santal Hul, 1855: A Retrospective Perspective from the 1890s

PETER B. ANDERSEN

INTRODUCTION

The Santals, a tribal people, left the *jangal* to settle on the plains at the end of the eighteenth century, but they were allowed to live only between the villages of the majority population and the *jangal*, and numerous ways of suppression kept them in a marginal social position. It may be said that the *jangal* became a metaphor for the

*Major parts of this paper are based on P.O. Boddings folkloristic collections, held in Oslo, and thanks are due to Santosh Soren, Copenhagen, Marine Carrin (with whom we are preparing selections from the archives for publication), and Harald Tambs-Lyche, who, with Marine Carrin, is working on the history of the Danish-Norwegian mission to the Santals. The Santali text of Durga Tudu has been prepared for publication by Soren and translated jointly by him and Peter B. Andersen. Parts of the present paper were read at the European Conference for Modern South Asian Studies, Edinburgh, 2000, in a workshop organized by Marine Carrin and Harald Tambs-Lyche; and at a seminar at the Anthropological Survey of India, Calcutta, 22 January, 2002, organized by The School of Anthropology. Regarding translations from Santali *sahib* is often translated as 'British', but outside direct quotes the British administrative system is mostly seen here as the East India Company, as it was not until 1858 that India became a Colony under the (British) Crown.

Santal dwelling wherever they settled, as the majority population considered that they brought the wilderness with them wherever they went.

As we shall see, the agrarian system at the end of the eighteenth and the first half of the nineteenth century put the Santal farmers in a situation where they were easy to exploit economically, and many ended up as debt slaves. This situation provides the background to the Hul, the Santal insurrection of 1855. This paper, however, will mainly consider how the East India Company's introduction of written records, in the administration of the Santals, created new ways of legitimizing claims for power, Raj, up to and after the Hul.

The documentation for this new mode of legitimizing of power draws on a well-known fact, which has, however, scarcely been considered by scholars: that two of the leaders, the brothers Sidho and Kanhu, were reported as literate in later Santal folklore, and that their schooling appears in retrospect, as a turning point in the remembered events.

Whether they ever went to school is an open question. I think that we have evidence that they did not, but the framing of the story as brought down to us offers clear indication that the Santals continued, in the last part of the nineteenth century, to elaborate on the legitimacy of the Hul as initiated by written orders received from God himself.

On the one hand we may see these indications against the background of mostly illiterate Santals struggling with the impact of colonial government by written records. Such a story has been told by Ajay Skaria (1996) in his painstaking analysis of the social context of a letter accompanying the refusal of the messianic Bhil and Naikda leader Joria Bhagat to surrender to the colonial troops in 1868. Skaria traces the social context of the evolution of writing in the local Dangi society from magical to monumental 'where the written text is subordinated to the process of the construction of a powerful symbol' (1996, 31). As much of his analysis concerns written records of exchanges between local leaders and timber companies cutting down the woods, the writing is set in the context of local power. The exchange is to the advantage of the locals as long as they can deny the importance of written records, but gradually changes to their disadvantage. In this situation, magical writing may become fetishized, in Skaria's terms, as when certain leaders were allowed to have their names written on their retainers' dress.

But we may also interpret the stress on the literacy of the Hul's leaders as evidence that the Santals had surpassed the levels of magical and fetishized writing, and were struggling to show that the leaders of the Hul were civilized people who could read and write like themselves. Read from this angle the story gives an insight into an early development towards a positive attitude to literacy and education among the Santals.

This would seem to prove that the Santals had accepted the acquisition of literacy as the great divide between civilized and non-civilized peoples. Such an acceptation would be in accordance with classical anthropological arguments like that of J. Goody.[1] But it is difficult to know whether they would agree with his assumption that precise logic and cognition become possible only with the invention of writing, since Goody assume that only the written word is able to fix the fluctuations in oral traditions. In this regard they would perhaps rather agree with Brian Street (1984) who maintains that literacy has many different forms and purposes, each of them with their own political, social, economic and religious implications. It is doubtful, however, whether they would agree with Street's critique of Goody for fixing the threshold of civilization at the invention of writing.

As will become clear, the participants in the Hul and the first generation of Santals that followed them, fought to reconciliate themselves with the events and the defeat, and in fact various interpretative strategies seem to have been at work. As we shall see the evidence, as seen from the end of the nineteenth century, stressed the legitimacy of the colonial power from the viewpoint of a tribal society on the margins of the *zamindari* (agricultural) system.

As of 1991 more than 5 million Santals were concentrated in the states of Bihar, Jharkhand, Orissa, Tripura and West Bengal, and found in minor pockets in many other places in northern India as well as in Bangladesh and Nepal.

Santali language is a Mundari language different from the Indo-European languages spoken by the surrounding majorities. Presently the Santals argue for a linguistic identity and demand that Santali should be granted special status as a minority language for teaching in schools and higher education.[2] But it seems that the linguistic aspect of identity was only of minor importance at the end of the nineteenth century, even if the bi-lingualism now common among the Santals was much less common then.

Today, as in the nineteenth century, Santals consider most Hindus, especially moneylenders (*mahajan*) and Brahmins, as *diku* which means a foreigner. The expression alludes to cats, seen as stealing food from humans, as in the proverb 'You may deceive a Santal, but not a Deko cat' (Bodding, 1934: II, 69). In spite of this established fact of ethnic categorization there have been important changes in the self-designation of confession among the Santals in the census figures over the years. Thus more than 95 per cent of the Santals reported themselves as Hindus in 1961, while only about 80 per cent did so in 1981. The change is not so much due to the Christian mission as to a change to different kinds of 'tribal religion' such as Saontar Dhorom (*dharma*), 'Santal Religion', or Sari Dhorom, 'True Religion', Sari Sarna (*sarna* or *jaher,* sacred grove), Adi Kherwal, 'original Kherwar (Religion)' (Census of India 1991: Religion).

The first mention of Santals in historical sources dates from British reports of the 1790s when the East India Company subjugated the eastern parts of central India. At that time the Santals lived in the jungles covering the plateaus of the present Jharkhand and adjoining areas in West Bengal and Orissa. In a retrospective study from 1868 W.W. Hunter reported that the Santal had been considered as pests to the adjacent lowlands until 1790.

> Every winter, as soon as they had gathered in the rice crop and celebrated their harvest-home, the whole nation moved down upon the plains, hunting in the forests and plundering the open country in the line of march. After three months' excellent sport they returned laden with booty to celebrate the February festival in their own villages. (Hunter 1868: I, 219)

They were then depicted as a people without caste, and it was generally stated that Hindus of higher caste did not allow them to stay in their villages, but placed them between the village and the jungle (O'Malley 1910). The reason that Santals moved down from the hills and settled in the Hindu area was the agrarian policy of the East India Company. The Company had acquired the function of collector of land rent—as a *diwani* under the Mughal in Delhi—in major parts of eastern India in 1765, and from the 1790s, initiated a change in the collection of land revenue. The Permanent Settlement made the right to collect revenue inheritable, and froze the rent at a fixed amount. The Settlement was based on the rather naïve idea that the collectors (*zamindars*) would invest in the land as soon as they knew that they could not be evicted, and this would then lead to an increase of the Company's revenue from other sources. But to ensure an immediate income the Company fixed the amount of rent many times higher than before the reform, and it was later increased at irregular intervals.

This meant that rent collectors had to bring virgin soil under cultivation and in the interior parts of the country they employed Santals for this task. They were employed as a group, under the leadership of a headman (*manjhi*) who negotiated the payment on behalf of all of them. The most common result was that the headman and the collector or his sub-collectors, agreed on a land rent which the headman was to collect from the rest of the group and settle on their behalf. After the Santals had cleared the jungle they laid out fields where they grew millet and, to a lesser degree, paddy. From a formal point of view, the Santals were allowed to cultivate the fields and could claim rights in the land at a later point. But the collector gave them no financial assistance for the first year, so they had to borrow against security in the land or the crop, to get through the long period from they planted the millet or first beds of paddy until they could harvest some four or six months later. Moneylenders moved into the area as fast as the Santals could get access to land. The mortgage bound the Santals to a situation very much like slavery, as the son interited the mortgage of the father, but when construction work on a railway began in 1854, the lot of the Santals seemed to improve as wage work allowed them to pay off their debts. But the moneylenders would not let them leave their lands to earn money so they could pay their debt, and this led to increased conflict between Santals and moneylenders.

THE HUL

Let us now turn to the Hul, as described in a number of sources. In most of these accounts the Hul is understood as a reaction to ruthless exploitation of the Santals by non-Santals through the rearrangement of the agrarian system. They were allowed to harvest the land cleared by them, but in many a case they were soon sent away, or they became poorly-paid landed workers devoid of any right to leave the land because of their mortgages.

In 1832 the government demarked an area in the northernmost part of the Rajmahal Hills (to the south of the Ganga River) with mason pillars, as reserved for tribals. This territory was called the Damin-i-Koh, and from some few thousand Santal settlers early in the nineteenth century, there were more than 80,000 in 1855.[3] This and other Santal settlements were considered as successful examples of how unruly groups might be changed into productive agriculturalists, and the social problems that accompanied the change went mostly unnoticed. But as Hunter reported, in retrospect,

> A family of new settlers required a small advance of grain to eke out the produce of the chase while they were clearing the jungle. The Hindu dealer gave them a few shillings' worth of rice, and seized the land as soon as they had cleared it and sown the crop. (...) From the moment the peasant touched the borrowed rice, he and his children were serfs of the corn merchant. (...) If the victim threatened to run off into the jungle, the usurer instituted a suit in the courts, taking care that the Santal should know nothing of it till the decree had been obtained and the execution taken out. (Hunter 1868: I: 229-30)

And,

> Hindu Merchants flocked thither every winter after harvest to buy up the crop, and by degrees each market-town throughout the settlement had its resident Hindu grain-dealer. The Santal was ignorant and honest; the trading Hindu was keen and unscrupulous. Not a year passed without some successful shopkeeper returning from the hill-slopes to astonish his native

town by a display of quickly-gotten wealth, and to buy land in the plains. The Santal country came to be regarded by the less honourable orders of Hindus as a country where a fortune was to be made, no matter by what means, as long as it was made rapidly. (ibid.: I: 228-9)

In 1854 conflicts broke out in the Damin-i-Koh and the houses of moneylenders were plundered and burnt down. Petitions—perhaps in writing—were sent to the government to apply for justice and rearrangement of the agrarian relations. As the government took no serious action, a demonstration march to Calcutta (Kolkata) was organized, under the leadership of the brothers Sidho and Kanhu, Chand and Bhairab who said they were acting according to the orders of god Thakur as his officiates, Subha Thakur. This designation must then have been understood, by the British, as a claim for the power of the Suba of Bengal which was the area from which the Great Moghul had allowed the East India Company to collect rents (as a *diwani*) in 1765. This seems to have been the interpretation in contemporary Anglo-Indian society, if one is to judge from newspaper reports, even if Hunter condemned the community's reactions and gave an emphatic description of the Santals in his later historical analysis (ibid.: I: 253). The group led by the brothers is estimated to have comprised about 10,000 persons, mostly Santals, and it soon took to looting. A police officer who tried to arrest the leaders was killed, and the government took severe action against what was consequently considered as a rebellion. About 30,000 Santals took part in the Hul, but not as a regular army and when 12,000-14,000 of the Company's soldiers attacked at the end of the rainy season in 1855 the insurrection was crushed.[4]

The only major challenge to this general depiction of the Hul is that of Ranajit Guha who in his gramscian analysis *Elementary Aspects of Peasant Insurgency in Colonial India* (1983) has argued for the substitution of a collectivity of peasants which unites different castes and tribes instead of the traditional emphasis on an ethnic group of Santals. The present argument, however, takes as its point of departure a minor part of Guha's argument, that the leaders of the rebellion argued their case from a so-to-say scriptural evidence. Or, in Guha's own words, arguing from the protocols of the court-case which ended with the sentence to death of the leaders by hanging:

> Both the *subahs* acknowledged, in retrospect, that their decision to launch the insurrection had been directly prompted by writing. But this was writing seen as divine intervention. As Sidu explained at the interrogation following his arrest, 'half a piece of paper fell on my head before the Thakur came and half fell afterwards. I could not read but Chand and Seheree and a Dhome read it, they said the Thakur has *written* to you to fight the Mahajans and then you will have justice'. This, he said, was the Thakur's order—an order given in *writing.* Kanhu was to confirm this later on when he, in his turn, was captured and related the circumstances leading to the revolt. Asked, What was the Thacoor like? He replied: 'Ishwar (God) was a white man with only a *dootee* and *chudder* he sat on the ground like a Sahib he wrote on this bit of paper. He gave me 4 papers but afterwards presented 16 more'. (ibid.: 54-5, parentheses added)[5]

As stated by Guha the authority of this apparition refers both to images of 'a supernatural being' and 'a white official', but when he continues his interpretation with 'a native scribe sitting cross-legged' (ibid.: 55) we may equally well think of the more sublime picture of a learned brahmin. The oscillation between Thakur and Ishwar is of minor importance as both may be seen as epithets of Shiva who in turn may be identified with Maran Buru, the main godhead of the Santals. What is important here, is that scriptural authority was already stressed in the court cases, just after the insurrection. Generally, such court cases form the most comprehensive material on the thoughts and lives of the lower classes at a time when they could not express themselves in writing. Such sources have been used systematically in a number of studies on European and North American heresy and withcraft cases, such as the well-known study of *Montaillou* by Le Roy Ladurie (1978), or *The Witches' Advocate* by Henningsen (1980). Both books are based on local archives of the European Inquisition. The Salem witchcraft cases known from Arthur Miller's play have been historically interpreted by Boyer and Nissenbaum (1974) where they utilize the court cases to distribute the accused among old and new settlers and analyse the cases with regard to the success of the recent settlers as opposed to the earlier arrivals.

In the Santal case their own reflections on the lost insurrection of 1855 are more meagrely presented in the court case materials even if glimpses allow us to recognize the contemporary religious legitimation of the Hul. The limited coverage of Santal thought may well be due to the fact that the court dealt with what was considered a political crime and not a crime regarding religious belief.

Some of the voices, however, of the Santals of the late nineteenth century have come down to us in a vast corpus of folklore collected by the Norwegian missionaries Lars Olsen Skrefsrud (1840-1910) and especially P.O. Bodding (1865-1938). Parts of the collections concern historical events in the Santal area and the Santals' own interpretation of them at a slightly later point of time.

These collections were made under the aegis of the Indian Home Mission to the Santals (later to become the SMNC, the Santal Mission of the Northern Churches; after Independence the Christians created the independent NELC, the Northern Evangelical Lutheran Church). It was founded in 1867 by Skrefsrud in collaboration with the Dane Hans Peter Börresen (1825-1901) and his German wife Caroline Börresen (1832-1914). They came to India with the Gossner Mission of Berlin for which they worked from 1863 to 1865 among the Kols of Chotanagpur, to the south of the Santal Parganas. But due to conflict they left the Gossner Mission. After three difficult years, later known as 'the Exile', Skrefsrud and Börresen were appointed as helpers to a Baptist missionary in the Santal Parganas in 1867. Next year Skrefsrud was baptized as a Baptist. In 1871, the Baptist missionary had to return home due to ill health, and in the following years Skrefsrud and Börresen gradually established themselves as an independent mission, which eventually turned more and more towards a Lutheran position, partly due to the founding of support groups of lay mission friends in Denmark, Norway, and other countries.

P.O. Bodding arrived in the Santal Parganas in 1890, when the mission had long been successfully established, notably by mass conversions during the famines of 1873 and the following years. He was soon assigned to administrative and scholarly tasks in close collaboration with Skrefsrud. After Skrefsrud's death in 1910 he led the mission until 1922, when he was sidetracked and assigned to scholarly tasks (Hodne 1992, Andersen 2002). Those tasks, however, offered him ample opportunities to continue the folklore collections initiated by Skrefsrud.

During the winter of 1869 Skrefsrud had collected the materials for *Traditions and Institutions of the Santals* from the venerable guru; Kolean (Kolean Haram). The text, of a couple of hundred pages, was published in Santali by Skrefsrud, and later translated into English by Bodding. According to Skrefsrud's own information he had taken the text down directly from the dictation of Kolean guru. Bodding inherited Skrefsrud's collections, and continued to build an immense collection of Santal folklore, myth and history. The catalogue of the collection (Soren 1999) comprises more than 3,000 numbered tales and stories in a thematic arrangement, and even though this includes fair copies of much of the collections, it is beyond doubt one of the major folkloristic endeavours of the nineteenth and twentieth centuries. Such work cannot be done singlehanded, and Bodding had a handful of dedicated Santal collectors assigned to the task, to whom he showed his gratitude in prefaces and books (Bodding 1919, Andersen 2002).

Dated letters show that the collections were already underway by 1893 and continued till at least 1925 (Soren 1999, 3-5). Bodding published a great number of folktales as well as analyses of witchcraft himself, but much of the historical material in the collection has never been accessible to the public though they have been used as sources for the publications of Bodding and a few other scholars. One of these stories is a history of the insurrection, *The Hul reak katha* narrated by Durga Tudu.

DURGA TUDU'S HISTORY OF THE INSURRECTION

In many ways the *The Hul reak katha* runs like an open-ended research interview, conducted by Bodding's interviewer, presumably his main collector Sagram Murmu. Murmu started by establishing the otherwise unknown Durga Tudu of the village Munda Am (the location of which is unknown to me) as an eyewitness who had participated in the insurrection in his youth, acting as a drummer for his own headman (a pargana or headman of 'a hundred villages' named Buka). His age is indicated by the information that he had only one child then. After some persuasion—the collector having promised him that, 'I will give you reward for the trouble, it will not be without remuneration'—Durga Tudu accepted to narrate his 'very long story' according to the proposed terms, 'from the beginning how the insurrection started and who started it first'.

Even if he does not stress it explicitly in these terms, Durga Tudu diligently distinguishes between what he has seen by his own eyes and what he has only heard about. In many ways, then, his story corresponds to present demands for collection of oral history within living memory (Vansina 1985)—a memory which in this case must have extended over a period of at least 36 or 39 years (if it was collected in 1893), but probably the time gap was somewhat longer as historical data had only a secondary priority in Bodding's objectives. Still, there are reasons to assume that it has been collected before Bodding wrote his contributions to O'Malleys *District Gazetteer for the Santal Parganas*, which was published in 1910.

It is not indicated whether Durga Tudu had converted to Christianity. He does narrate the story of the insurrection in a moral framework, as utilized in his explanation of the defeat, but this kind of moral interpretation had definitely spread well beyond the Christian Santals by the 1890s and the first decennia of the twentieth century (Andersen 2002).

Durga Tudu tells us how his headman, Buka, did not join the camp of Sidho and Kanhu before they asked him to do so, and he describes how the Subha Thakurs plundered and raped, setting a bad example which was followed by the other Subha Thakurs when they joined the insurrection. How (in the autumn of 1855),

> The British soldiers suddenly met us (after we had plundered a big village). We started to fight. We did not win, many Santals were shot and killed, some were hacked down and killed, some were carried away by the Mor river and died, and some of us were saved by running away. I carried the kettle drum on my head and ran away along the river bank. And, when the pargana (his headman) saw me, he also ran behind me. In this way we were saved. (Tudu n.d., parentheses added)

Durga Tudu also narrates how the village headmen and chiefs

of hundreds of villages surrender to the British and accept to help them capture the insurrectionists by spying, 'otherwise who knows (whether the British soldiers could have caught them)?'. Tudu's conclusion puts the Company's administration in a positive light, 'Thus the British people brought peace to the country.' This conclusion may well be understood in relation to the concrete initiatives taken by the Company in creating the new district of the Santal Parganas, centred around the Damin-i-Koh, where the Company at least tried to remedy some of the Santals' grievances. They gave the Santal headmen special prerogatives and opened direct access to the Company's administrative system, thereby circumscribing the importance of non-Santal middlemen. According to Durga Tudu, the two leading Subha Thakurs Sidho and Kanhu,

> extolled themselves in vain. They only caused others' lives to be destroyed. That is not right. Where and in which matters were they successful? Not even for one day they were kings, or, not even for one year they collected rents. They only caused the lives of other people to be lost. That is in a nutshell the matter, otherwise they did not accomplish anything. People were offended just by looking at their bad behaviour. Owing to this reason, the Sun god did not appreciate their work.

But they could have won, had they stayed chaste—as in fact God had demanded of them when he entrusted their quest on them—and to Durga Tudu, 'the real sin (*pap*) is the fornication (*lotghuti*)—to take the wife of another man (. . .) Although the man does not know you, yet the Sun god can see you from the above. He can see through all your deeds. Because of this, you are sure to fall into sin.'

SCHOOLING AND THE QUEST FOR REFORMS AND A SANTAL RAJ

Durga Tudu stresses that he knows about Sidho and Kanhu's background only from what he has heard. They were the sons of the wealthy village headman Bhogon of the village Bhognadi and his first wife; Bhogon had four more sons with his second wife: Chand, Bhaero, Soso Sonkhor and Podo Kuar. Because of his wealth 'he agreed with a brahman guru of Badhait Bazar for a sum of money as payment' and sent the two sons 'of his first wife to learn reading and writing'. And here, 'It is said that these two lads learned a little and could at least write their names'.

But they did not remain in the brahmin's school for long, for on the way to the school they met god and he entrusted them with the task of negotiating the land rent with the Raj (i.e. the Company), and if unsuccessful, to assume power themselves.

That it was god—Jagannath—is evident from the way he appeared to them, and to no one else. The events took place at a certain tree on their way to school. Here, the deity first appeared as a man lying on the ground, 'he had no arms, no legs, but had heads in both ends'; on the second day 'he had legs in both ends, but had no head and no arms'; on the third day they found him sitting like a man, and he called them to him, 'Please! Do come here, I will give you a blessing', and when they sat by him he said,

> The blessing (*bhor*) is that they have imposed a heavy rent upon you. Send a letter about this matter to your Raj so that the people ploughing with cows should pay a rent of two annas, and those ploughing with bullocks a rent of four annas, and those ploughing with buffaloes a rent of eight annas. Proclaim this message. And, if your Raj does not listen to it, you make yourselves kings. I will extend my assistance to you.

In spite of this gracious blessing the brothers hesitated since they were not fit for the task, due to their lack of the necessary knowledge, 'How can we make ourselves kings? We do not know how to read and write. With our ignorance, we cannot govern a country. Please! Then teach us your knowledge.' And Durga Tudu relates, that 'they did not go to the school, instead they learned sorcery from him. Within some days, who knows how many, they reached attainment.' It is evident, here, that administrative skills in government, i.e. writing and sorcery, are competences so closely interrelated that they become indistinguishable, different terms only for the same kind of powers, which in turn legitimize any government in the eyes of Durga Tudu. On the other hand he is constantly wondering how far Sidho and Kanhu really achieved these skills. When god ordered them to 'write a letter to your Raj so that you Santal people become kings'. Durga Tudu continues,

'Somehow they wrote a letter', and he proceeds by narrating the more traditional way of preparing a message to call for marriage, meetings, or war, by winding a thread around a small fork of branches, 'and by seizing it with pincers made of twigs they sent it to its destination by having passed it from village to village'. His retrospective distance to the legitimacy of the lost insurrection is also evident in his statement that 'they pretended to be mad' as a way to introduce the fact that 'They began to make some sacrificial offerings and called themselves Subha Thakur'. But even in his doubt Durga Tudu gives evidence of his belief in the governmental power which might be achieved by any Raj through the ability to read and write along with other means of sorcery.

On the factual level Durga Tudu seems to have been right in his doubt as to whether Sidho and Kanhu ever learnt to read and write, as we know that the letter Durga Tudu refers to was actually received by the collector of Beerboom, a certain R.I. Richardson, who reported on it in a letter to colonel Burney, in military command at Suri. Richardson's letter makes it evident that the letter he received was in accordance with the traditional Santal form of announcements as to when one was expected to arrive somewhere or when invited guests were expected to attend an event such as a marriage. It is evident, too, that Richardson did not dream about negotiating with the brothers or any other of the Santal leaders at that point of the Hul. He states,

I have the honour to report for your information that I yesterday received from the Police Zemadar at Nugger, a Saul twig, with 3 leaves upon it.

The twig had been sent to the Zemadar, from a person calling himself the Soobah Baboo [Mr. Subah] with a request that he should forward it to the authorities at Sooree [Suri], whom he was shortly coming to see.

I have enquired among the Sonthal prisoners in the Jail, as to the meaning of this symbol, but they are either unwilling or unable to give any information in the matter, except that the three leaves express the intention of the sender to come at the third day. Under the above circumstances, I beg you will make whatever arrangements you may consider called for, I for my part, shall send no answer to the message it being my intention to put the Soobah in irons on his arrival.

The question as to whether he is about to come in peacefully to submit, or to try his strength with us, must remain for the present, a matter of doubt. (The full text of the letter, quoted from Tarapada Ray, *Santal Rebellion, Documents*, 1983, 24, parentheses added.)

The court reports indicating that Sidho and Kanhu argued their legitimacy from the letters they had received, show that writing was seen, by then, as legitimizing claims for government. But the growth of such legitimizing in the oral traditions about the Hul, reveals the importance assigned to writing at a later point. In the areas inhabited by Santals this legitimacy of writing refers to a conflict of hegemony more relevant at the end of the nineteenth century and the beginning of the twentieth than by the time of the rebellion half a century earlier. Then, the ability to read and write was only gradually becoming a qualification deemed important for rulers. This is clear from reply of the Panchet Raja to the government in 1838 (4 April) where he stresses that he does not want his sons to learn English and Persian since his ancestors never learnt these languages, and he continues to state that his sons could hardly read and write Hindi and Bengali, but were learning to do so (Jha 1979: 134-8). Reading and writing did not yet belong to the kind of sorcery needed to govern—even if they would soon become so. The latter fact is quite evident from the conflicts of access to learning among different tribes and castes in the second half of the nineteenth century.

COMPETITION FOR EDUCATION BETWEEN ETHNIC GROUPS

Early missionaries as well as government reports on public instruction tell us of conflict between Santals and other groups over access to the educational system with the implied prospects of improving their position. This is clear from the following quote from McAlpin's report of 1909, constructed as a typical kind of reply in Santal villages of Bankura district:

> No one in the village can read or write. We do not send our children to school. There is a school a mile off. It has a *Dikku* (Hindu) master. We do not send our children to it. It is too far. We cannot pay the fees. Our boys are frightened by the *Dikku* boys. They also are required as labourers. Yes, we recognize that education will help us against the *mahajan* [moneylender].

> If there is a school close at hand, a Sonthal school-master and no fees, we would send our children to school. (McAlpin 1909/1981: 55, spelling as in original, parentheses added)

The Santals' fear of the Hindu boys and the Hindu schoolmaster, referred to in McAlpin's report, might be seen as a reflection of their own poor situation. But there is also evidence which points to an explicit strategy, devised by the Hindus, of competition for education. This may be inferred from a statement by an old Santal recorded by Culshaw in the 1930s:[6] 'The *Deko* say to us, "You cow-eaters, if you learn to read and write you will go blind", and many of our people, being simple, believe them' (Culshaw 1949: 166).

Letters and the ability to read them are part of a magic, but in the case of the Santals, magic is turned against them, as they will go blind if they learn to read. On the one hand such statements allude to the fact that low castes were denied access to brahmin texts and rituals; on the other hand they refer to the fight for control in an administrative system based on written records. The blend of the power of magic and the power of secular knowledge is evident from McAlpin's report, where education is seen as a skill to be used against the moneylenders' deceit. When interviewed, then as later, Santal elders accept that the skills acquired in school are important, but feel that the obstacles in acquiring them may be insurmountable.

We hear the echo of these conflicts between brahmin teachers and Santals in Durga Tudu's relation of Sidhu and Kanhu as school dropouts who sought magical means to achieve knowledge.

SANTAL EDUCATION

Formal education among the Santals may have been started by Christian missionaries in 1852, but it was only after the suppression of the insurrection that permanent efforts for schooling and evangelization were initiated.

One of the major programmes was run by the Rev. Droese and the Church Missionary Society, who received a government grant for their school programme from 1862. Their annual reports show that they had started 12 schools with 345 Santal boys as early as in 1858, and in 1864, the first year where the Santal Parganas are reported separately, there were 300 pupils (most presumably Santals) in the mission's 11 schools of the district.

In the following period there were ups and downs for the schools. 'Downs' were often caused by bad harvests, cholera and smallpox, and when one goes through the annual reports on *Public Instruction in Bengal*, bad harvests seem to be closely followed by epidemics. Over the years there was an increase in the number of Santal boys (and much fewer girls) attending school.

During the initial phase of Santal education the medium of instruction was not their own language, but one of the majority language , usually Hindi or Bengali; but the reports on *Public Instruction in Bengal* stressed, from an early point onwards, that this strategy was wrong and that instruction should be carried out in their mother-tongue. The missionaries were the first to attack this problem systematically, but from 1884 onwards, the government schools adopted a special system that enabled Santal pupils to be taught in Santali by Santal teachers during the first years of school (lower primary school).

The first schoolbooks in Santali came out when the government system of instruction in Santali was first introduced; though perhaps not before the end of the 1880s. The schoolbooks written by the group of missionaries around Skrefsrud and Bodding may have been the first to appear (Hodne 1966: 307-13). These books together with the collections of Santal folktales and the religious tracts that the missionaries had published, laid the foundation for a printed Santali literature.

Some general figures of attendance to the mission schools and the government schools are available. In the Santal Parganas there were 2,612 pupils in 1881, 5,922 in 1882, 8,086 in 1884, but 800 less the following year. After this, it is difficult to follow the figures on Santals for a long period, but in 1927 there were 9,527 Santal pupils in all of Bengal, a number which had increased to 12,477 by 1932.

In the 1904 report it was calculated, for all the aboriginals of

Bengal, that about 15 per cent of their children of school age attended school. If these 15 per cent had actually completed their schooling it should have led to a massive increase in literacy, but in fact it seems to have had only a very small impact.

On the basis of the 1911 Census it was calculated that the literacy among the so-called 'animistic'[7] population of Bengal was 0.45 per cent for the males and 0.031 per cent for the females (*1907-08 to 1911-12, Fourth Quinquennial Review*).

These figures might lead one to conclude that the process of access to administrative powers, which would of course have meant empowerment to any educated Santal, had not even taken off after half a century. But in retrospect we know this conclusion to be wrong. It was indeed those who had been schooled in the last part of the nineteenth century who laid the foundation for higher education among Santals and opened the Indian Civil Services for their participation. It was also Santals of that period who successfully reformulated the aims and objectives of Santal culture in ways which came to fit the modern democratic, national union. Even if Durga Tudu may have looked askance at the education of the leaders of the insurrection, his very doubt shows how Santal culture had managed to adopt and expand under changing circumstances.

Sidho's letter of demands was leaves fetched to twigs, but it was constructed at a later time as a written letter, as were the letters he received from god. All these letters may be understood as literacy in the magic sense, written by subdued people claiming the legitimacy shown by the ability to handle the letters of power. The typologies of literacy offered by Skaria does indeed help us understand the meaning of incomprehensible letters and revelations. On the other hand, the Santals continued to work on the traditions concerning the letter and they endeavoured to show that the great leader of the Hul was a civilized man who regrettably lost, not because he lacked the necessary skills to govern, but because he could not control his lust. A sad story, but also one that shows that colonial subordination through writing had been appropriated by the Santals as their own means of legitimization and in this way they were and are in agreement with the colonizers' argument for governing through written records.

As a last remark we may wonder why it was Sidho who was the one to learn to read and write, and not Chand, as might have been assumed from the statements of Sidho during his interrogation. I suppose that this is because the ability to read and write had to be attributed to Sidho and Kanhu, to legitimize their leadership of the Sidho insurrection. After primary educational programmes had run for more than 30 years in the Santal Parganas, that ability had to be bestowed upon the two famous brothers themselves and not on any others—neither any Dom nor any brother of their fathers' second wife. In this as well as in other regards Durga Tudu's relation of the events during the insurrection shows how education had taken root as a means for legitimization of power among the Santals at the end of the nineteenth century.

NOTES

1. Goody published his first presentation of the argument in Goody and Watt (1963), but the most comprehensive version is by Goody alone (1987).
2. And in this regard it is an important success that Santali was included in the Eighth Schedule of The Constitution of India by The Constitution (Ninety-Second Amendment) Act, 2003 [7 Jnauary 2004].
3. Estimated at no less than 83,265 in the Damin-i-Koh alone in 1851 (L.S.S. O'Malley 1910: 99).
4. There are many accounts of the Hul. The present account is based largely on Nyhagen (1990, I: 37-42), who in turn bases his account on W.W. Hunter's (I: 1868) early account though they stress different points.
5. Peter Worsley (1970) might have taken Sidho's statement as evidence for his critique of Weber's concept of charismatic leadership since it shows a division between the decisions carried out by those who read the message, and the charismatic leader who receives it from God. Such division of leadership is not present, however, in Kanhu's answers to the interrogation.
6. Presumably also from Bankura district, as most of Culshaw's collections were carried out there.
7. Animistic was then a term for the tribal population. In total the animistic population constituted 4.5 per cent of the total population of Bengal.

REFERENCES

Manuscripts

Tudu, Durga (n.d), *Hul reak katha,* History of the Rebellion, Manuscript, Oslo University Library, Ms. 8vo 1448-0 and Ms. fol. 1686-II-1, *Santalia* nos. 0432 and 1969.

Printed Sources

Andersen, Peter B. (2002), 'Revival from a Native Point of View: Proselytization of the Indian Home Mission and the Kherwar Movement among the Santals', in R. Frykenberg (ed.), *Christians and Missionaries in India: Cross-Cultural Communication Since 1500,* Grand Rapids, Michigan and Cambridge, U.K: Eerdmans/Routledge, pp. 119-32.

Boyer, Paul and Stephen Nissenbaum (1974), *Salem Possessed: The Social Origins of Witchcraft*, Cambridge, Massachusets: Harvard University Press.

Bodding, P.O. (1919), *Sona: En kristen Santalkvindes Liv og Gjerning*, Köbenhavn: Den Nordiske Santalmission.

———(1934), *A Santal Dictionary*, vol. II, Oslo: I kommisjon hos Jacob Dybwad.

Census of India 1991, Series 1, India, Part IV-B (ii), Religion (Table C-9).

Culshaw, W.J. (1949), *Tribal Heritage: A Study of the Santals*, London: Lutterworth Press.

Government of Bengal (selected years of the reports of), *Public Instruction in Bengal*, from the year 1872-3 to 1947-8, including the *Quinquennial Reports* starting with the *Review of Education in Bengal, 1892-3 to 1896-7, Being the First Quinquennial Report in which is Incorporated the Usual Information Given Yearly with Annual Reports*, until the *Report on Public Instruction in Bengal For the year 1947-8*. Printing initiated at Calcutta, the Bengal Secretariat Press, last reports printed by the Superintendent, Government Printing, Bengal Government Press, Alipore, Bengal (the titles are slightly changing).

Government of India (2004), *The Constitution of India (Supplement to the Fourth Edition) [The Constitution (Seventy-ninth Amendment) Act, 1999 to Constitution (Ninety-Second Amendment) Act, 2003]*.

Goody, Jack (1987), *The Interface Between the Written and the Oral*, Cambridge: Cambridge University Press.

Goody, Jack and I.P. Watt (1963), *The Consequences of Literacy, Comparative Studies in History and Society*, vol. 5, pp. 304-45. [Reprinted in J. Goody (ed.), 1968, *Literacy in Traditional Societies*, Cambridge.]

Guha, Ranajit (1983), *Elementary Aspects of Peasant Insurgency in Colonial India*, Delhi: Oxford University Press.

Henningsen, Gustav (1980), *The Witches' Advocate: Basque Witchcraft and the Spanish Inquisition (1609-14)*, Reno, Nevada: University of Nevada Press.

Hodne, Olav (1966), *L.O. Skrefsrud: Missionary and Social Reformer Among the Santals of Santal Parganas: With Special Reference to the Period Between 1867 and 1881*, Oslo: Forlaget Land og Kirke.

———(1992), *Santalmisjonens Historie*, vol. III, Oslo: Den Norske Santalmisjon.

Hunter, W.W. (1868), *The Annals of Rural Bengal*, vol. 1, London: Smith, Elder & Co.

Jha, Jata Shankar (1979), *Education in Bihar 1813-59*, Patna: K.P. Jayaswal Research Institute, Historical Research Series, no. XVII.

Le Roy Ladurie, Emmanuel (1978), *Montaillou: Cathars and Catholics in a French Village, 1294-1324*, London: Scholar Press.

McAlpin, M.C. (1981), *Report on the Condition of the Sonthals in the Districts of Birbhum, Bankura, Midnapore and North Balasore*, Calcutta: J. Mukherjee, Firma Mukhopadhyay (1st edn., Calcutta, 1909).

Miller, Arthur (1980), *The Crucible*; text and criticism ed. Gerald Weales, Harmondsworth: Penguin Books.

Nyhagen, Johan (1990), *Santalmisjonens Historie*, vols. I-II, Oslo: Den Norske Santalmisjon.

O'Malley, L.S.S. (1911), *Bengal District Gazetteers: Santal Parganas*, Calcutta: The Bengal Secretariat Book Depot.

Ray, Tarapada (1983), *Santal Rebellion: Documents*, Calcutta: Subarnarekha.

Skaria, Ajay (1996), 'Writing, Orality and Power in the Dangs, Western India, 1800s-1920s', in *Subaltern Studies IX, Writings on South Asian History and Society*, ed. Shahid Amin and Dipesh Chakrabarty, Delhi: Oxford University Press, pp. 13-58.

Soren, Sagram Santosh Kumar (1999), *Santalia, Catalogue of Santali Manuscripts in Oslo, NIAS Report Series*, no. 41, Copenhagen: Nordic Institute for Asian Studies.

Street, Brian V. (1984), *Literacy in Theory and Practice*, Cambridge: Cambridge University Press.

Vansina, Jan (1985), *Oral Tradition as History*, London: James Currey and Nairobi: Heinemann Kenya.

Worsley, Peter (1970), *The Trumpet Shall Sound: A Study of 'Cargo' Cults in Melanesia*, London: Paladin.

7

Marginal Mendicants: The Jādopaṭiās of Bengal

HANS HADDERS

INTRODUCTION

The Jādopaṭiās live in West Bengal as well as in the border areas of Jharkhand and Orissa.[1] The size of their population is uncertain, but the French anthropologist Rosita de Selva has estimated the total population in India at approximately 6,000 to 7,000 (de Selva 1997: 27). These male picture show men are of Bengali origin[2] but operate mainly in the tribal villages where they show their scrolls in return for a measure of rice.[3] During the last century many of these Bengali scroll painters moved out into the fringes of the Bengali society due to conflicts or socio-economic changes in that society. On two occasions Jādopaṭiā informants have reported instances of migration from Bengal *c.* 60-80 years back in time, due to conflicts between Hindus and Muslims in the district of Bankura and the industrialization in the area of Asansol in West Bengal (Faivre 1980: 111).

The Jādopaṭiās generally live on the outskirts of a Santal village or in close proximity. Their mother tongue is Bengali, but they also speak Hindi and the Munda dialects of their patrons with great ease. They have another service too, which they render in return for rice as well as other items and money. When they hear of a death that has taken place within their professional territory they go there and perform a mortuary ritual called *cokhodān* 'the gift of the eye'.

Due to their adaptive skills they have created a niche for themselves as funerary priests and performers among the neighbouring tribal populations. Within the tribal population the Jādopaṭiās have gained some respect, whereas within the Bengali society they are perceived as low caste.

At present some Jādopaṭiās leave the strenuous professional undertakings established by their forefathers and opt for small business or manual labour on a contract basis, whereas others still continue their navigation through the changing professional habitat amongst the tribal population, trying not to lose their footing. The precarious trail traversed by these scroll-painters, moving their identities along with the socio-economic and political tides, is a reflection of the greater struggles fought out between central and peripheral forces on the Indian subcontinent. The Jādopaṭiās have always been in a marginal position, in several respects, and thus they have been bound to balance carefully their performance at any given time among their potential clients in order to survive.

In what follows, I take a closer look at descriptions of the Jādopaṭiās which have appeared in print over the last hundred years. These descriptions mirror their struggle to survive as a professional group, as well as the prevailing ideas of academics and authors concerning the Jādopaṭiās and their relationship with the tribal groups. Comparing these descriptions to my own data, I try to illuminate the nature of the relationship between the Jādopaṭiās and the Santals.[4] In this article I also want to explore some of the dynamics involved in the socio-cultural mediation performed by the Jādopaṭiās, as they navigate and adapt themselves skilfully to the various marginal situations and contexts where they appear. Those I met in the field mainly worked among the Santals. Thus I shall focus mainly on the interaction between them and the Santals, and the nature of the relationship between these two groups.

THE SANTALS

The Santals with their cheerful disposition and love for hunting, singing and dancing, lead freer, less inhibited lives than do Hindu and Muslim cultivators. They speak their own pre-Dravidian language of Santali, worship their own Santal *bongas* or spirits, regulate their village life in a democratic manner and celebrate their own Santal festivals with dancing and feasting. (Archer 1977: 15)

The quote from Mildred Archer, above, evokes an image of 'the noble savage', the perfect target for an ethnographic account. However, as we ought to know, old categories enslave us, and our conceptual tools capture us in an epistemological straightjacket. I will aspire here to transcend some of the old categories, placing them in a historical context, though aware of the danger of being trapped by new conceptions.

The Santals,[5] the largest tribal[6] community on the Indian subcontinent numbers some 5 million people (Gautam 1998: 14). They are scattered throughout north India as well as in Nepal and Bangladesh. In India they are found mainly in the states of Bihar, Jharkhand, West Bengal, Orissa and Assam. They are endogamous and speak Santali, which belongs to the Munda group of Austro-Asiatic languages (ibid.). The Santals prefer to call themselves *hor* (human being, a common term in all Mundari languages) or adivasi (Skt: original settler). According to Andersen (1986: 7f) the Santals have been recognized as a separate ethnic group since the end of the eighteenth century. A rich documentary source of material can be found about them. The earlier works are found in Troisi's Bibliography (1976). Various accounts are available in works by Christian missionaries, colonial administrators, anthropologists and social scientists. The missionary work among the Santals started around 1850 and gradually the missionaries adopted a Roman transcription of the Santali language (Andersen 1998: 22). Among their work, that of Lars Olsen Skrefsrud and Paul Olaf Bodding stands unrivalled. Both concentrated their data collection around Dumka in the Santal Parganas.[7] Skrefsrud and Bodding worked on an astonishingly wide range of topics including grammar, lexicography, folklore and anthropological descriptions. One of their most precious legacies is Bodding's *Santal Dictionary*, published in five volumes between 1932 and 1936. It is based on Skrefsrud's vocabulary of 13,000 words, more than doubled by Bodding. The dictionary contains impressive information about the Santals, as Bodding did not limit himself to translations, but offered ethnographic descriptions of various kinds in the articles (Andersen 1998: 22f). To get a better understanding of the coexistence between Santals and Jādopaṭiās we must look at the character of their relationship in the light of the Santal struggle for greater autonomy.

HORO-MITAN: FRIENDS AND FOES

The anthropologist Raheja notes the political nature of ethnographic knowledge and literature produced in the colonial era: 'The discursive reifications of caste (and tribes), intimately tied at their genesis to the politics of colonial rule, later became the foundation of much anthropological and historical writing on Indian society' (Raheja 1996: 508). During the last three decades there have evolved several major academic attempts as a reaction against the trend described by Raheja.

Advocating the concept *Horo-Mitan* (lit.. Man-Friend) P.P. Mahato, research officer at the Anthropological Survey of India, has given us a concept to describe the friendly and symbiotic relationship that exists among the 'indigenous tribal' (the *kheroals* or *hor*) and the peasants and 'folk-artisan' groups of Jharkhand[8] (Rycroft 1996: 96). The *Horo-Mitan* society is seen as rooted in the pre-colonial condition, and the effort to write or rewrite its history associated with the project of Subaltern Studies, advocated by Ranajit Guha (1982) and others.[9] Thus, Mahato's project is part of the 'decolonization' of cultural identities in Jharkhand. Since the 1930s, political strife for autonomy, known as the Jharkhand movement, has united tribes under the common name adivasi, 'aboriginals' (Andersen 1998: 41). I stress that the artisan groups, designated as *mitan* above, have united with the adivasi or vanavasi (forest dweller) in the struggle against the oppression of outsiders. Who are these enemies ?

In opposition to the dyad *Horo-Mitan* stands *Hor-Diku*. In his *Santal Dictionary*, Bodding writes; '*deko*, n. A Hindu or Bengali (of the better class, not low-caste Hindus as e.g., *Doms*, *Bauris*, *Hadis* . . .' (Bodding 1934: 69). The term *diku* has a derogatory slant to it. With its negative associations *diku* has been applied by the Santals to moneylenders, rajas, landowners and landlord's servants (Guha 1983: 281-2). The strong derogatory associations of the term is also linked to the tribal peasant insurgency (*hul*) against British Colonial rule in 1855, and its aftermath (ibid.: 111, 281). However, *diku* is also used in a more neutral sense to designate any non-autochthonous such as Hindu, Muslim, European or any foreigner (ibid.: 281). Carrin (1991) notes that the upper caste Hindus, viewed as oppressors, are known as *maran diku* (the great *diku*), opposed to lower caste Hindus, like artisans seen as close neighbours, who are known as *hurin diku* (the small *diku*). Thus the dichotomy of *diku*—an oppressor—versus *mitan*, an ally or a friend, is not absolute. Relationships between the Santals and other groups should rather be conceptualized as placed along an axis from close affinity characterized by symbiosis (*mitan* or *hurin diku*), to distance characterized by parasitism (*maran diku*). To what extent can the relationship between the Santals and the Jādopaṭiās be included in the *Horo-Mitan* type of relationship? Statements by informants show that this inclusion is supported by mutual acceptance. Once when I recorded an interview with a Jādopaṭiā in his village in Santal Parganas, he asked me to turn on the tape-recorder once more, so he could include a final message. When I did so he explained why the name of this forested area was Jharkhand. Finally he included his passionate support for the cause of the Jharkhand movement as proof of his fraternity with the Santals.

THE SCROLL PAINTERS OF BENGAL

In Bengal the main group of scroll painters are called *patuās*[10] (from *paṭa* meaning canvas or cloth [Sanskrit]) or *chitrakars* (*citrakār*, from *citra*, picture in Sanskrit). Scrolls made by such village artists have been common in West Bengal in the districts of Bankura, Birbhum, Burdwan, Hooghly, Midnapore and Murshidabad. However, according to Beatrix Hauser there is only a small number of practising *patuās* today, mainly in the districts of Midnapur and Birbhum (2002: 108).

Thanks to the passionate 'folk art' collector Gurusaday Dutt (1882-1941), we have rich data about Bengali scroll painters and their scrolls. Dutt studied law in England and was later appointed to the Indian Civil Service. During the 1930s he was a District Magistrate in Birbhum and had ample opportunity to study the *patuā*. In his paper 'The Art of Bengal'[11] he notes that each scroll ends with representations of the king of death and of the last judgement. In the paper 'The Tiger's God in Bengal Art'[12] Dutt gives one of the first comprehensive accounts of the Jādopaṭiās,[13] their art and trade (Dutt 1990: 76, 79-82). The anthropologist Binoy Bhattacharjee has made an in-depth study of the *patuās* in Birbhum. He focuses on the changing and ambiguous religious identity of the *patuās*, as oscillating between Hindu and Muslim identity (1980). During the nineteenth century many *patuās* who where sponsored by the Muslim rulers in Bengal—to propagate their faith—converted to Islam. During the first half of the twentieth century, fierce riots between Hindus and Muslims broke out in the struggle that preceded India's Independence. In the later part of this period most *patuās* tended to side with Hinduism (ibid.; Hauser 2002: 114). Today most of them again follow Islam. But in addition to their Muslim identity and name they still keep their Hindu name, and use it when they perform Hindu myths for their—exclusively Hindu—patrons. Hauser points out that 'they practise their rites of passage according to the Islamic rules, albeit in an unorthodox manner' (Hauser 2002: 110). According to Bhattacharjee, scroll painting is not a monopoly of the *patuās*, though it is regarded as their 'caste calling'. They have a number of occupations but claim scroll painting, scroll exhibiting and idol making as their traditional caste occupation (Bhattacharjee 1980: 1). Regarding the relationship between *patuās* and Jādopaṭiās, Bhattacharjee makes an important statement which agrees with my own field data.

> Although there is no difference in socio-religious practice and social position or even in physical features, between the Patuas and Jadu Patuas, the Patuas of Birbhum emphatically denied any relationship with the Jadu Patuas. One informant said that in the past probably the two were one and the same caste. I also feel that Patuas and Jadu Patuas originated from the same stem. (ibid.: 11)

Bhattacharjee relates how he searched at length for information about the Jādopaṭiās, from Santals in particular, without much success. Finally he managed to make contact with a group of them in the Bolpur area, just before daybreak. They had halted under a tree for the night and intended to leave early in the morning. They denied any relationship with the *patuās*. Bhattacharjee notes that the Jādopaṭiās have a nomadic habit and that they have become an endogamous community working among the tribal groups (ibid.: 11-12). The Jādopaṭiās I met confirmed Bhattacharjee's find, and told me they are divided into four exogamous 'clans' (*paris*), each with their own 'totem'; *paramāni*—turtle, *heṭmuriā*—pig, *khāsphul/palās*—flower or leaf (*Butea frondosa* Koenig), and *balāhāri/balā*—leaf (compare Singh 1998: 1323, below).

In opposition to a benign understanding of the relationship between the Santal and the Jādopaṭiā, Bhattacharjee states that 'The Jadu Patuas specialized in exploiting the Santali people in this area and had earned a bad reputation for this' (Bhattacharjee 1980: 11).

DESCRIPTIONS OF THE JĀDOPAṬIĀS

One of the earliest references to the *Jādopaṭiās* which I have found occur in the *Bengal Census Report* of 1901 (O'Malley 1901: 413ff), to which Bhattacharjee and Dutt also refer. In the *Bengal District Gazetteer* (1911) O'Malley quotes his own entry in the *Census Report* with some minor alterations. It is an intriguing passage, which provides a valuable starting point for illuminating the development and change of the attributions of religious and occupational identity to the Jādopaṭiās.

The Jadupetiās are a community found only in this district and in Manbhum (i.e. today; Purulia) and the Santal Parganas, who occupy a place midway between Hinduism and Muhammadanism. They say they are the descendants of a Muhammadan *fakīr* by a low caste Hindu woman. They believe in Allah, but worship Kālī, Manasā, Devī and other deities of the Hindu pantheon. Hindu priests sometimes officiate when they offer sacrifices to Kālī. They practise circumcision and bury their dead. On the other hand, many of them kill animals as the Hindus do, by severing the head from the body, and shave off their beards. Many again bear

Hindu names, and their married women mark the parting of their hair with vermilion. Some also abstain from beef. They have a Kāzī who officiates at their marriages, but not necessarily at their burial services. By profession they are brass-workers and make trinkets, gongs, weights, etc., of metal. Some again are mendicants; they draw pictures of persons recently dead and exhibit them to the bereaved relatives who give them presents.

(O'Malley 1910: 38f)

First of all we may note the ambiguous religious identity of the Jādopaṭiās described here. It reminds us of the *patuās* of Bengal. But whereas the *patuās* have tended to turn to Islam to gain status, most Jādopaṭiās have sided with Hinduism. In fact, all Jādopaṭiās I met vehemently claimed Hindu identity and I did not find anything in their behaviour that contradicted this claim. Thus they slaughtered chicken as Hindus do, by severing the head of the animal. However, there are still some Jādopaṭiās who follow a number of Muslim ritual codes in praxis, but claim Hindu identity in public.[14] One of my Santal informants confirmed this, telling me he had noticed that the Jādopaṭiā who sacrificed a chicken at his house had killed it in the Muslim manner (*al-Halal*), by cutting the throat, severing the jugular veins (santali; *jabe*). In the *Bengal Census Report* statistics of 1901, 238 males and 240 women were listed as Hindu Jādopaṭiās (ibid.: 218ff), whereas only 39 males and 44 women were listed as Muslim (ibid.: 276ff). Thus, in spite of O'Malley's entry about Jādopaṭiās being placed midway between Hinduism and Islam, the *Report* tells us that 91 per cent of them were Hindus, and only 9 per cent Muslims at the time. Are these statistics based on self-attribution or ascribed status? In the Appendix VI of the *Report* there are abstracts of caste tables with short explanatory remarks. In the list of the Jādopaṭiās (XXXV) we find; 'A mixture between Hindus and Mohammedans. Many are brass-workers.' I presume that the Jādopaṭiās would not openly describe themselves as having an ambiguous religious identity.

O'Malley gives some information about the occupational identity of the Jādopaṭiās. In the *Census Report* of 1901 they were listed as either brass-workers or mendicants that draw pictures of persons recently dead. I shall compare these references with those by Campbell[15] in his *A Santali-English Dictionary* (1899), by Bodding in his *A Santal Dictionary* (1932-6), and with Gausdal's description (1960), as well as with my own findings from the field.

Campbell writes: 'Jadopaṭia. A caste of Hindus who deal in enchantment and profess to hold communication with the spirits of the dead' (ibid. 1899: 249). '*Kere kore.* An aboriginal tribe who work in brass and bell-metal. The number of this tribe is very small. They have no settled habitation, but go about from place to place exercising their craft' (ibid. 1988: 398).[16] Bodding writes: 'Jadopaṭia, n. A Hindu caste. There are two kinds, some support themselves as braziers (also called: *kere kore* or *lurka*) and some who profess to have communication with dead people and make "pictures" of them to take to relatives and cheat them for money. (H. *jādav-pati,* one of Krishna's titles)' (Bodding 1935, vol. III: 218). Further in Boddings dictionary; '*lurka,* n. Those who make *lurka* and bore holes in the ear for them. Here the Jadopaṭia, q.v., are also called so' (ibid., vol. IV: 192). Bodding also comments on the word *doroson*, which is very close to the word *dorson*, to see, to look, to visit a sacred shrine, to see a vision (Campbell 1988: 205).

> *doroson,* n. Supposed images of dead people, of witches, and bongas, etc. These 'pictures' are prepared by people of the Jadopaṭia caste. When a person is dead, they paint a picture supposed to represent the person dead. They take this to the house of the deceased, say that he (or she) has shown himself to them (the picture being of the one seen by the painter) and complained that he is in want of this, that or the other. People who believe this story will give the Jadopaṭia what he mentions. These same people also prepare 'pictures' of spirits, marriage ceremonies, etc., etc.; taking these round to show them to people and ask for money. . . . (Bodding 1934, vol. II: 115)

In his account[17] which deals with the sub-clans of the Santals, Gausdal (1960) gives the following explanation of the word *lurka*:

> The word *lurka* has several meanings. It may be a kind of ear-ring which is said to be very seldom seen among the Santals, and it may be used about those persons who bore holes in ears for such rings. That type of work is mostly done by *Jadopaṭias* in the Santal villages. (ibid.: 130)

During my own fieldwork in Santal Parganas (Dumka subdivision) I had an experience that tallies with O'Malley's, Campbell's, Bodding's, and Gausdal's descriptions above. At an early stage, when I was searching for the scroll-painting Jādopaṭiās, someone told me that I could find a small settlement of them on the outskirts of a distant tribal village. When I arrived there some inhabitants confirmed that there was one household of Jādopaṭiās nearby. As I reached that house I spotted a group of non-Santal people in the yard. I talked to them and realized that they were not scroll painters but brass-workers, when they willingly showed me their metal ware. This is the only instance when I came across Jādopaṭiā brass-workers in the field. Their women confirmed that they pierce the ears of the Santal children. They had Hindu names and the women mark the parting of their hair with vermilion. However, they did not wear the shell bracelets, customary for Hindu women. They told me they were Muslims and that a *kāẓī* (Muslim priest) officiated at their weddings and funerals. One of the men told me his full name followed by the title Jādopaṭiā.[18] When I left their house they responded to my Muslim greeting. Later I talked to some Hindu Jādopaṭiās (scroll-painters) about these brass-workers. The scroll-painters said the brass-workers belonged to another 'sub-caste' (*jāt*); *lurka*/Muslim, and had nothing in common with them. One day the wives of these scroll-painters told me they pierce the ears of Santal children. They wanted to sell me some of the earrings they had in store.

The data I have, cannot suffice to judge if these brass-workers and the scroll-painters could have a common history. But the fact that these two groups are called, and call themselves Jādopaṭiās, points in that direction. When it comes to their religious identity, as either Hindu or Muslim, I would like to comment. The communal trend, with increasing polarization between Hindus and Muslims in contemporary India, also reflects upon the religious self-attribution of the scroll-painting Jādopaṭiās. The fact that all I met, claimed Hindu identity was confirmed by the scarcity or absence of any 'Muslim' themes in their scroll paintings. These informants also denied visiting Muslim villages. My findings contrast with those reported by Mildred Archer (1977) and Faivre (1980): Several of the Jādopaṭiās they describe painted and displayed Muslim themes and visited Muslim villages.[19]

Why is it then that the brass-working Jādopaṭiās have been alienated from the scroll-painting Jādopaṭiās and have turned to Islam? Unlike their scroll-painting 'cousins', the brass-workers neither tried to gain status as *chitrakars* in a Hindu artisan tradition, nor did they work as Hindu funerary priests or pose as some kind of brahman (see below). In the same way as the *patuās*, I suspect the brass-workers turned to Islam to escape being ill-treated as low caste Hindus, in favour of a more humane treatment as brothers and sisters in the family of Islam (Hauser 2002: 110; Ghose 1981: 77).

One of the most recent references I have found to the Jādopaṭiās occurs in the series 'People of India' (Singh 1998) published by the Anthropological Survey of India. Here they are listed as Jadupetia/Jadupati. As for their religion, as Hindus, and their social organization, Singh's comments tally with my own observations. But he says nothing about their profession as scroll-painters or exhibitors of scrolls. Thus we may assume that this group of Jādopaṭiās have abandoned their traditional occupation. I have seen this trend among the younger generation I met during my fieldwork.

> A community of Bihar, they are also referred to as Chitrakar by their neighbouring communities, and Jadababa by the Santal. They speak khotta [a dialect of Hindi] among themselves and Hindi with others and use the Devanagari script. . . . They are divided into a number of [exogamous] clans, such as Kashfule, Hetmure, Mejasthane, Bourahari, Mundhantanga and Matabaha. . . . Most of them work as agricultural labourers while some work in the collieries. They profess Hinduism, though some influence of an indigenous faith is still prevalent. An iron rod with a branch of the *simul* tree (mohangiri) is considered to be the family deity while the *sal* tree with a stone (*gaondevata*) is worshipped at the village level. (ibid.: 1324f)

In an earlier publication by the Anthropological Survey of India (Singh 1996), the 'Jadupetias' are said to have come from Bengal, and live presently in Deogarh district of the current Jharkhand (ibid.: *Appendix A*, p. 413). In the 1998 publication, it is noted that other communities call the Jādopaṭiās 'Chitrakar'. Thus, as the name *chitrakar*, implying a Hindu scroll-painter, is still used by others, it cannot have been long ago that they have given up scroll-painting. But since they no longer speak Bengali they must have been out of touch with their past Bengali-speaking environment for many generations.

In addition to showing their scrolls in the tribal villages the Jādopaṭiās have another source of income. They await the news of death occurring in a Santal household. Then they visit that house and perform a mortuary ritual focusing on an act known as *cokhodān*; 'the gift of the eye'. This act has lent its name to the entire funeral ritual performed by the Jādopaṭiās.

COKHODĀN IN THE TEXT OF THE ETHNOGRAPHER

As far as I know, the first detailed account of this ritual appears in Gurusaday Dutt's paper 'The Tiger's God in Bengal Art' (1932). This passage gives us several important clues to how Dutt conceived these doings:

> Whenever a Santal man, woman or child dies, the *Jādu Patuā* appears at the house of the bereaved family with a readymade sketch of the deceased drawn from his own imagination. There is no attempt at verisimilitude, but the picture merely represents an adult or a child, a male or a female, according to the age and sex of the deceased. The *Jādu Patuā* presents the picture, wholly drawn in colour, with one omission only, viz., the iris of the eye. He shows the picture to the relatives and tells them that the deceased is wandering about blindly the other world and will continue to do so until they send gifts of money or some other articles through him, so that he can perform the act of *chakshudān,* or bestowal of eye-sight. The Santals believe this to be actually true and give themselves up to weeping at the misery of their deceased relative wandering about blindly in the other world. They protest that they have already given him gifts on his death, but the *Jādu Patuā* sticks to his point and tells them that King Yama has taken away the gifts made earlier, and so they must send the deceased more things through him in order to satisfy his needs. So the relatives are persuaded to make presents of money or some articles of domestic use to the *Jādu Patuā* for transmission to the deceased. He then puts the finishing touch to the picture by performing the act of *chakshudān*. It is perhaps from this semi-magical practice that the *Jādu Patuā* derives his name (*jādu* = magic; *patuā* = painter). (Dutt 1990: 80)

Dutt's account has gained great authority over the years. Many writers refer to the passage when they write about Jādopaṭiās.

Another civil servant who took a similar interest in Indian popular painting, folk culture, and art, was W.G. Archer. He was Deputy Commissioner of the Santal Parganas from December 1942 onwards, and after two and a half years was placed on special duty to record and codify Santal civil law. He held this post until June 1946. During these years he worked among the Santals, learnt Santali, organized a collection of Santal poetry, legends, stories and addresses. Archer also collected invaluable ethnographic material, published in *The Hill of Flutes* (1974), one of the best known accounts of the Santals. A brief passage about Jādopaṭiās appears in chapter XX, where he gives us a detailed description of funeral practice and ceremonies.

> While these ceremonies are proceeding and sometimes even on the day of death itself, the house of the dead person is visited by a jadupatua, a humble member of a Hindu painter caste. This individual combines the roles of itinerant minstrel and funerary beggar. He brings a few scrolls of paintings depicting the Santal myth of creation, the Baha festival, life in Death's kingdom and sometimes the goddess Kali and the Krishna cycle. He squats in the courtyard, unrolls his pictures, entones a recitative and finally produces a sketch in which the dead person is shown with blank and sightless eyes. In the corner of the drawing is a picture of a cow, a fowl, a bowl or a brass plate according as the jadupatua assesses the wealth of the family. At the end he exacts the animal or utensils as his tribute for restoring sight to the dead and only when it is given does he put the eyeballs in the sketch and leave the house. (Archer 1974: 335)

This passage is Archer's only reference to the Jādopaṭiās. One indication of how little fuss the Jādopaṭiā makes of himself, avoiding any attention to his person, is that many ethnographic accounts of the Santals do not mention him at all. The plain reason for this negligence is that most authors never noticed the Jādopaṭiā. It is notable that Archer gives them the epithet humble. This contrasts with the common notion of the manipulating Jādopaṭiā who forces the Santal to comply with his demands. However, Archer also refers to him as a funerary beggar. He is the first to mention the exact time when *cokhodān* is performed. His account seems to imply that he had some rapport with the scroll-painters. Between 1943 and 1945 Archer and his wife Mildred obtained a fine collection of scroll-paintings from Jādopaṭiās of Santal Parganas with whom they had regular contact. Later, Mildred published *Indian Popular Painting in the India Office Library* (1977), which contains information on the Jādopaṭiās in general and minute details about the scroll-paintings, their themes and content. It also contains some valuable details about *cokhodān,* and an illustration of a 'mortuary' picture (1977: 64, nos. 45, 46). Her account tallies with her husband's, but is longer and more detailed.

It is noteworthy that Mrs Archer refers to the same rationale for the name Jādopaṭiās (i.e. magic painters) as Dutt does, though she puts it somewhat differently. 'This act was supposed to involve *jadu* or magic and for this reason the artists were called jadupatuas or magic painters' (Archer 1977: 7). My own data differs from Dutt's and Archer's accounts. All my informants (both Santal and scroll-painters) denied that the name of the painters was Jādopaṭiā. They claimed that it should be Jādopaṭiā, Jādobābā, or simply Jādo.[20] Incidentally they also call themselves, and are called, *chitrakar,* 'painters', in a Bengali or Hindi-speaking context. All I met called themselves, and were called, *chitrakar* or Jādopaṭiās by the members of their group. I should stress that they never refer to themselves as *chitrakar* in the Santali context, or when they speak Santali. They then use the same designations as the Santals do.

At this point we may ask how did the Santals perceive the Jādopaṭiā and the work he does after a death has occurred? We have seen that Bengali society seems to regard him as a charlatan. Archer calls him a funerary beggar, but other authors call the Jādopaṭiā a priest. 'Originally the Jadu Patuas were a class of tribal priest painters whose art was intimately connected with magical mortuary rites' (Sanyal 1984: 134). However, none of these authors gives any evidence from the field for giving them this status.

The first persons known to have lived among the Jādopaṭiās for some time are Jean-Baptiste Faivre and his friend Utpal Chakraborty. Faivre was an artist and ethnographer, and Chakraborty is an art historian. From December 1978 to March 1979 they did fieldwork in the Santal Parganas (Faivre and Chakraborty 1980). I cite part of the English abstract:

Two traditions meet: that of the Patuas, 'painters' with a 'noble' repertoire, and that of the Jadupatuas, 'painters-magicians'. . . . Though the Jadupatuas know how to amuse and entertain, the concern to impress and even threaten (they live almost entirely by gifts) is never absent. One of their main activities among the Santals is a parody of the funeral ceremony through an assumed image of the deceased. These proceedings, which are accompanied by often considerable 'honorariums' are doubtless at the origin of their name of magicians (jadu or jado) and the Santals persistent distrust of them. (Faivre 1980: 111)

Faivre distinguishes between two traditions of scroll-painters, 'noble' *Patuas* and fraudulent *Jadopatuas*. It is clear that Faivre had no doubt about the origin of the epithet *jādo* as being magic.[21] In the heading to his paper and in the abstract, he writes 'jadupatuas'. In his text he sticks mainly to the term *chitrakar*. 'The terms chitrakar and jadupatua are not synonymous and stand for two distinctive statuses (still we use them here without distinction for commodity)' (ibid.: 111).[22] It is not clear what Faivre means here. Is he talking about attributed, or of self-ascribed status? We must take both into account. Faivre lets us know that the Jādopaṭiā himself refuses the explanation that *jādo* means magic. He says that a scroll-painter rejected this, and claimed that *jādo* was the Santali translation of *chitrakar* (ibid.: 112). The rejection of the denomination magician is an important issue here.

'As part of an attempt to raise themselves in the social scale, a number of jadupatuas had recently discarded this name and had taken to calling themselves chitrakar (painter)' (Archer 1977: 16). Mildred Archer here describes an observation from the field.

That the Jādopaṭiās have discarded their former name among the Bengalis and adopted the name *chitrakar* is related to several factors. We shall consider how scroll-painters have been classified in Sanskrit texts. Then there is 'Hinduization' due to conflicts between Hindus and Muslims. Finally we must consider how the Jādopaṭiās have been classified by collectors and art historians such as Dutt and the Archers. Dutt's revivalist and modernist, nationalist project, where 'folk art' and 'folklore' played central parts, also created an impetus for the use of the term *chitrakar* for a scroll-painter (Korom 1989, Hauser 2002). By using the term *chitrakar* (painter/artisan) the Jādopaṭiās associate themselves with one of the nine guilds (*navaṣāka*) mentioned in Sanskrit treaties, as the Bengali *Paṭuās* do. 'The Chitrakars were explicitly mentioned in the thirteenth century text *Brahmavaivartta Purāṇa* (Skt.) as one of the nine sons of the celestial architect *Viṣvakarman*. These nine sons became the 'Nine craftsman-guilds' (Hauser 2002: 113). This category of artisans has a higher status than the 'sub-castes' that the Jādopaṭiās are usually associated with (*Māl* or *Bediyā*) (Bhattacharjee 1980). *Chitrakar* is thus used as a 'title' or 'surname' (*padabi*). Thus the scroll-painters gain status through a practice similar to what Srinivas coined 'Sanskritization' (Srinivas 1952: 30), by calling themselves *chitrakars*.

The issue of the designation of scroll-painters as either 'chitrakars' or 'jadupatuas' is complicated. Ray, in *The Tribes and Castes of West Bengal*, makes a point of distinguishing the *patuās* (or the 'chitrakars') from the *Jādu-patuās* (1953: 307). Now, this would seem to be a proper distinction, as it mirrors the views of the painters themselves, as we have seen. But I shall comment on the reasons Ray gives for his distinction.

He distinguishes the scroll-painters whom he associates with the 'nine recognized caste groups' (*chitrakars* or *patuās*), attached to the mainly Hindu, Bengali population inhabiting the 'plains', from the tribal group of artisans (Jādopaṭiās or *Paṭkars*) living among 'the Santals, the Bhumijs and other backward classes' in the *jangal* or 'hills' (ibid.: 302). We note that when Ray wrote, most *patuās* had turned to Hinduism. Further, the Jādopaṭiās are typically associated with the budding of the basic arts, primitive techniques (i.e. *cire-perdu* casting) and the tribals with their belief in magic and 'animism'. On the other hand the so-called 'recognized' chitrakars or *patuās* are associated with 'organic and complicated stages of progressive art' (i.e. 'high proficiency in mould-casting which is not known at all to the tribal group'), and the 'socially advanced' (*samajik*) Bengali population practising 'proper' Hinduism (ibid.: 302-9).[23]

Ray's 'evolutionist' discourse was printed and published while the Jādopaṭiās in the field were busy attributing themselves as *chitrakars*, in order to gain status in the eyes of the Bengali society, in accordance with the logic of the discourse presented by Ray.

Thus while the self-conscious Jādopaṭiā have tried to get rid of the derogatory status as magicians for decades, the institutionalized practice of seeing the 'primitive' *Jādopaṭiā* as a magician 'of the jungle'—started by Dutt, the Archers and Ray—is still continued by many authors and ethnographers today (for example Sharma 1993; de Selva 1994, 1997; and Rossi 1998).

Faivre's article includes several photographs of the scroll-painters and their habitat, and a rich ethnographic description of their art, craft and doings among the Santals. In his account they are portrayed with their personal names. He comes closer to them than any of the earlier accounts. One of his informants says; 'The chitrakar is the priest "Brahman" of the Santals.' (Ray 1993: 112).[24] The rationale behind this statement was explained by the informant in the following way; 'as we are present after a death, and our women pierce the ears of the Santal children after birth, we are their priests/brahmans' (ibid.: 112). This is the first time we get this kind of statement directly from an informant. It is an intriguing claim that becomes a vital part of Faivre's exposition. It provides an important clue to understand why the majority of the Jādopaṭiās who work among the tribals have opted for Hinduism. Several of Faivres' informants compared the traditional salary (*dān:* Bengali; gift) of the brahman at the funerary ceremonies to the payment the Jādopaṭiā receives from the Santal after his mortuary work (ibid.: 120). Thus, we see how the Jādopaṭiās use various elements tied to an idea of some kind of brahman when they strive to legitimize their status as priest (*purohit*). They refer to their work with mortuary rituals, and to expiation. At the time of death, the brahman, mahabrahman or *agradānī* must 'digest' the sin of the deceased and serve as a vehicle for the transmission of his moral impurity. Among Hindus the performance of this task is a defiling activity (Parry 1994; Quigley 1993: 61-4).[25] We may note that such brahmans—who have close communication with the *pret* or ghost—are in many contexts treated like untouchables. One of their major roles is to atone for the sins of the dead by accepting gifts, often belongings of the deceased, on behalf of the ghost, so it can finally become an ancestor. The practice by the funeral priests in a Hindu context is similar to some of the actions performed by the Jādopaṭiā at the time of *cokhodān*. Among the Santals or the Soras, possession is a common occurrence (Elwin 1955; Carrin-Bouez 1986, Vitebsky 1993). Thus the Santal is compared to the patron (*jajmān*)[26] of the brahman and the *purohit*. The Jādopaṭiā borrows Hindu categories and glosses his professional role with concepts from a Hindu context.

The Jādopaṭiās I talked to claimed that the sins of the deceased Santals would be reduced by the performance of *cokhodān*. This statement has several implications. It connects the doings of the Jādopaṭiā with the judgement and punishments meted out by Yama in hell.[27] It also introduces the Hindu concepts of 'sin' (*pāp*). The concept of 'sin' is connected to the law of cause and effect (*karma*), and intimately linked with the Hindu eschatological notions of reincarnation (*samsāra*) and liberation (*mokṣa*). How does the Santal make sense of this allusion to 'sins' of their deceased relatives? Carrin-Bouez makes this comment:

> Death is the privileged subject of faith, since death is a problematic theme, poorly defined for the Santal who lack a proper eschatology. This problematic theme is, so to speak taken over by the Hindu thinking, through the mediation of the jadu patua (Jādopaṭiā) who paint the picture of the Santal dead, as well as concepts related to 'ethics', such as the notion of merit or fault, modalities of the karma, theory of individual fate. (Carrin-Bouez 1986: 181. English translation by Philippe Mainçon)

Among the Santals the notion of impurity is connected to the dangers inflicted by, and attracted by, the deceased and death itself. The dead pose a potential threat to the living and it is of utmost importance that mortuary rituals are performed properly, to ensure that these 'poisonous' dangers are purified and neutralized. We must keep in mind, that, among the Santal, as well as in Hindu society, there are many parallel ideas about the destiny of the 'life principle' or soul, and afterlife in general. One reason for this, in Hindu society, is the wealth of textual sources and an abundance of ideas from different periods of time. In the article 'The After-Life in Indian Tribal Belief', Fürer-Haimendorf (1953) gives us some examples:

> Many a Hindu of today believes that a dead man's *jiv* (life principle) manifests itself in the crows which eat the food offerings put down at the

cremation-ground, and if no crows touched the food it is taken a sign that the Departed is angry or distressed. At the same time he believes that the *jiv* must go before Yama's court of judgement, and if able to show sufficient accumulated merit or karma, will be admitted to the company of the sainted dead or *pitri*. Yet he also believes that a dead man may be reborn in a grandchild; and besides holding all these apparently inconsistent beliefs, he acknowledges his duty to perform for his deceased father a series of rites, known as *sraddha*, which are aimed at providing and sustaining a new, ethereal body for the departed. (Fürer-Haimendorf 1953: 47)

Hindu and Santal society have probably influenced each other mutually as to the understanding of soul-concepts and eschatological belief (ibid.: 44). Some regional facets of this complex issue of co-existing models and variations in practice are reflected in the professional discourses and doings of the Jādopaṭiā.[28] The reader will have realized that the distinction I make between 'Hindu society'/'Hindu context' and 'Santal society'/'Santal context' is an abstraction made for the sake of clarifity. In the field, the boundary between these two spheres is often blurred and unclear. It is in these marginal areas that some of the Jādopaṭiās' successful mediations for survival as a professional take place.

Let us now look more closely at the nature of the professional relationship between the Jādopaṭiā and the Santal. Do Santals acknowledge being the patrons of the Jādopaṭiā, and to what extent can this relationship be described in terms of the *Horo-Mitan* concept?

THE SANTAL AS A CLIENT/PATRON

How does the Santal perceive the Jādopaṭiā's claim that the Santal is his *jajmān*? Among the Indian authors who have written about the Jādopaṭiā, Gautam and Gupta differ in their more positive description of the relationship. The folklorist Sankar Sen Gupta presents an interesting picture of this kind of scroll-painter in Purulia district of Bengal, where they are known as *pattikars* or *paṛkars*.

The *pattikars* in the district of Purulia call themselves as patua brahmin. They have their *jajmans* in the manner the brahmins have their clients. No one is allowed to disturb other's clients. These *patuas* are not as neglected in their society as the Hindu or Mussulman *patuas*, rather they have a dignified position. A Santal, a *Bhumij* and the type of people think that the *pattikar* has some supernatural power and he himself too claims so at the time of painting the Supreme God *Marang Buru*. When a *patua* comes to his clients a *Majhi Haram* or the village chief will always oblige him with a *dhuti* (a loin cloth) and a *Pargana Haram* or the chief of a few villages will offer him more than a *dhuti*. (Sen Gupta 1973: 49. Data supplied by P.P. Mahato [see ibid.: 47])

Sen Gupta and Gautam (1977: 38) characterize the relationship between the *pattikars* or *paṛkars* and Santals as friendly. The relationship can certainly be characterized as a *Horo-Mitan* type, as suggested by Mahato. In contrast to high caste Hindus and landowners, considered as outsiders by the Santals, the Jādopaṭiā are described as one among many groups of low caste artisans and service-rendering professionals (like the barber), who live in symbiosis with Santals. Gautam categorizes these groups as 'Santal cognates'. The Santals include them in their history and tradition. Thus, Gautam relates that the Jādopaṭiā, like other service-rendering groups, receive customary dues (*paona*) at the time of feasts, festivals and harvest, in the common manner of a priest-client/patron relationship (i.e. *jajmān*) (ibid.: 148). The Jādopaṭiā has been described as having such status among the Santals in other areas of Bengal as well. Rycroft relates the existence of such symbiosis between the scroll painters (*paṛkars*) and the tribal people of Purulia district of West Bengal (1996). However, none of the Santals whom I asked acknowledged a '*jajmāni* relationship' between themselves and the Jādopaṭiā. In contrast, the Jādopaṭiā who frequented their villages, adamantly claimed such a relationship with them. 'Certainly they are our *jajmān*. Our grand-fathers and great-grand-fathers have visited these areas. . . .' Budhesvar Citrakar told me. He also explained that Jādopaṭiās from other villages than his own would not venture into his territory. Budhesvar's statement describes the pragmatic organization of the funerary market of the Jādopaṭiās rather than a formalized '*jajmāni* relationship'. One possible reason why some scroll-painters have developed a closer tie with their patron might be that they live in close proximity to them. The majority of Santals

I talked to, live far away from the villages of the Jādopaṭiās who visit them.

As we have seen Gautam describes the relationship between the Jādopaṭiās and the Santals as friendly (1977: 38). He categorizes Jādopaṭiās along with other scheduled castes:[29] Paharia, Mahli, Mal, Pal, Turi, Dom, Tanti and others, calling these groups 'Santal cognates' in opposition to high caste Hindus. The latter are seen as *dikus* (ibid.: 38-9). This dichotomy is similar to Mahato's, *Horo-Mitan* vs. *Hor-Diku*. Concerning the Santal attitudes to the 'cognates' Gautam includes this statement by a Santal teacher:

> These groups, except the Paharia, immigrated to the Santal Parganas with us. They were brought in by the Santal for their help. Since then along with us they have also suffered the ups and downs of life. (ibid.: 38)

Further, Gautam relates how the friendly relations are based on mutual respect and assistance. In opposition to this the relationships with the *dikus*, the high caste Hindu outsiders, are based on exploitation rather than a sense of common welfare. Gautam also notes that there are groups that fall between these two categories, and who try to be as neutral as possible (ibid.: 38). Kelkar and Nathan (1991) also describe a symbiotic relationship existing between adivasi and the artisan and service castes in Jharkhand. They make some interesting comments that apply to the Jādopaṭiā.

> For the past few hundred years the adivasis of this area (i.e. Jharkhand) have lived in a symbiotic relationship with various artisan and service castes, referred to as *sadans*, who now constitute up to 50 per cent of the population. In many revolts in the area, the *sadans* too participated in large numbers. Though these *sadans* are often of the same castes as are found in the adjoining plains, yet there are little contact between Jharkhandi castes and their corresponding castes outside. Marriage, which is a very good indicator of the existence of social relations, is, even for these castes, confined to Jharkhandi circles. (ibid.: 21)

There are some interesting remarks here concerning the relationship between Patuas and Jādopaṭiās. They do not intermarry, but recognize each other as different groups. I have hinted at their possible common heritage. The comments made by Kelkar and Nathan, concerning the *sadans*, point in a similar direction. Rather than conceptualizing the Jādopaṭiā and the Patuas as groups of completely different origin as Ray and Dutt does, one may visualize the scroll painters as belonging to a larger group that has developed different professional niches over time. Since the nineteenth century we have a number of examples of such niches, for instance, the Jādopaṭiās as brass-workers, as scroll painters or funerary priests, the Patuas as the so-called Kalighat painters of Calcutta, and the 'ethno-art/tourist-art' producing scroll painters of today, patronised by the Crafts Council of West Bengal who provide scrolls for an urban elite and the growing tourist market (Hauser 2002). Lately the Jādopaṭiā have been invoked at various internet locations as the painters, representative of the folk culture of the state of Jharkhand (see e.g. *jharkhand.nic.in/about/culture.htm*).

From the data presented here it becomes clearer how the Jādopaṭiā can find a grounding for his claims to be the brahmin of the Santals. In the eyes of Santals he is definitely regarded as some kind of priest with special powers. But the stigma attached to the funerary priest in the Hindu or Bengali context does not seem to apply among the tribal population. On the contrary Mildred Archer, among others, noted how the Jādopaṭiā is treated with respect and received accordingly in Santal households; 'On arriving at the house, he would be politely welcomed, given a cot to sit on and supplied with tobacco . . .' (Archer 1977: 16). I, too, have seen how the Jādopaṭiās are received with respect, offered a seat and tobacco whenever they call at a Santal household. Many of the Santals I talked to claimed that the Jādopaṭiās had been with them from 'the beginning of time'. The myths told by the Jādopaṭiās, in the form of picture recitations, of how the first Jādopaṭiā became a painter-priest among the Santals, places the beginning of their professional relationship in primordial time. As a matter of fact, the Jādopaṭiās plant themselves firmly within the myth of creation. The first Jādopaṭiā usually occurs in their picture scrolls after the death of the two original human beings, Pilchu Haram and Pilchu Budhi. Thus the Jādopaṭiā, created by the god Maran Buru or Sin bonga, appears in the scrolls shown to the Santal audience as conveniently included in the creation of the Santal social order.

Some salient features of the identity construction undertaken by Santals are connected to the primeval past, and the notion of a golden age following the creation of Santal society. Thus the myth of creation is a central locus for Santal identity construction. According to Marine Carrin the Santals have produced a symbolic answer to dominance in order to resist oppression by other powerful groups.

> Since the nineteenth century, the Santals have produced symbolic answers to dominance in order to resist oppression. I shall analyse paradigms of Santal identity, to show it is rooted in the consciousness of a distinct past, linked to particular places, such as the old forts (*mare ghar*) of their mythical kingdom Champa in Hazaribagh. . . . Their historical experience is reflected in the way Santals act in different social and political contents, as members of a scheduled tribe, as adivasis or as Jharkhandis.[30] (this volume: 144)

We have seen that the Jādopaṭiās have managed to gain some kind of professional relationship with their Santal clients. I have shown that many authors and ethnographers describe the Jādopaṭiās in unfavourable terms and view them as charlatans, magicians or exploiters of the Santals. In this article I have striven to illuminate the character of the relationship between Jādopaṭiās and Santals in order to gain a more nuanced understanding of their coexistence. Nevertheless, I want to emphasize that, though the Santals generally do accept the Jādopaṭiās, they are far from uncritical about them and their work.

CONCLUSION

As a mediator between a number of different domains and spheres, such as 'tribe' and 'caste', life and death, purity and impurity, the Jādopaṭiā may well be seen as a somewhat ambiguous figure functioning in marginal situations. The Jādopaṭiā functions in a space where various domains meet, and sometimes blur into each other. He has created a professional niche in the space between Hindu and Santal society. The Jādopaṭiā appears when death has struck a household. He makes little fuss about himself. Suddenly he stands at your doorstep. Mostly he comes unannounced like death itself. He is a respected guru of death, as well as a feared person. The work he does takes place during a transitional phase, characterized by fluidity, when the deceased gradually attains the status of an ancestor. The Jādopaṭiā, who has the power to assist the deceased through 'the gift of the eye' can also bring misery to the household through the curse of the 'evil eye'. Death among Santals and Hindus is fraught with danger and pollution. Anyone who deals with death is treated with some caution. However, as we have seen, the creative Jādopaṭiās seem to have planted their scroll performance and themselves solidly within the Santal myth of creation. Among the Gonds of Andhra Pradesh, the Pardhans have established a similar niche as professionals, bards and guardians of tribal tradition and mythology (Fürer-Haimendorf 1979: 152-62). However, the tie between the Gonds and the Pardhans is much closer than between the Jādopaṭiās and the Santals.

The activities and discourses of the Jādopaṭiās challenge many of the preconceived ideas that as anthropologists, we may have, about Indian society. The socio-cultural transgressions of the scroll-painters show us that boundaries between several spheres in the Indian socio-cultural fabric are much more permeable and plastic than we might expect. In a recent article Parkin (2000) refers to the contemporary anthropological trend to focus on identities and identity formation. As for ethnic identity Parkin, citing Barth (1969), points out that in recent anthropological conceptualization such identities are conceived as fluid, malleable as well as being manipulated and under constant negotiation. Even though these 'postmodern' identities may appear fixed to those who hold them, this does not stop some anthropologists from treating them as arbitrary (Parkin 2000: 49). Parkin also reminds us that 'However we may treat such terms (i.e. "tribal" or "ethnic" identities), making irresolvable epistemological problems out of them, indigenes and their spokespersons are quite willing to treat them in a positivist (i.e. "essentialist") and unproblematic fashion' (Parkin 2000: 51).

The concept *Horo-Mitan* is helpful in establishing a more fluid and plastic conception of the social realities that we meet in the field. We ought to be careful about the attributions we make, and the designations we give to phenomena and groups encountered in the field. One way of securing a solid ground for attributions, self-attributions and designations, is to connect them to their respective spokespersons in their respective historical socio-political contexts.

NOTES

1. The Jādopaṭiās live in Bengal in the districts of Bankura, Bardwan, Birbhum, Midnapore and Purulia, and in Jharkhand, in the districts of Dhanbad, Singbhum and Dumka, and in Orissa in the district of Mayurbhanj.
2. No Jādopaṭiā I met could tell me anything about a migration by their forefathers from Bengal. Other authors suggest that the Jādopaṭiās 'belonged to a purely aboriginal stock but subsequently converted to Hinduism' (Dutt 1990: 80), or that they 'are perhaps tribals who have only become identified with these castes (i.e. as Jādopaṭiās) in the past few generations' (Parkin 1992: 41).
3. Usually one *pao*, a measure equal to about a quarter of a *ser* (by weight or dry measure). One *ser* is equal to about one kg (these measures vary with locality). The Santals measure their rice in brass measures made by artisans known as Jādopaṭiās, Lurkas, Kere Kore or Dhokras. Brass utensils are made by the 'hollow casting' method (*cire perdue*) (Reeves 1962: 36-54).
4. I thank the 'Institute for Comparative Research in Human Cultural' in Oslo for financial support of the six months of fieldwork upon which this paper is based. Many themes in this text are discussed more fully in my M.A. dissertation 'The Gift of the Eye' (Hadders 2001). I am indebted to Marine Carrin and Harald Tambs-Lyche.
5. Santal was not an emic term originally. Later on it has been incorporated in the Santali language. There are several theories about the origin of the term (see Gautam 1977: 9ff and Andersen 1986: 8). However, as Santal is used in most literature I will use this term. My Santal informants used the term *hor* or adivasi. My Jādopaṭiā informants used the term adivasi or *mānhjī* (which is a word of Indo-European origin and means 'chief'). The latter is a polite form of address used within the Santal community, as well as by non-Santals addressing Santals (Andersen 1986: 8).

6. The category 'tribe' is a British colonial construction that has been further reified in ethnographic works. Peter B. Andersen, following Cohen, suggests that we ought to abandon this category and use the term ethnic instead of tribal (Andersen 1998). He traces terms like 'tribe' and 'animist', applied to the Santals, to the 'evolutionism' of the nineteenth century (Andersen 1986: 8). I will use the expression 'Santal society'.
7. L.O. Skrefsrud from his arrival in 1867 up to his death in 1910, and P.O. Bodding from his arrival in 1890 until he returned to Scandinavia in 1934.
8. Jharkhand became a separate state in 2000. Geographically, it is situated mainly on the Chotanagpur plateau, with an extension into Santal Parganas (Kelkar and Nathan 1991: 21). The name Jharkhand (*jhar:* grove, *khand:* country), is an old Mughal name of the region covering the bordering area of the present states of West Bengal, Bihar, Orissa, and Madhya Pradesh (Andersen 1998: 42).
9. In the light of recent critique of 'orientalism', the Subaltern Studies aim at showing how the colonised speak back in a post-colonial situation (confer Inden 1990). Guha follows a Gramscian line of theory, and utilizes the term 'subaltern', coined by Gramsci, as a heading for the quest of writing their history.
10. *Patuā* is the transliteration of the spoken Bengali version of this word in English language texts. The transcription of the written Bengali version is *paṭuyā*. In my text I follow the standard transliteration of Bengali, as used by Anderson (1962), with minor modifications. For instance *cokhodān* is not transcribed *cakṣudān*, which follows the 'Sanskritized' written form. The reason is that I want to stay closer to the colloquial pronunciation of my informants. Where other authors are cited, I use their transcription. When Santali words are concerned I have been less consistent.
11. First published in *Modern Review*, May 1932.
12. Ibid., November 1932.
13. I stick to the convention of calling the scroll painters Jādopaṭiās in my text, as that is one term all my informants used. Why I differ from some of the authors I quote will become clear from the text.
14. Personal communication with Sitansu Mukhopadhyay, June 1998. Mukhopadhyay got his Ph.D. in art history from Visva Bharati University in 1991. His thesis focuses on the Patuās and Jādopaṭiās of West Bengal, and is based on extensive fieldwork. I tried to get a copy of

his thesis, but I was unable to do so. The thesis is written in Bengali and deals with 'The Jadu Patuas and Patuas of West Bengal'.

15. The Rev. A. Campbell (1845-1919) was a Scottish missionary among the Santals. He was stationed at Pokhuria in the Manbhum district (current Purulia), not far from the Santal Parganas.
16. Quoted from the third edition of the revised version by Macphail (1953).
17. Gausdal belonged to the Lutheran Santal Mission and spent some 40 years with the Santals. He based much of his book *The Santal Khûts* on ethnographic data collected by Bodding and Skrefsrud (1960: 1, 4f).
18. A Hindu landowner standing next to us told me to write this man's first name followed by *sheik* (a Muslim title [*padabi*]). However, the brass-worker told me to write Jādopaṭiā.
19. The Muslim festival of *Muharram* uses *tāziyas*, symbolic of the tombs of Hasan and Hussain, the martyrs of Kerbela, in their processions. Barekhan Gāzir, a Muslim *pir*, holy man, worshipped by both Hindus and Muslims as a protector against tigers (Archer 1977, Faivre 1980).
20. This type of scroll-painter is also known by other names as *jangli paṭuā* (jungle), Ṣantali *paṭuā* and in Purulia district he is known as *paṭkār* or *pattikar* (de Selva 1994: 63; Rycroft 1996: 72; Sen Gupta 1973: 49). My Jādopaṭiā informants also used *jādobābā, jādoṭhākur, jādoguru* and *jādoharam* (among others).
21. Compare Ray (1953) on magic further on in my text.
22. Philippe Mainçon has undertaken all translations from French.
23. Ray's distinction between Patuās and Jādopaṭiās also echoes the distinction made by Emile Durkheim in *The Elementary Forms of Religious Life* where he distinguishes between proper institutionalized religion united by the church, and the individual magician with his clientele. '*There is no Church of magic*' (Durkheim 1995: 4ff. Italics occur in the original).
24. The Jādopaṭiās I met also made similar claims.
25. Parry says that the word *pāp* (sin) and *doś* (fault) are used for sin in this context. But the most common term is the Hindi word *prayāshchitt*, which stands for expiation or atonement of sin. Parry also stresses that the term *prayāshchitt*, used colloquially by the Banaras sacred specialists, also has the sense of the 'sin' which is expiated, and is

used interchangeably with *pāp* and *doś* (Parry 1994: 281, n. 3). My Jādopaṭiā informants used the Bengali *prayāścitta* as a term for the action of purification from 'sin', or as a general purification from something inauspicious.

26. *Jajmān* is a patron of a ritual specialist, especially of a brahmin priest (Parry 1994: xxiii). The Hindi (or Bengali) term *jajmān* derives from the Sanskrit term *yajamāna*, 'patron of the sacrifice', for whom the priest performed the ritual. In parts of northern India, the term *jajmān* has been extended to cover 'patron' in a more general sense (Fuller 1990: 39). In the contexts discussed in this paper, the term *jajmān* refers to a relationship between patrons and artisans/priests prevalent in northern Indian villages, where payments or dues (*paona*) for a service rendered is paid in kind. These types of relationships are more or less formalized over time (Fruzzetti 1982: 43). The description of the term *jajmān*, given here by me, mirrors my informants' use of the term. For a discussion and a critique of anthropological understanding of the *jajmāni system* see Fuller (ibid.: 33-63), and Parry (1994). In the later part of this paper I will return to the claim that the Santals are the *jajmān* of the Jādopaṭiā.
27. The theme of king Yama and the punishments in hell is one of the major themes on the scrolls of the Jādopaṭiā that he displays in the Santal village.
28. A penetration of this grand issue of origin of the notion of *karma* is beyond the scope of this article. However, for an extensive discussion of the origin of Karmic Eschatology in the Indian setting see Erik A. Edholm 1988 and Fürer-Haimendorf 1953.
29. Scheduled (listed) Castes (SC) is an official designation used by the Indian government, parallel to the designation 'Scheduled Tribes'. In a move of 'protective discrimination' these groups are considered 'Backward Classes' and given safeguards for their 'social welfare' (Devalle 1980: 22). One of my Jādopaṭiā informants told me he was entitled to such subsidies as a member of a Scheduled Caste. However, as far as I know, the Jādopaṭiās are not listed as a Scheduled Caste by the Anthropological Survey of India (confer Singh 1995). Nevertheless, in practice it is quite possible that the Jādopaṭiās get such subsidies all the same.
30. Jharkhand exists as a political entity recently recognized by the Indian government. Geographically Jharkhand region is situated mainly in the Chotanagpur plateau, with an extension into Santal Parganas (Kelkar

and Nathan 1991: 21). The name Jharkhand, which mean 'forested area' is an old Mughal name of this region that covered the bordering area of the present states of West Bengal, Bihar, Orissa, and Madhya Pradesh (Andersen 1998: 42).

REFERENCES

Andersen, B.P. (1986), 'Ritual Friendships as a Means of Understanding the Cultural Exchanges Between Santal and Hindu Cultures', *Temenos,* vol. 22, pp. 7-20.

———(1998), 'Ethnicity, Ritual Integration and Literature as Illustrated by the Karam Ritual Among the Santals', Ph.D. thesis, Institute of History of Religion, University of Copenhagen.

Anderson, J.D. (1962), *A Manual of the Bengali Language,* New York: Frederick Ungar Publishing Co.

Archer, M. (1977), *Indian Popular Painting in the India Office Library,* London: Her Majesty's Stationery Office; the Alden Press.

Archer, W.G. (1974), *The Hill of Flutes: Life, Love and Poetry in Tribal India—A Portrait of the Santals,* London: Allen & Unwin.

Barth, F. (ed.) (1969), *Ethnic Groups and Boundaries: The Social Organization of Cultural Difference,* Oslo: Universitetsforlaget.

Bhattacharjee, B. (1980), *Cultural Oscillation,* Calcutta: Naya Prokash.

Bodding, P.O. (1932-6), *A Santal Dictionary*, 5 vols, Oslo: Det Norske Videnskaps-akademi.

———(1994), *Traditions and Institutions of the Santals*, Delhi: Bahumukhi Prakashan (1st pub. 1942, Oslo: Oslo Ethnographical Museum Bulletin: 6.).

Carrin-Bouez, M. (1986), *La Fleur et l'Os: symbolisme et rituel chez les Santal.* Paris: EHESS.

———(1991), *Inner Frontiers: Santal Responses to Acculturation,* Bergen: Chr. Michelsen Institutt.

Campbell, A. (1899), *A Santali-English Dictionary,* 3rd edn. ed. R.M. Macphail. Reprint by Firma KLM, Calcutta, 1988.

Dasgupta, B. (ed.) (1985), *Samsad Bengali-English Dictionary* (revd. and enlrgd. 2nd edn.), Calcutta: Nabajiban Press.

Datta, S. (1993), *Folk Paintings of Bengal,* Delhi: Khama Publishers.

De Selva, R. (1994), 'Contraindre ou le rôle funèbre du Jadu Patua, peintre-magicien (Bengale, Inde)', *Le deuil et ses rites III,* Systèmes de Pensée en Afrique Noire, 13: 43-87.

———(1997), 'Patua et Citrakar du Bengal: définition. statut, organisation sociale. Une Mise au Point', in *Aspects de l'Art Populaire Indien. Jean-Baptiste Faivre et Les Peintres Santals*, Mantes-La-Jolie, Musée de l'Hôtel-Dieu, pp. 26-30.

Devalle, S. (1980), *Multi-Ethnicity in India: The Adivasi Peasants of Chotanagpur and Santal Parganas*, Copenhagen: IWGIA, Document 41.

Durkheim, E. (1995), *The Elementary Forms of Religious Life*, New York: Free Press.

Dutt, G.S. (1932), 'The Art of Bengal'. *The Modern Review*, Calcutta, May, pp. 519-29.

———(1990), *Folk Arts And Crafts of Bengal: The Collected Papers*, Calcutta: Seagull Books.

Edholm, E.A. (1988), 'The Colours of the Soul and the Origin of Karmic Eschatology', in C. Cederroth et al., *On the Meaning of Death: Essays on Mortuary Rituals and Eschatological Beliefs*, Uppsala: Almqvist & Wiksell International, pp. 95-111.

Elwin, V. (1955), *The Religion of an Indian Tribe*, Bombay: Oxford University Press.

Faivre, J.B. and U. Chakroborty (1980), 'Rouleaux Peints des Chitrakars ou Jadupatuas des Santal Parganas: Etat du Bihar (Inde)', *Objets et Mondes*, vol. 20, 3, pp. 111-22.

Fruzzetti, L.M. (1982), *The Gift of a Virgin: Women, Marriage, and Ritual in a Bengali Society*, Delhi: Oxford University Press.

Fuller, C. (1990), 'Misconceiving the Grain Heap: in J. Parry and M. Bloch (eds.): *Money and the Morality of Exchange.* Cambridge: Cambridge University Press.

Fürer-Haimendorf, C. Von (1953), 'The After-Life in Indian Tribal Belief', *The Journal of The Royal Anthropological Institute*, vol. 83, pp. 37-49.

———(1979), *The Gonds of Andhra Pradesh: Tradition and Change in an Indian Tribe*, London: Allen & Unwin.

Gausdal, J. (1960), *The Santal Khûts: Contribution to Animistic Research*, Instituttet for Sammenlignende Kulturforskning, Serie B: Skrifter L, Oslo: H. Aschehoug & Co. (W. Nygaard).

Gautam, M.K. (1977), *In Search of an Identity: A Case of the Santal of Northern India*, Leiden: Author.

———(1998), 'Tribal Material Culture: The Santal of Northern India', *IIAS Newsletter No 15, Winter*: 14.

Ghose, B. (1981), *Traditional Arts and Crafts of West Bengal: A Sociological Survey*, Calcutta: Papyrus.

Guha, Ranajit (1982), 'On Some Aspects of the Historiography of

Colonial India', in *Subaltern Studies,* I, Delhi: Oxford University Press, pp. VII-VIII.

——— (1983), *Elementary Aspects of Peasant Insurgency in Colonial India,* Delhi: Oxford University Press.

Hadders, H. (2001), *The Gift of the Eye,* Trondheim Occasional Papers in Social Anthropology, no. 8, Trondheim: NTNU-trykk.

Hauser, B. (2002), 'From Oral Tradition to "Folk Art": Re-evaluating Bengali Scroll Paintings', *Asian Folklore Studies,* Spring issue.

Inden, R. (1990), *Imagining India,* Oxford, U.K., and Cambridge, Mass.: Blackwell.

Kelkar, G. and D. Nathan (1991), *Gender and Tribe: Women, Land and Forest in Jharkhand,* Delhi: Kali for Women.

Korom, F.J. (1989), 'Inventing Traditions: Folklore and Nationalism as Historical Process in Bengal', in Dunja Rihtman-Augustin et al. (eds.), *Folklore and Historical Process,* Zagreb: Institute of Folklore Research, pp. 57-82.

Macphail, R.M. (1953), *An Introduction to Santali,* 3rd revised edn., Benagaria: Joint Santali Literature Board.

Mukharji, R.B.S.C. (1938), *Bihar District Gazetteer, Santal Parganas,* Patna: Government Printing (1st edn. by L.S.S. O'Malley, 1910).

O'Malley, L.S.S. (1902 [1901]), *Bengal Census Report,* Calcutta: Bengal Secretariat Press.

———(1910), *Bengal District Gazetteers, Birbhum,* Calcutta: The Bengal Secretariat Book Depot.

Parkin, R. (1992), *The Munda of Central India: An Account of their Social Organization,* Delhi: Oxford University Press.

———(2000), 'Proving 'Indigeneity', Exploiting Modernity, Modalities of Identity Construction in Middle India', *Anthropos,* vol. 95, pp. 49-63.

Parry, J.P. (1994), *Death in Banaras,* Cambridge: Cambridge University Press.

Quigley, D. (1993), *The Interpretation of Caste,* Oxford: Clarendon Press.

Raheja, G.G. (1996), 'Caste, Colonialism, and the Speech of the Colonized: Entextualization and Disciplinary Control in India', *American Ethnologist,* vol. 23, 3, pp. 494-513.

Ray, S.K. (1953), 'The Artisan Castes of West Bengal and their Craft', in A. Mitra (ed.), *The Tribes and Castes of West Bengal,* Calcutta/Alipore: Land and Land Revenue Department.

———(1961), *The Ritual Art of the Bratas of Bengal,* Calcutta: Firma KLM.

Reeves, R. (1962), *Cire Perdue Casting in India,* Delhi: Crafts Museum.

Rossi, B. (1998), *From the Ocean of Painting: India's Popular Paintings 1589 to the Present,* New York and Oxford: Oxford University Press.

Rycroft, J.D. (1996), 'Born from the Soil: Indigenous Mural Aesthetic of Kheroals in Jharkhand, Eastern India', *South Asian Studies,* vol. 12, pp. 68-81.

Sanyal, H. (1984), 'The Nature of Peasant Culture in India: A Study of the Pat Painting and Clay Sculpture of Bengal', *Folk*, vol. 26, pp. 21-178.

Sen Gupta, S. et al. (1973), *The Patas and Patuas of Bengal,* Calcutta: Indian Publications.

Sharam, S.K. (1993), *The Indian Painted Scroll,* Varanasi: Kala Prakashan.

Singh, K.S. (1995), *The Scheduled Castes,* Delhi, Anthropological Survey of India and Oxford University Press.

———(1996), *Communities, Segments, Synonyms, Surnames and Titles: People of India,* National Series, vol. VIII, Delhi: Anthropological Survey of India and Oxford University Press.

———(1998), *India's Communities, People of India,* National Series, vol. V, Delhi: Anthropological Survey of India and Oxford University Press.

Srinivas, M.N. (1952), *Religion and Society among the Coorgs of South India,* Oxford: Clarendon.

Troisi, J. (1976), *The Santals: A Classified and Annotated Bibliography,* Delhi: Manohar.

Vitebsky, P. (1993), *Dialogues With the Dead: The Discussion of Mortality Among the Sora of Eastern India,* Cambridge: Cambridge University Press.

8

The Agency of the Colonial Subject: Claims and Rights in Forestlands in the Early Nineteenth-Century Nilgiris

GUNNEL CEDERLÖF[1]

The sub-collector's question to the Toda pastoralists in the Nilgiris Hills in south India seems reasonable enough. The Toda of Caundalmund had earlier asked the Government of Madras to regain full control over the land that had been forcefully taken from them by a wealthy banker, Sir William Rumbold, in 1831. The government had already agreed to return this land to the Toda; the question remained 'but why do you now claim, in addition, lands which have been included in the Cantonment, and have been occupied, without, as appears, any objection on your part'?

The Toda who had been summoned in 1836 to give a deposition and explain their claims also to lands within the military cantonment, replied:

> All the ground which we have now pointed out has always belonged to Caundalmund, we did not sell it to Sir W. Rumbold by our own consent, we were taken to the Cutcherry and they wrote whatever they liked as the boundaries. We are ignorant whether the ground which we wished to reserve and which is not within the limits of Sir W. Rumbold's property, is included in the Cantonment or not. We believed up to this time that it was our own. We now only understand it after Your Honour has explained to us. We must have the ground which we showed, because if we sell it we shall undergo great inconvenience, if our buffaloes enter into it, and this [is] the reason of our wishing to keep the ground.[2]

In the early nineteenth century, in south India, when the major wars were over and the British East India Company began establishing sovereign rule over land and people, the issue of rights was a core question. Since the Company lacked resources to found their rule by means of physical violence they depended much on negotiating agreements with local rajahs and chieftains or, at least, avoiding pushing Indian rulers to the edge of what was politically possible. On the rich teak forests that were located on the western side of the mountain range bordering on the Malabar and the Coimbatore districts the demand was high. The Bombay and the Madras governments as well as the many private contractors who supplied the timber from the forests sought to secure these resources, either by settlements, contracts and treaties, or by establishing direct control. However, the British counterparts under debate in this paper were not rajahs. The negotiations on the Nilgiri plateau itself are less well known and were of a different character and were carried out with people who first had to learn the language of Law, and ways to find support for their claims within the newly established colonial administration. In the Nilgiris Hills, the counterparts to the colonial administration were pastoralists and shifting cultivators. To the British, they were the Todawar and the Burgher, more commonly known as the Toda and the Badaga.

The region has often been described as an enclave on a mountain top where limited groups of defenceless tribals fell victim to colonial conquest. However, this conquest took at least 20 years to establish and, looking closer at the documentation, the local population appears surprisingly skilled at local politics, while at the same time, the colonial administration was torn by inner conflicts of interest. Even though they were on hugely uneven terms, the multifaceted conflicts created space for the Nilgiri population to influence the proceedings by various forms of negotiation. As the conflicts escalated in the 1830s, the local population acquired means that were introduced by the colonial administration in order to establish control over the territory, i.e. the legal institutions. They both utilized the means of petitions and appeal as well as the new, legal terminology by which they formulated their claims to the land. This was the land that constituted part of their lives and livelihoods, from the grazing grounds for their cattle to the notion of the 'afterworld' beyond the hills on the horizon. By this, the Toda and, later, the Badaga could obstruct government initiatives and renegotiate access to land and resources that had been taken from them by private individuals and the East India Company administration.

When the Toda met the sub-collector in 1836, they had just realized that the land they had allowed the new settlers to occupy for about a decade had, in fact, been lost. In the following years of dispute, their claims to the land were tried by the legal institutions that had been introduced by the colonial government. However, not only did negotiations take place between local population and different levels of administration, laws also were to a certain degree shaped as the disputes over land developed. As will be argued, also in a highly asymmetrical relationship as that between a colonial government and a small population in marginal forest tracts, the latter had the capacity to influence the proceedings.

Rights are contested domains in history. Whenever a claim to a right appears, it is hardly ever derived from a legal code, ready to apply in situations of conflicting interests. This is particularly so in situations of conquest when the new rulers aim at determining and establishing entitlements. South India in the early nineteenth century witnessed constant negotiations where claims to both customary and formal rights were articulated and contested. This article focuses on the settlement of rights in land and natural resources in the forests of the Nilgiri Hills in 1819-43. It deals especially with how people in the Nilgiris acted to secure rights that they perceived had always belonged to them once they realized that these were under threat. Land disputes had begun several years before William Rumbold began establishing his Nilgiri-estate in 1831, but it was at this time that conflicts scaled up.

This period of the history of the Indian subcontinent has important characteristics that distinguishes Company rule from Crown rule. Within Indian environmental history, the distinction has only lately begun to be recognized. The period has rather been understood as the long drawn-out beginning and escalation of imperialism without any major, significant characteristics apart from those connected with imperial rule. Thereby, there has been an underlying assumption of interventions into forest tracts by a modern state institution which represented colonial interests and acted as a fairly singular unit also in the early nineteenth century. In consequence, conflicts in forest tracts tend to be analysed in dichotomous, oppositional pairs—the forest dwellers *versus* the colonial state—without further problematizing the various and contradictory interests within such large units.[3]

I will argue that the lack of a well-established, centralized state together with the presence of the specific and different interests encompassed by the East India Company made the settlement of rights in the local contexts more open to negotiation. Further, I will argue that the settlement of rights depended much on the classification of land in combination with the classification of people as communities. A major characteristic of rights in land and resources as they were established by the colonial administration, is that they were communal rather than individual, and particularly in the sense that certain rights were granted certain groups of people. Only thereafter would a title to land be assigned to an individual person. However, when the British officers negotiated the settlement of such rights these rights were not negotiated in a completely open agenda but within a discourse where ideas of property dominated.

Finally, when people locally responded to European violations of local norms of land management and control, the response did not come in the form of an open revolt against colonial administration but as various forms of resistance that took on many shapes. As the documentation reveals, such local communities as, for example, the Toda did not act on a community basis, either as Todas or together with other communities as one big, subaltern community against the colonial administration. The documentation rather reveals a situation where resistance was located in kinship groups and settlements. Further, when people acted to secure the land they once controlled, it turns out that they often utilized the legal sphere, for example, in petitions to the district or presidency administrations. Hence, they acted in a sphere that was defined and imposed on local society by the dominant colonial power, and resistance came to be expressed in the discourse of the dominant. In spite of the uneven power relations, the outcome was not immediately predetermined.

CONFLICTS OVER LAND

The local communities in the Nilgiris were among the first populations living in the hill and forest-tracts on the continent, to receive visits by officials from the colonial government. After two decades of not very successful investigations in the fringes of the Nilgiri region, colonial officers arrived in 1819 and already within a couple of years, they decided to stay permanently. Soon, a small European settlement, Ootacamund, began to grow and proprietary rights in land became an urgent question for the government. One may assume that when Europeans built houses and claimed Toda land, the situation would escalate into a conflict between the two and colonial power would enforce their rule on local people by military means. One of the first government constructions was, in fact, the military cantonment, which meant an important presence of military and civil officers. History of later periods from east, north and north-east India also tends to emphasize the violent conquest and organized resistance in the forest regions.[4] However, there are no records of physical violence in the take-over of lands in the Nilgiris. The purpose of the cantonment was primarily to provide a sanatorium for military officers so that they could regain their health in a good climate without having to travel to Mauritius or the Cape. Local resistance to this land-grabbing was not lacking, but was mostly unorganized while, initially, the Toda does not seem to have perceived the European presence as a threat to their own dominance in the region. However, in the early 1830s, when more substantial land claims were made, the situation created divides within the administrative body and land settlement turned into lengthy disputes that came to run through several decades. The most diverse interests collided. Local communities saw their grazing lands, sacred grounds and fallows being appropriated by the newcomers. In contrast, the district authorities and individual European and East Indian entrepreneurs realized ways to enlarge their own domains *vis-à-vis* the Government of Madras, while the government itself was eager to establish sovereign rule over both territory and people.

The Toda men whom the sub-collector had gathered in the administrative office in 1836 seem somehow to have been taken by surprise. As can be seen in their reply, quoted earlier, they had obviously just realized that lands which they believed to have been under their own authority were no longer theirs. Now, they objected that they would no longer be able to graze their cattle on the grounds. Ootacamund had expanded right next to two of their own settlements and the Europeans' land claims included the entire settlement of Caundalmund. However, even though the Toda had been remunerated a few times for land that had been occupied by others, this is the first instance when the documentation reveals that they had realized that such payment implied that they could no longer control the management of that land.[5]

The district collector, John Sullivan, was one of the three individuals who had paid the Toda for land and received government authorization. His lands were, however, exceptionally large, as in 1822 they came to include an enclosure of 1,900 acres to be used for agricultural experiments. This made him the largest landowner in the Nilgiris beyond comparison. Within a few years, the government began to perceive the increasing number of unauthorized settlements as a problem, and took up discussions about forms to legalize them while, at the same time, they would establish control over both land and people. They were increasingly critical of Sullivan's independent way of running the district administration. Simultaneously, Sullivan began to voice a strong support for Toda proprietary rights in land. He argued that, if uncontrolled, the European settlements were to become a threat to both the environment and to local inhabitants. Therefore, the Toda land rights needed legal protection. He explained that the Toda had absolute rights in property that were founded in their ancient origin in the Nilgiris. They were 'aboriginal' (i.e. the first to settle on the land) and, further, acknowledged as superior among other local communities who substantiated their relationship by the contribution of *gudu*. *Gudu* was a kind of social tribute or gift within a socio-economic and ritual system of interdependence between people and communities in the Nilgiris. It was mostly given by Badaga shifting cultivators as a share of the produce to the Toda who held authority over the particular piece of land they cultivated.[6]

Sullivan was not the only civil servant who acknowledged the Toda's authority in the Nilgiris. The early ethnographies all testify to their rights as lords of the soil. The Madras Government, however, never accepted these claims as they threatened the Company's sovereignty in the region. The fact that Sullivan himself had paid for his lands later became a tool for the government, when they began to intervene in the administration of the Nilgiris. While Sullivan forcefully argued that the Toda were the first settlers in the Nilgiris and, thereby, should be given proprietary rights in land, the Madras Government refused even to take a discussion on this issue. In 1828, they fixed the same amount that Sullivan had paid the Toda for land in 1822 as the sum by which the Toda should be compensated for loss of land. The choice of legal terminology was important. The Madras Government made sure to exchange the words 'purchase money', as suggested by Sullivan, for 'compensation for the usufruct of land'. This exchange of terms was crucial, as a purchase would have indicated that there, in fact, existed an owner. By the 1828 resolution, the notion of usufruct had entered the legal discourse. It was also a first step to secure government sovereignty in the region.[7]

It should be noted that this resolution was passed in the year following on the Governor Thomas Munro's death. Munro had throughout his career and against strong opposition within sections of the East India Company argued for the *ryotwari* revenue system. According to the 'Munro system', there were to be no middlemen between the cultivator and the government, and the district collectors were vested with comparatively strong powers. Being a close friend and keen supporter of Munro, John Sullivan found himself facing Munro's major adversaries when the governorship was passed on to Stephen R. Lushington in 1827 and the 1828 resolution reflects a changed policy.[8]

But resolutions took long to take effect. John Sullivan had left office when William Rumbold appeared in the hills in 1831 and the major part of the Nilgiris had been shifted to the jurisdiction of the Malabar district. Rumbold had the vision to establish a hotel in Ootacamund and he desired a portion of land that included the Toda settlement of Caundalmund and some lands that were used by Badaga cultivators.[9] R. Crewe, the commander of the military cantonment, supervised and facilitated the purchase. The correspondence caused by this land transaction is quite extensive but perhaps the most interesting narration of the early events has been given by a man named Venkat Soobayen, the acting *peshkar* of Ootacamund. He was the low-level district official who claimed to have used 15 days to persuade the Toda to accept the transaction. In 1832, he filed a petition defending himself against accusations of corruption. Now, the same Toda men had taken him to be judged by the Madras Government.[10]

This petition is one of those documents that open a window to local society, which is rarely represented in the colonial files. Soobayen was the kind of official who carried out the details of the rule of a colonial administration. Mostly, only the result of such day-to-day work ended up in the files in more summary documents that were signed by a British official. But since Soobayen was brought to trial, his reality becomes visible when he explained his unfortunate situation as caused by local politics. Suddenly, people who elsewhere were defined community-wise (as, for example, 'Toda') are here individuals with interests and an agency of their own.

Soobayen explained how he, by the order of the District Collector A.F. Hudleston and Commander Crewe, had assembled the 'owners' of the Caundalmund land, Addy Tothawan and Nairry Tothawan, and the *monigar* Koondan Kallan who was the lowest-level government official and represented a link between the colonial administration and an individual locality.[11] Soobayen was ordered to persuade the Toda to sell the land to William Rumbold who, apparently, first had originally offered Rs. 700 (only later to bring down the offer to Rs. 350). However, they refused to accept the deal since their tutelary deity resided on the land. Not even Crewe in person could convince them to sell. Crewe then ordered Soobayen to make sure for himself whether or not there were any images of the deity on the land. Soobayen reported:

I accordingly accompanied by Kistnayar, the Talook First Goomastah [clerk], and Kolkars Shaik Boodan and Shaik Omood proceeded thither, and saw in a small house, 4 or 5 pots filled with milk, curdled milk, ghee, butter and such other things. The Tothawars assured me that these were considered as their Gods, and about 30 persons, men, women and children, came crying and requesting me not to cause the land to be sold, of all which I made a faithful report to Major Crewe, and sent also a report to Mr Hudleston who sent an order in reply directing me to desire the Tothawars to remove their Divooms [gods] to some other part, to purchase the land, and make my report when I had done so. I again sent for the Tothawars and communicated to them the purport of the order, but they positively refused to sell the land at 350 Rupees. I reported the circumstances to Major Crewe, thro' the Head Manager of the Commissariat Department, who told me in answer that, that officer would give something more on my communicating this to the Tothawars, both in a good and harsh manner, they still stated many objections. At last I took the abovementioned Nairy and Addy Tothawars and Koonda Kallen the Manigar, and also a stamped paper of the value of one Rupee, to the Commissariat office. When the manager told me that Major Crewe had desired him to get a deed of sale executed in the name of Sir William Rumbold, and had given orders for the payment of that sum. As the Tothawars complained very much that the sum of 400 Rupees was not enough, the Deputy Cutwall Baala Krishnayan and some other persons observed to them that in consequence of Nunjah Cawnden having refused to receive the price offered him for a tract of land which was required for the Government Garden at Kartee, the price was not paid him, but that the land was taken and added to the garden. Upon which the Tothawars consented to the Deed of sale being executed for 400 Rupees, and it was accordingly written in the name of Sir William Rumbold, and they received the sum of 400 Rupees in the presence of the witnesses who affixed their signatures to the Deed. I then got back from the Tothawars one Rupee, being the value of the stamped paper, returned to the Cutcherry and reported immediately the circumstance to the Principal Collector.[12]

It is well worth taking note of the terminology that Soobayen used. Addy and Nairry are called the 'owners' of the land, and they were asked to sell it. Commander Crewe wanted a 'sale deed' to be signed at the payment of Rs. 400. The government's elaboration of the legal terminology in 1828, where 'purchase payment' turned into 'compensation payment' and ownership was never acknowledged to the Toda, had obviously not filtered down in the administrative echelons.

After his description of the sequence of events that led to the sale of Caundalmund, Soobayen goes on to defend himself against the charges of having kept Rs. 100 of the 400 for himself. His argumentation is a bit thorny, including accusations of corruption against other officials and the allegation that the Toda 'are a people who will kill their enemy out of revenge, it was through their evil propensity and the evil disposition of the Nellialom Rajah that they entered into a conspiracy against me'. The full documentation gives the image of a *peshkar* who resorted to quite unscrupulous methods to carry out his mission. In a similar case, Collector Hudleston carefully instructed him not to forcefully deprive anyone of land unless they freely consented to the transfer. Resulting from the Toda's charges against him, Soobayen was eventually discharged from office in 1833.[13]

Until the Toda filed their petition, their only way of objecting to losing authority over land was by refusing to accept the payment offered. Filing the petition changed this discourse. When a district official was charged with corruption, the case had to be dealt with by the presidency administration and the Toda's petition entered therefore the Madras Revenue Board's agenda. The Board found that 'the case to which the Board allude appears to them to have been one of great injustice to the Todawars'. However, the Board continued, 'it appeared to the Board that the primary object of the Todawers in preferring their complaint was not so much to accuse the *peshkar* of extortion as to obtain the assistance of the higher authorities in recovering the possession of land which had been wrested from them against their will'.[14]

In this way, the Government of Madras came to protect Toda land from intrusion, which would have been the outcome if the district and local administrations had handled the case. However, the dividing line between the district and presidency policies begins to dissolve as one looks at their implementation. For example, the governor of Madras, S.R. Lushington, a man known for his opposition to all claims of Toda proprietary rights, had sent instructions both to Commander R. Crewe and the Collector A.F. Hudleston, where he told them to cooperate and facilitate the settlement of Indo-Britons on wastelands outside the Nilgiri cantonment.[15] The interpretation of 'wasteland' was apparently generous as it included a Toda *mund* and Badaga fields. The procedure was also a bit lax. The Revenue Board later found that William Rumbold had neither enclosed the land according to the Resolution of 1828, nor had he applied for a government grant. He had, assisted by Crewe and supported by Hudleston, simply requested the *peshkar* to arrange the purchase of land from the Toda of Kandelmund. The *peshkar*, in turn, bargained the price and threatened the Toda that land would be lost with or without payment. The Toda's way out of this clinch was to turn against the *peshkar*, and a regionally strong man, the Nelialom Rajah, assisted them in filing the petition.

It has occasionally been argued that in disputes such as these, people in forest and hill tracts sought primarily to secure high payment for their lands, which would occasionally cause them to delay and renegotiate agreements. However, the situation in the Nilgiris does not support such a conclusion. The transaction of money appears rather to have had a symbolic value while land itself did not represent a commodity. But such a logic is rarely maintained in the colonial administrators' reports. A passage in an investigation made by Hudleston's successor as district collector, F.F. Clementson, has been much referred to. He explains how the Toda had become more aware of the value of money during the presence of Europeans in the hills. No longer would Rs. 10-15 for a piece of land suffice to satisfy them. 'The Todawars are a simple race and till our arrival on the Hills were unacquainted with the use of money of any description, but they have now become fully aware of its value, have learnt to assert and protect their own rights on all occasions and never fail to make a good bargain in disposing of their lands.' This passage has been quoted both in the late nineteenth century, imperial historiographies, and by present-day scholars who, in turn, often quote the imperial historiographies. However, the Nilgiri documentation, in which Clementson's report to the Revenue Board is only one among a great number of document, shows that Clementson is quoted quite partially and that the Toda did not want to act in that arena at all.[16]

In this particular case, not even when they were offered Rs. 700 did they accept to yield the control of their land. Clementson had explained that 'motives of religious prejudice' had made them unwilling to part with it. What he referred to was the small temples next to the Caundalmund settlement. These were sacred places of the Toda's highly ritualized buffalo-cult.[17] The former Collector Hudleston's poor understanding of the Toda's religious life had caused him in 1831 to suggest the *peshkar* that the temple should be moved to some other land. 'Should you find there any image, you should send for a Brahmin and consult him to carry the same to such other spot the people may wish to have it removed to, affording every assistance to perform any ceremony that may be required to that end.' But as the Toda gods lived on the land and could not be carried off to some other spot, and Brahmins had no part in Toda cults, the Toda could not accept this suggestion since they 'dreaded the malediction of their deity' as they explained to an officer in Ootacamund.[18]

INSUBORDINATION UNDER EMERGING STATE POWER

The conflicts over land that the Toda experienced in the Nilgiris, occurred when the British East India Company had only begun to move more firmly into the Indian forest tracts. Actors with strong and, sometimes, contradictory interests went eagerly in search of timber and land. In analysing the first European penetrations of the Nilgiri Hills, I will concentrate on three points. First, there is a need to emphasize the specificities of a situation in which there is a lack of a formal state. Second, in the process of settling land and revenue, there was no immediate transfer and implementation of legal codes into the region by which land could be granted to individual holders. Rather such codes were shaped in the course of conflicts, and rights in land and resources came to depend on classifications of people into communities. Third, once the Toda confronted the settlers' and government's claims to their lands, resistance was voiced in the legal sphere that had been imposed on them by the colonial administration.

Much of the earlier works in the broad field of environmental history have focused on the management of forests while the questions of authority and ownership have been quite overlooked. Or perhaps it is more correct to say that the studies have centred on the mismanagement of the forest resources with regard to a sustainable environment, managed by the local population and with a preserved bio-diversity. This focus may be due to the fields' roots in ecological and environmental studies from where a large number of useful insights have grown.

This perspective has also left imprints on the understanding of nineteenth-century history. However, there is a tendency to submerge into the larger arguments about management regimes the specificities of interactions in the early, European intrusion into the resource-rich forests. For example, Ramachandra Guha focuses the impact of industrialization and colonialism on Indian forest tracts and describes these processes as an onslaught on the forests, leading to an ecological crisis, which magnitude marks a turning point in history. In this perspective, the 'landmark in the history of Indian forestry' is a technical one—the building of the railways—which led to a management regime that destroyed the accessible forests. To him, the presence of a strong, colonial state and its administration plays an important role in submerging nature and people to its demands of resources and control. Hence, the growing state machinery and its advancing forestry policies and management practices are contrasted to the organized resistance it faced from forest communities. This results in a strong emphasis on the later part of the nineteenth century.[19]

However, throughout the conflicts that led to the 1843 resolution of Toda rights in land, the larger question was that of proprietary rights rather than of the management of resources. Further, a major characteristic was the relative lack of unified state policies.

In fact, Indians and Europeans in the Nilgiris faced a lack of a formally unified state. The term 'Company state' is sometimes used to distinguish the state-like institutions of the early British colonial rule from the later 'colonial state'. The distinction is important and the term useful, but only to the extent that it does not conceal the ambivalent nature of the Company's administration in India.

K. Sivaramakrishnan is one of the few authors in the field of Indian environmental history who structures his argument around the difference between Company rule and Crown rule. He characterizes the early administration as a state in being or 'in the making'. Even though regionally specific variations are at the core of his argument—centrally laid management plans could be diverted and abandoned once they faced the local, diverse situations—there is an important transition from a Company government that basically saw forest as a limitation to agriculture and a government under the British Crown that enforced a stricter, centralized control in forest conservation management. Like Bernard Cohn, he problematizes the creation of the colonial state and how it acquired its attributes. But where Cohn puts emphasis on the British project which attempted to create a system of rule within the legacy of indigenous institutions, Sivaramakrishnan points to the cooperation that state-making required from state agents and political communities at the local level.[20]

Thomas Munro's stand on the level of government intervention in the forest tracts is quite interesting and points to the paradoxical situation in which John Sullivan as the collector-in-charge of the Nilgiris found himself in the late 1820s. Over a period of time, Munro argued for both Company sovereignty and indigenous private rights in land. He found the best forms for administration in adopting the existing, ancient Indian laws and customs. He assumed that Indian rulers had, at all times, been regarded as sole landlords, hence sovereigns, with immediate relationships to individual tenants at will on small farms. Consequently, the *ryotwari* system was built on the legacy of the Indian rulers' sovereignty. As a strong protector of the Company, in 1813 Munro argued forcefully in Parliament for Company monopoly in the overseas trade. In the Charter Act of that year, Parliament also made no real attempt to weaken the Company's monopoly over many of the Indian valuable products. However, only a few years later, Munro criticized the Company's monopoly in the Indian timber trade and argued for the protection of private property in the Malabar forests. The conservation of these forests had had the objective to secure timber for the Bombay shipyards and the Conservator had acted as the agent of the Bombay Government. To ensure a sustained supply of timber for the Marine Board, the Company had enforced a far-reaching monopoly that, in fact, had deprived the *jenmi*[21] landowners of their rights to utilize their property. This policy was also in line with the Company's increasingly militarized rule. It had however, caused much local resentment. Munro argued that a free market together with the owners' fond concerns of the timber yield would make up for any government restrictions for the protection of the forests where the timber monopoly would only destroy good relationships with the owners. However, already within a year after abolishing the monopoly and the office of Conservator of Forests, in 1824 the Collector of Malabar reported that there had been a rush into the market which cleared it of timber felled for public purposes and left the Government empty-handed. In 1840, when the office was reopened, the collector claimed that Munro's high opinions of the owners' concerns for forest conservancy had been 'utterly disproved by the last 17 years experience' when large tracts had been clear-felled.[22]

In the Nilgiris, John Sullivan had been left quite undisturbed by government interference into his administration during Munro's governorship and Munro's ideas of free trade within India and indigenous property rights suited Sullivan's administration well. He compared Toda Rights to those of the Malabar *jenmi* landlords. If the Toda were granted proprietary rights it meant that land was free to purchase and the same rights would pass on to the new owners. Sullivan also realized the benefits of free trade. When the Government wanted to introduce fixed prices in the Nilgiris in order to curb the rising prices on food grains, vegetables and other consumption goods, he argued that 'I have just as little right to regulate the prices of articles at Dimhutty, as in the market at London'.[23]

However, once the Lushington administration in Madras took over, the meaning of sovereign rule altered and came into conflict with Sullivan's arguments for Toda property rights. Thus, by the 1830s, the strong and independent collector of the Munro model, the 'princes of large provinces' according to one of Munro's subordinate officers, was sharply questioned, both in words and in government deeds. The administrative structure of Madras was now shifting away from being 'one of form, private interest, of rise of seniority, a corporation government of senior merchants, junior merchants and factors . . . [and] Collectors . . . with unbound authority' (the subordinate officer again). The administration of the Nilgiris from the 1830s onwards on the other hand revealed the implementation of a sovereignty that implied more immediate government control and the 'respect for indigenous institutions' no longer allowed a collector to include pastoralists and hill cultivators. Thereby the Toda lost room for manoeuvre they had found within the conflict-ridden, former, colonial administration.[24]

As indicated earlier, the settlement of land in the Nilgiris took almost a quarter of a century, which is a surprisingly long time considering the small size of the region, its limited population and the lack of armed rebellion or forceful resistance against colonial rule.[25] Partly as a result of competing interests within the administration, partly of skilful local politics, the battle over land came to be fought in the legal sphere. This sphere was not externally defined or transmitted, either from Europe or from other parts of British India to be implemented as a package in the Nilgiris. The formulation of legal codes brought together a multitude of influences—different interests, legal principles, and customary and formal legal practices—in the complex processes in which regulations of rights in nature were shaped. A significant feature of the settlement of rights in land and resources was rather that arguments, procedures and laws were shaped alongside the conflicts. Ideas about people and perceptions about land, landscape and resource use, merged into these disputes and came to define the rights that were assigned in land.

To establish territorial control under the Company does not seem to have been the most urgent aim when the Europeans first moved into the Nilgiris in the early 1820s. John Sullivan's first reports to the revenue board dealt with the assessments that he thought had been much neglected. But in the following years he paid less attention to the Nilgiri accounts. In general, correspondence and reports described the amazingly beautiful landscape and the tall, athletic and self-assured herders—the Toda—whose appearance turned the Europeans' thoughts in the direction of ancient Rome or of the bold British peasantry, and to ideas of liberalism in quite an impressive mix. Being as much on a mission of surveying the hill tracts as of finding a Britain-away-from-home, the civil servants and the scholar-administrators who collected ethnographical and environmental data appear to have found what they searched for when they arrived in the Nilgiris.

The new settlers' impressions of the local population were almost entirely positive. The people were undoubtedly perceived to be living under simple conditions, but the descriptions were not attached with the derogatory judgements that became common some 20 years later. However, the influence of the contemporary ethnological works and the academic debates about the origin of mankind is evident throughout the entire period from 1819 to 1843 with the passing of the resolution on Toda rights. The perception of the population as divided by communities, distinctly defined as different from each other became a principle, which later deepened into legal categories. The settlement of rights therefore received a particularistic rather than universal character, and rights were in the first instance dependent on the community rather than on the individual.[26]

However, over time and in concurrence with the different arguments, the notions of people changed. Immediately in the discussions that led to the resolution of 1828, the Madras Government confronted Sullivan's argument that the Toda, as a consequence of being a socially-elevated people and aboriginal in the region, were to be acknowledged as having absolute property rights in the soil. Both the government and the Revenue Board questioned the Toda's status as aboriginals and, in the revenue files, the terminology denoting the population, began to shift from 'native' and 'inhabitants' to 'tribe' and 'race'. When the 1843 resolution was passed, the earlier ambition to secure Toda rights as aboriginal inhabitants had watered down to securing their rights as subjects of the supreme government. The legal terminology stated that they had never been 'proprietors' but mere 'occupiers' of land. As cattle herders, they had therefore no need for property rights, only for access to grazing grounds. In this way, notions of land and of people came to relate to, and influence the establishment of legal rights in nature. As I have developed this argument elsewhere, I will not go further into it here.[27]

When the Toda men sat down for negotiations with the sub-collector in 1836, as was related in the beginning of this article, they faced quite a confused situation. For more than a decade, they had received the new European and East Indian settlers on their grazing grounds in the heart of the land where they were in undisputed authority.[28] Throughout numerous generations in large parts of the Nilgiris, Toda pastoralists had shared this land with others. Within a complex socio-economic relational system, the Toda allowed shifting cultivators to use portions of the land in rotation. However, their authority over the land had remained. Now they realized that even though they had managed to make the local European authority bow to the foreign government and return what William Rumbold had forcefully purchased, the government also had claims to Toda land. There were suddenly new boundaries, invisible to the Toda but transparent to the honourable sub-collector and the powers he represented, which had entered their landscape; boundaries that threatened to transform not only the environmental landscape but also the social, political and cultural landscapes.

As I will show, in a period when rules for land management and land control in the forests faltered and the local administration had been built up in ways that conflicted with the government principles of the 1830s, the Toda managed to delay and distort the enforcement of a governance policy based on principles of sovereignty. John Sullivan and others had argued that the Toda had 'aboriginal' rights and, hence, phrased Toda authority in ethnological language for legal purposes. Thereby, they argued for absolute property rights in a district in which they also had interests to secure and protect from government interference. For the Toda, the 1830s opened up a sphere where they both realized and confronted the threats to their lands in the discourse of the dominant.

Two debates on insubordination, rooted in the mid-1980s, have inspired the study of situations such as those in the Nilgiris. Both appeared simultaneously and even though different—one focused on rebellion and the other on everyday resistance—the discourses merge in their concern for the agency of the subordinate or the oppressed. Both centre on the conflictual relationship between an oppressive state and subordinate subjects or citizens and the ways in which the subordinate or subaltern responds to oppressive rule and structures.

Among the major contributions to this debate are of course those by Ranajit Guha and James Scott.[29] Both authors focus on the means by which relatively powerless groups create their own agendas of confrontation and fight back with the 'big arms' of insurgency or the 'small arms' of non-cooperation. Ranajit Guha's work on peasant insurgency in colonial India (1983), with its ambition to 'rehabilitate the subject' and bring forth the main aspects of peasant rebellion, tends to give priority to insurgency once it comes out into the open as uprisings. His work has inspired a great number of studies where oppressed groups of people are explained as having found ways to organize across caste and kinship boundaries as a subaltern community. When Guha suggested a re-reading of the colonial archives he aimed at rectifying misinterpretations of organized peasant rebellion against colonial rule that in earlier historiographies had been described as communal protests, sectarian attitudes or unorganized riots. Such 'elitist' interpretations of peasant history, where the terminology of the colonial officers is uncritically transferred into historical analyses was one of the main targets of the early writings in subaltern studies. This is certainly a relevant criticism to apply also to the many works on the Nilgiris that rather uncritically have relied on the imperial historiographies of the Nilgiris produced from 1880 onwards. However, paradoxically, Guha's methodological suggestion to read the colonial files by way of reversing the values that texts contain, in order to find the mind of the rebellion, seems to work best when it is applied to more general reports of the colonial officers. In these, the reports are more often written from the perspective of the colonial project as a single mission of conquest and rule in which rebels become 'thugs' and uprisings are termed 'riots'. This is also where the people to be ruled are singled out as communities, like the Toda in the Nilgiris. But once the analysis is taken beyond these reports and into private correspondence, petitions and depositions, the diversity becomes visible and the 'voice of the subaltern' perceivable.[30]

In contrast to Guha, Scott focuses the small arms used by people who cannot risk the consequences of a direct confrontation with government authorities and ruling power but who give voice to their resistance in more subtle ways. Such protests need not be made by people conscious of their wider, ideological implications but are part of common behaviour and shared values. Scott does not confine peasant politics solely to resistance but argues that it is also expressed in compliance with authority. Since at the core of peasant rebellion are, mostly, the peasant households' basic survival needs, self-interest or 'everyday compliance' is as vital to insubordination as is resistance. In this way, Scott's understanding of the insubordinate peasants grasps both their more forceful provocations of authority—that which, in the case of colonial India, would end up in summary government reports—and their less noticeable expressions.[31]

The drawback of both perspectives is that they portray better the conditions of subordinate groups in more solidly institutionalized states than those in the more unclear situations of the establishment of a new regime after conquest. The Nilgiri situation proves an apparent lack of open confrontation since governance was fractured and there was no clear, single policy to oppose. Similarly, the subtle resistance of foot dragging, false compliance and sabotage in 'everyday resistance' may rather be the response to a situation where people perceived themselves as oppressed, perhaps even structurally oppressed, and knew whom they were up against. In the case of the Nilgiris, settlers and colonial administrators arrived in a region with a locally functioning, social system that was not immediately suppressed or crushed by warfare. The local population in the hills, like the Toda who met with the sub-collector in 1836, only slowly became aware of the extensive claims of the new rulers, the scale of their rule and its capacity to penetrate the society known to the Toda. This may partly explain why people never jointly organized to confront the government's claims and authority.

FRACTURED LOCAL POLITICS

Less than four months after the Toda deposition in 1836 the conflict deepened. Initially, it all seemed to follow the government's plans. The sub-collector had prepared a document to be signed where the Toda *puttadars*, or landholders of the settlements concerned (called *munds*) and the *monigars* of the sub-district Malnaud would give up their rights in land within the military cantonment in return for compensation payment. On 13 March, 26 Toda men signed this document. However, the sub-collector had thought it necessary to obtain additional signatures from other 'influential Todas' to prevent disputes over the agreement in the future. This was disclosed by him when he wrote to the collector by the end of the month and explained why the whole mission had eventually failed. Apparently, when these influential men arrived, they refused to sign the document but let the sub-collector know that 'We have heard of the arrival of the money we are unwilling to accept it . . . and we will never agree to accept it hereafter.' Their explanation, given in yet another deposition, was that the document had been signed 'at the instigation of Goondoocul who, being a Circar servant was interested in doing so'. Goondoocul was a *monigar* and thereby, so to speak, on the government payrolls. The Toda apparently thought that his loyalties were more with the government than with them. This time they expanded their reply as they explained how the land transaction would interfere not only with their needs for grazing ground but would pose a threat to the most fundamental aspects of life and livelihood:

> . . . within this last fortnight after the signing of the Kararnamah, eight

of our people have departed this life and some of us have been seriously warned by our Deity in their dreams, that those who sell the Ground shall be deprived by him of all their prosperity, that they and their Buffaloes shall be brought to the brink of destruction. In consequence of this we are now subject to the loss of plenty of our Buffaloes, and those surviving amongst them are dry and do not give milk as before.[32]

However, their pleas did not soften the government's mind. The Toda's refusal to accept money compensation for land was met by the Revenue Board's decision to keep the sum in deposit for one year and, if the Toda did not change their minds and accept the payment within that period of time, the money as well as the land would be lost.[33] However, this time the Court of Directors interfered. Communication between Madras and the Company's executive board in London took a long time, but once the news reached London, the Court refused to sanction the procedure. They sympathized with the practical problem of moving the entire military cantonment away from Toda land but declared that 'the original occupation of the land to which the Todas had a prescriptive right is not to be justified', and that putting the Toda under such pressure as to deposit the compensation until they yielded was 'in fact a mere arbitrary exercise of power'. This, the Court feared, would 'shake the confidence which the simple fact of their obstinate refusal to transfer their rights, shows that the Todas now place in the justice and moderation of our Government'.[34] The Court's conviction of the Toda's faith in their government was perhaps a bit too optimistic, but the Toda definitely acted in accordance with the recently introduced 'rules of Law' and administrative procedures.

The divisions in the colonial administration are evident. The Court of Directors, getting their decisions sanctioned by the Board of Control, had a major influence on policy issues and appointments within the East India Company. Several individuals connected with the administration of the Nilgiris had direct links to members of the Court. Among those were William Rumbold and the brothers C.M. and S.R. Lushington. But the geographical and time distance left the Court without immediate influence on the day-to-day decision-making. Similarly, the government of Madras and the Revenue Board had initially a limited influence on the collector's administration of the Nilgiris. In the 1820s, they were more concerned with the administration of the western side of the hills, where securing the timber of the Malabar teak forests was a major worry. But their overall interest in this marginal forest tract became clear when they began to investigate and overrule decisions made by the district administration in the late 1820s. The conflicts go deeper the closer one gets to the Nilgiri district itself. While the district or, in fact, the Nilgiri administration argued for private initiatives on a market free from government intrusion, the Madras government enforced their rights as sovereign rulers. This immediately had consequences for the Toda who had turned to the government in order to get their land back. Eventually, they did regain control over some of the lands that had been occupied by the cantonment and William Rumbold. But they were never acknowledged as proprietors. What they received in the end was a right of occupation as pastoralists on account of revenue payments to the sovereign state.

An unavoidable question is why there is no evidence of a large-scale organization among the Toda of the entire Nilgiris against the intrusions on Toda land. What happened in central Malnaud to the Toda of Caundalmund and Manjacalmund in the 1830s came to set a precedent for the legal regulations of land rights and would inevitably influence the rights of all Toda. The 1830s became a period of conflicts when the Toda began to realize the consequences of the European presence. But when it came to the question of land, it seems that each *mund* and clan acted more or less on its own. The British were puzzled by the Todas' social organization that was unfamiliar to them. It is interesting to read Coimbatore Collector Drury's report where he both described the Toda land management system and translated the information into a familiar terminology. Thereby, *mund* is termed both *mund*, *moort* and *baste*, and land under the control of family or kin is described as having been entered into an individual Toda's *pattah* or land deed. The collector writes:

Each Mund or Moort has its separate grounds, including woodlands and pastorage and I understood from the Todawars of the Khodanaud Munds that they do not consider themselves as proprietors in common with other

Todawars, that their rights in their own Munds are independent of other Munds and each family held its own right in the Mund which was invariably respected. The Todawars drive their herds backwards and forwards from one of their own Munds to another, to seek better pastorage without interruption, the Mund vacated by one family of Todawars is never occupied by another, nor do the cultivating classes attempt to take possession of the lands of the Mund while it is vacant. Lands are sometimes exchanged by one family of Todawars with another but no land belonging to one baste[35] is transferred to the people of another. In Ootacamund and Munds in its immediate vicinity, it is understood that any Todawar may sell the portion of the Mund entered in his own Puttah,[36] without reference to the Todawars of the same Mund, he is however obliged to obtain the consent of his own family and relatives.[37]

From the investigation of 1835, in which the collector's report is enclosed, can be concluded that the part of the Nilgiris that forms the plateau was considered to be under exclusive Toda authority. This was where the European settlement Ootacamund had been established. Outside this portion of the Nilgiris, the Toda received *gudu* from the Badaga when they cultivated Toda grazing lands. This was not a general gift that was shared by all Todas, but remained with the Toda in the extended-household settlement that held authority over that piece of land. So, when the Europeans negotiated to purchase the rights in the land that was occupied by the cantonment and by William Rumbold, they did not negotiate with the whole Toda community but with those that resided in Caundalmund and Manjaculmund. There are no signs in the entire process of legal settlement of Toda rights that all Todas in the Nilgiri Hills united as a community to prevent the loss of land under the authority of one Toda *mund*.[38]

When the Toda of Malnaud faced losing their lands, their claims were very precise. These claims were also confirmed by the Badaga cultivators who, in turn, had more problems defining their own claims to land. As shifting cultivators, they left a field after three years' cultivation, not to return to it for a considerable length of time. When the eastern portion of Rumbold's estate was surveyed with the help of the Badaga claimants, it required lengthy discussions on the land itself, where the old boundary stones had been removed, until they could all agree on the extent of the old fields. But the Toda were never vague about the land they considered to be under their authority.[39]

In earlier historiographies of the Nilgiris, the Toda have mostly been described as having been dependent on the backing of the collector John Sullivan. They have rarely been described as having acted on their own account. Investigations relate how they have been 'instigated' by somebody else or have signed petitions drafted by somebody who used the Toda for his own aims. Certainly, all the lengthy minutes and letters signed by Sullivan had an impact on events. The Court occasionally, and to the annoyance of the Madras Revenue Board, commended him for his insight in Toda society and his well-founded suggestions.[40] But during the events we are discussing here, he was for a long period out of both office and country.

However, many historiographies of the Nilgiris have been so dependent on accounts made by British officers of rank that they have failed to see the impact of local politics. For example, there is an interesting reference to a local rajah who is said to have acted in support of the Toda in the early 1830s. The reference appears in Venkata Soobayen's defence against accusations of corruption, quoted earlier. In the midst of floods of counter-accusations against other low-level, colonial servants, the Nellialom rajah appears. He was one of the local rulers in neighbouring Wynad who tried to keep up a level of autonomy when the Government of Madras claimed sovereignty over the Wynad forests. In his petition, Soobayen accused the rajah and the Toda of Caundalmund of having entered into a conspiracy. He further goes on to question one of the *monigars*' behaviour. The sub-collector of Dharwar had instructed Soobayen to arrange for the purchase of another piece of land from the Toda of Kotahkaad when their *monigar* absconded and could not be found for three months, for which Soobayen as the acting *peshkar* was blamed.[41] Apparently, the Toda were not just passive victims incapable of defending their lands. Narratives such as those in Soobayen's petition help to open up a field of local politics in which the Toda were active participants.

CONCLUSION

The significance of Toda resistance to colonial domination in the 1830s that I want to point to, lies in the ways in which they interacted and negotiated with superior authority. Local politics mattered and the Toda were apparently skilled in the art. In spite of their weaker position, they made use of divisions and fractions within the colonial administration and utilized the means of appeal and petition. In this way, the discourse of the colonial rulers partly shaped the subordinates' struggle. Simultaneously, the emerging colonial rule was locally drawn into the discourse of its subjects. Either, as in the case of the Collector John Sullivan, who throughout his own disputes with the Madras Government brought in local notions of Toda superiority or, as in the case of the low level, Indian colonial servants, who became the means by which the Toda could reach higher levels of the ruling, colonial government. Compared to the insurrection in the forests of north, north-east and east India half a century later, or to the Santal uprisings throughout the century, the subjection of these southern forest tracts under Company rule shows important differences.

Once the Madras Government began investigating the local administration of the Nilgiris, lands and resources were taken control of by means of law. The government was expected to establish its rule in a just way, where rights were tried and arbitration took place in front of a judge. This procedure was certainly not just in any universal sense of the term, but defined from within the interests of trade, commerce, revenue and colonial government control. However, the legal sphere that had been imposed on to Nilgiris society by the colonial government and was used by them to redefine local rights became an arena for resistance. The struggle stood over access to and control over land and resources, which means that the different interests in nature and perception of the landscape came to shape the arguments. Likewise, the British also surveyed and classified people as communities with different relationships with nature. In consequence, definitions of both land and of people who lay claims on the land became crucial.

In the academic debates on Indian forest history, studies of land

and people have often been kept apart. On the one hand, there are a great number of studies on the expansion of colonial rule as generated by interests in material resources, especially timber and revenue, and the need to secure state control over forest tracts or tracts in their immediate vicinity. On the other hand, there are ethnographic and anthropological studies of people—tribals, indigenous people, adivasis, aboriginals—that also trace a prehistory to their present predicaments back to the treatment of a people during the establishment of the colonial state. Of course, all studies do not fall into either of these categories, but rarely do researchers engage in the intricate ways in which the classification of land and that of people corresponded and interacted in the determination of rights in forestlands under early colonial rule. Corresponding with the establishment of British rule in India, from the late eighteenth century onwards, the growing interest in the origin of mankind developed a broad field of ethnological studies where people were defined, classified and ranked.[42] In the early settlement of forestland, the way in which a people was defined, tended to influence its rights in land and natural resources. Taking the Nilgiris as an example, if a community was found to be 'aboriginal', which implied being original settlers, they had the proprietary right in the land. If, however, they were found to have been under the sovereign rule of a state, which in the case of the Nilgiris would have been under Mysore rule, all such claims lost validity, and the colonial state could replace the former rulers and take on their rights and authority over the region. As is evident from the above analysis, the Madras Government enforced their agenda of being a sovereign state. This argument constantly confronted claims from, among others, John Sullivan, that the Toda were the aboriginal settlers on the hills and respected by all local communities for their indisputable rights as lords of the soil. This concurred with arguments in support of the sanctity of private property. The discussions were clearly not as simple as this but in a two-sentence summary, this tended to be the general logic.

This situation also indicates another characteristic of the settlement of land, which, in fact, was a settlement of rights. When such rights were established, they were basically communal, not individual. Particular rights belonged to particular communities. Government reports and correspondence reflect the continued attempts to pin down what was a right and who had such a right. Only thereafter was a title to land granted to an individual person. This interrelationship between the rights in land and resources and the rights of a certain people is one of the most interesting aspects of the early period of the process in which the colonial government achieved control over the forestlands in the Western Ghats of south India. This is the context in which property and proprietary rights were established in these forest tracts.[43]

If we assume that the Toda perceived the prospects of overthrowing authority as extremely limited, the documentation reveals that they made use of the possibilities given within the colonial administration to achieve the best outcome possible in a bad situation. Also representatives on all levels of the administration had interests that, in the short run, coincided with those of the Toda. Firstly, when the Collector John Sullivan strove to keep the European enterprises free from government intrusion, he brought in the need to protect Toda proprietary rights as aboriginal inhabitants. The European settlers in the Nilgiris would rather negotiate land with the Toda as landholders than with the government as the sovereign ruler. Second, when the Government of Madras wanted to acquire control over the private entrepreneurs who did not conform to sovereign rule, the effect was that the Toda found protection from land-grabbing within the government administration. Finally, the Court of Directors were keenly aware of the need to protect the rights in property of all subjects to British rule, European as well as indigenous Indian. The Toda, even though only a small 'tribe' on a mountain top, were also subject to this logic as its implementation in the Nilgiris had implications in other parts of the growing empire. There were also other reason for the European concern with the Toda, 'this interesting race', to quote a Court despatch that has to do with ambitions to protect 'aboriginal tribes' from extinction under the onslaught of merchant and industrial interests. But at this point, it is sufficient to emphasize the ways in which the Toda were able to navigate within the local exercise of colonial rule, with the ambition to retain their rights and secure a society carried by norms and values that were common to the local communities of the Nilgiri Hills.

In most of the surrounding, south Indian society, the British colonial state had begun to establish its rule. However, in the 1830s, it was still much contested and, locally, its hold on development was still weak. This provided the Nilgiri communities with room to manoeuvre. Having said all this, it needs to be emphasized that this seemingly ambiguous and fractured, colonial authority ultimately held the upper hand in relation to communities such as the Toda. All administrators were part of colonial rule in which no enclaves of self-sustaining, local, socio-economic systems could remain intact. The Toda chose to resist more than to confront superior rule.

It could be further investigated whether similar situations existed elsewhere in Indian forests but have so far been neglected by research, while priority has been given to the more violent, rebellious insurgencies where colonial armed forces met with armed rebellion by groups and communities, who had put inner conflicts aside to meet the threat of enforced state power. The more low-scale conflicts, as well as low-scale resistance in the Nilgiris show an immediate complexity in the divisions among the conflicting parties and an ambiguity with regard to the implementation of the colonial state policy. With a colonial administration being divided by conflicting interests, one may conclude that there was no larger colonial project or colonial-*ism* enforced locally. However, irrespective of support from a district collector, protection from land-grabbers by the government of the Presidency and the preferences given to indigenous, colonial subjects by the Court of Directors, the outcome remained: the Toda lost access to land and resources. Ultimately, a strong colonial administration was established also locally and local society was engulfed by the larger market in which land and resources became commodities. To confront superior power, the Toda entered into negotiations with its representatives, European as well as Indian. Such resistance of the forest dwellers may have been weak compared with the powers that they were up against. But in delaying the process and reconstructing its conditions, it was relatively powerful.

NOTES

1. I am grateful to the Swedish Collegium of Advanced Study in the Social Sciences, Uppsala University, and Queen Elizabeth House, Oxford University, where I have benefited greatly from the research environment and discussions with fellow researchers. Beppe Karlsson and Inger Österdahl have made useful comments. The work is part of the project 'Claims and Rights: Processes of Negotiation over Nature in India' funded by the Bank of Sweden Tercentenary Foundation and the Swedish Council for Research in the Humanities and Social Sciences (HSFR).
2. Caundalmund (or, today, Kandelmund) is the name of the Toda settlement in Badaga language while, in Toda language it is called Kashmund. Cutcherry means administrative office or court house. OIOC, Madras Revenue Proceedings, 27.12.1836, no. 43, pp. 7079-84, Translation of Deposition given before E. Smith Esquire sub-collector of Malabar by the undersigned Malnaud Todavars under the date the 7 December 1836.
3. K. Sivaramakrishnan's recent work on state-making in eastern India is an exception to this general treatment of nineteenth-century history, where he specifically contrasts the period of Company rule with that of Crown rule. Sivaramakrishnan 1999.
4. See, for example, Sundar 1997 and Ramachandra Guha 1989.
5. Ootacamund was established in between Caundalmund and Manjacalmund within the division of Malnaud. A 'mund' was a Toda settlement. The spelling of names and place names follows that of the documentation.

   There are a few records on early remuneration. At the most, three individuals had paid the Toda for land. OIOC, Madras Board of Revenue Proceedings, 23.10.1828, to the Board of Revenue from John Sullivan, Collector, 11.10.1828, para 5.
6. Spelt 'goodoo' in the government documents. OIOC, Madras Revenue Proceedings, 26.2.1835, to the Pl. Coll. of Malabar from John Sullivan, former Principal Collector of Coimbatore, 16.1.1835, pp. 2237-43, no. 1, para 4, Walker 1989, p. 196.
7. Sullivan later modified this claim that the Toda were the first settlers when investigations showed that Todas did not recognize archaeological remains as theirs. Thereby, it was generally concluded, there had been other people living on the Nilgiris before the Toda arrived. At this point,

Sullivan argued that the Toda were definitely the first settlers among those living in the region in the present day, which still proved their proprietary rights. OIOC, Madras Revenue Proceedings, 26.2.1835, no. 1, to the Pl. Coll. of Malabar from J. Sullivan, formerly Pl. Coll. of Coimbatore, 16.1.1835, pp. 2237-43, para 2. OIOC, Madras Revenue Proceedings, 17.9.1822, no. 15, pp. 2422-3, and OIOC, Madras Board of Revenue Proceedings, 23.10.1828, pp. 10687-9, to the President and Members of the Board of Revenue, from John Sullivan, 11.10.1828, para 5, OIOC, Madras Board of Revenue Proceedings, 27.11.1828.

8. Stein 1989: 167-8, 306-10.
9. According to investigations made between 1834 and 1837, there were originally nine Badaga 'occupants' who cultivated the lands which were included in the farm land assumed by the government in 1831. OIOC, Madras Board of Revenue Proceedings, 6.11.1834, pp. 11903-5.
10. OIOC, Madras Board of Revenue Proceedings, 5.8.1833, no. 5, Arzee of Venkata Soobayen Acting Peishkar of Ootacamund, pp. 9687-8, OIOC, Madras Board of Revenue Proceedings, 21.1.1833, pp. 791-801, no. 1, to the Board of Revenue, The Petition of Venkata Soobyen, late Peishkar of Ootacamund in the Neilgherry Talook in the Zillah of Malabar.
11. The major part of the Nilgiris was transferred to the administration of the Malabar district in 1830. John Sullivan introduced the office of *monigar* (*manigar*, *monivar*, etc.) at an early stage of his administration of the Nilgiris Hills. In the Nilgiris, the *monigar* was a member of a local community of a certain *nad*, whom the administration could relate to in public matters. The *monigar* received pay or, at times, rent-free land in lieu of pay.
12. OIOC, Madras Board of Revenue Proceedings, 21.1.1833, pp. 791-801, no. 1, to the Board of Revenue, The Petition of Venkata Soobyen, late Peshkar of Ootacamund in the Neilgherry Talook in the Zillah of Malabar.
13. OIOC, Madras Board of Revenue Proceedings, 5.8.1833, no. 5, to A.Fr. Hudleston Esq, Principal Collector of Malabar from Venkat Soobayen, Acting Peshkar, n.d., and no. 10, to Venkatkoopayen, Acting Peshkar at Ootacamund from Fr. Hudleston, Principal Collector of Malabar, 10.10.1832.
14. OIOC, Madras Board of Revenue Proceedings, 20.11.1834, para 2.
15. Stephen Rumbold Lushington was governor of Madras from 1827-32.

OIOC, Madras Board of Revenue Proceedings, 5.8.1833, nos. 6 and 7.

16. In the same document, Clementson explains that the Toda in Caundalmund never wanted to part with their sacred grounds and that 'Repeated entreaties and the offer of a large sum of money (from four hundred Rupees) at length induced them to yield though reluctantly as acknowledged by the Peshkar himself.' OIOC, Madras Board of Revenue Proceedings, 5.8.1833, paras 2, 3 and 6. Quoted, for example, in the Manual of Nilgiri District by Grigg 1880, p. 332, who, in turn, is quoted by the Anthropologist Anthony Walker in Walker 1989, pp. 243, 246.
17. The cult of the sacred dairies has been discussed in many studies of the Toda. For an insight into how it has been described at two different points in time, see Rivers 1906, pp. 38-181, 231-48 and Walker 1989, pp. 27-33.
18. OIOC, Madras Board of Revenue Proceedings, 5.8.1833, no. 4, pp. 9585-7, to the Acting Peshkar of Neilgherry from A.Fr. Hudleston, Principal Collector, 8.9.1831, OIOC, Madras Board of Revenue Proceedings, 20.11.1834, p. 12791, no. 1, Collector's letter 8.7.1833.
19. Guha 1989, pp. 37-9, Guha 1983, pp. 1883-4.
20. Cohn 1997, pp. 60-2, Sivaramakrishnan 1999, pp. 4-9, 149-51. Other studies that have aimed at deconstructing the state as an actor and focused conflicts between different levels of administration, different departments and different regions and time periods have mainly dealt with the late colonial period or post-Independence India. See, for example, Saberwal 1999 and Skaria 1999.
21. *Jenmi, jemnum*, sovereign proprietary right in land. Parliamentary papers, session 1812, vol. 7, *Fifth Select Committee*, App. 23, Extracts from reports respecting land tenures and assessments, in Malabar, para 179.
22. Gleig 1830, vol. 1, *Memorandum on Opening the Trade with India to the Outports*, 1.2.1813, pp. 386-7, 390; Gleig 1830, vol. 2, App. XI, *Minute on Monopoly of Timber at Malabar, 6.12.1822*, particularly para 15, OIOC, Madras Board of Revenue Proceedings, 27.7.1840, App. A, para 6; Grove 1995, pp. 399, 417-19, Rangarajan 1996, pp. 20-2; Stokes 1959, p. 39; Washbrook, 1999, pp. 402-3.
23. OIOC, Madras Board of Revenue, 24.5.1827, in Morrison 2000, p. 20.
24. The subordinate officer was William Thackery who had worked under Munro, loyal to his ideas since the settlement of the Ceded districts in

1800. Stein 1989, p. 167; Grove 1995, pp. 396-7; Stokes 1959, p. 141, Washbrook 1999, pp. 402-5.

25. On several occasions, the European surveyors attempted to count the Toda population but with results varying from 326 (in 1826) to 600 who attended a Toda funeral in 1832.
26. OIOC, Thomas Munro Collection, Box 28, from John Sullivan to T.M., Neelgerry Hills 8.1.1819, OIOC, Madras Despatches, 22.5.1818, OIOC, Madras Board of Revenue Proceedings, 15.3.1819, Hough 1829, pp. 64-5, Harkness 1832, p. 6.
27. Compare, for example, OIOC, Madras Board of Revenue Proceedings, 15.3.1819 and OIOC, Madras Despatches, Revenue 19.4.1837, OIOC, Madras Despatches, Fort St. George Revenue Department, 21.6.1843. Cederlöf 2002.
28. The Malnaud district of the Nilgiri plateau.
29. Ranajit Guha 1983 and Scott 1985.
30. Ranajit Guha 1983. Interesting contributions and critical comments in the subaltern discussion about resistance can be found in Haynes and Prakash 1991. See also Cederlöf 2002 and Cederlöf 1997, pp. 166-9.
31. Scott 1985, p. 295.
32. OIOC, Board's Consultations, 9.5.1837, Letter from E. Smith, Sub-Collector, to Clementson, Principal Collector of Malabar, 31.3.1837.
33. OIOC, Board's Consultations, 9.5.1837, Board's resolution, signed A.P. Onslow, Secretary.
34. OIOC, Madras Despatches, Madras Revenue Department, 10.4.1839, para 49.
35. *Bustee*, a hamlet, small village, in this case a mund.
36. Land deed, title to land.
37. George Dominico Drury was Collector of Coimbatore district 1833-41. OIOC, Board's Collections 63.953, State of the Todawars on the Neilgherry Hills, Extract of Revenue Consultation, 6.10.1835.
38. Captain Henry Harkness wrote in 1832 in his extensive report from travels in the Nilgiris: 'At present, each burgher, hamlet, or village, pays to the family of the Tuda in whose district it is, basides their annual and occasional offerings to the Tir-ir-is, eight measures [about two quarts each] of whatever grain they grow on each field or plot of land.' The latter was the *gudu* payment. Anthony Walker correctly observes that the European settlements in Ootacamund were established in the vicinity of ten Toda munds, nine of which belonged to one single

patriclan, the Kash clan. Early British dealings did not involve the whole Toda community. OIOC, Board's Collections 63.953, State of the Todawars on the Neilgherry Hills, Extract of Revenue Consultation, 6.10.1835, Harkness 1832, p. 108. Walker 1989, p. 243. See further Keys 1812, Macpherson 1820 and Ward 1821.

39. D. Eliott, third member of the Revenue Board, surveyed these lands, helped by the tahsildar and Cutcherry servants, the *curnums* (village accountants) of Todanad and Maiknaud, the *monigar* and the Badaga claimants together with others from the neighbouring villages. OIOC, Madras Board of Revenue Proceedings, 12.1.1837, report on the lands composing the Farm at Kaitie; D. Eliott, pp. 410-32, para 7.
40. See, for example, OIOC, Madras Despatches, Revenue 19.4.1837, para 38.
41. OIOC, Madras Board of Revenue Proceedings, 21.1.1833, pp. 791-801, no. 1, to the Board of Revenue, The Petition of Venkata Soobyen, late Peishkar of Ootacamund in the Neilgherry Talook in the Zillah of Malabar.
42. See, for example, Prichard 1855 (1843), Pels and Salemink 1999, and Stocking 1988.
43. See further Cederlöf 2002

REFERENCES

Archive

Oriental and India Office Collections (OIOC).

Unpublished

Board's Collections.
Madras Board of Revenue Proceedings.
Madras Despatches.
Thomas Munro Collection.

Published

Parliamentary papers.

Secondary Literature

Cederlöf, Gunnel (1997), *Bonds Lost: Subordination, Conflict and Mobilisation in Rural South India c. 1900-1970,* Delhi: Manohar.

———(2002), 'Narratives of Rights: Codifying People and Land in Early

Nineteenth-Century Nilgiris', *Environment and History*, vol. 8, 2002, Isle of Harris: The White Horse Press.

Cohn, Bernard (1997), *Colonialism and Its Forms of Knowledge: The British in India*, Delhi: Oxford University Press.

Gleig, George Robert (1830), *Life of Major General Sir Thomas Munro*, London (3 vols.).

Grigg, H.B. (1880), *The Manual of Nilagiri District*, Madras: E. Keys, Government Press.

Grove, Richard (1995), *Green Imperialism: Colonial Expansion, Tropical Island Edens and the Origins of Environmentalism, 1600-1860*, Cambridge: Cambridge University Press.

Guha, Ramachandra (1983), 'Forestry in British and post-British India: An Historical Analysis', *Economic and Political Weekly*, vol. 18, nos. 44 and 45.

———(1989), *The Unquiet Woods: Ecological Change and Peasant Resistance in the Himalaya*, Delhi: Oxford University Press.

Guha, Ranajit (1983), *Elementary Aspects of Peasant Insurgency in Colonial India*, Delhi: Oxford University Press.

Harkness, Henry (1832), *A Description of a Singular Aboriginal Race Inhabiting the Summit of the Neilgherry Hills or the Blue Mountains of Coimbatoor, in the Southern Peninsula of India*, London: Smith, Elder, and Co.

Haynes, Douglas, and Gyan Prakash (eds.) (1991), *Contesting Power: Resistance and Everyday Social Relations in South Asia*, Delhi: Oxford University Press.

Hough, James (1829), *Letters on the Climate, Inhabitants, Productions, etc., etc., of the Neilgherries or Blue Mountains of Coimbatoor, South India*, London: John Hatchard & Son.

Keys, William (1812), 'Topographical Description of the Neelaghery Mountains', H.B. Grigg (1880), pp. xlviii-li.

Macpherson, Evans (1820), 'Report Submitted to John Sullivan, Collector of Coimbatore', in H.B. Grigg (1880), pp. lv-lx.

Morrison, Alexander (2000), 'Creating a South Indian Hill Station: Ootacamund and the Nilgiri Hills 1818-37, unpublished undergraduate dissertation, Oriel College, Oxford.

Pels, Peter and Oscar Salemink (eds.) (1999), *Colonial Subjects: Essays on the Practical History of Anthropology*, Ann Arbor: Michigan University Press.

Prichard, James Cowles (1855 [1843]), *The Natural History of Man*, London: H. Baillière, 4th edn.

Rangarajan, Mahesh (1996), *Fencing the Forests: Conservation and Ecological*

Change in India's Central Provinces 1860–1914, Delhi: Oxford University Press.

Rivers, W.H.R. (1906), *The Todas,* London: Macmillan and Co.

Saberwal, Vasant K. (1999), *Pastoral Politics: Shepherds, Bureaucrats, and Conservation in the Western Himalaya,* Delhi: Oxford University Press.

Said, Edward (1979), *Orientalism,* New York: Vintage.

Scott, James (1985), *Weapons of the Weak: Everyday Forms of Peasant Resistance,* New Haven and London: Yale University Press.

Sivaramakrishnan, K. (1999), *Modern Forests: Statemaking and Environmental Change in Colonial Eastern India,* Delhi: Oxford University Press.

Skaria, Ajay (1999), *Hybrid Histories: Forests, Frontiers and Wildness in Western India,* Delhi: Oxford University Press.

Stein, Burton (1989), *Thomas Munro: The Origin of the Colonial State and His Vision of Empire,* Delhi: Oxford University Press.

Stocking, George W. (1988), *Bones, Bodies, Behavior: Essays on Biological Anthropology,* London: University of Wisconsin Press.

Stokes, Eric (1959), *English Utilitarians in India,* Cambridge: Cambridge University Press.

Sundar, Nandini (1997), *Subalterns and Sovereigns: An Anthropological History of Bastar 1854–1996,* Delhi: Oxford University Press.

Walker, Anthony R. (1986), *The Toda of South India: A New Look,* Delhi: Hindustan Publishing House.

Walker, Anthony R. (1989), 'Toda Society Between Tradition and Modernity', in Paul Hockings, ed., *Blue Mountains: The Ethnography and Biogeography of a South Indian Region,* Oxford: Oxford University Press.

Ward, B.S. (1821), 'Geographical and Statistical Memoir of a Survey of the Neelgherry Mountains in the Province of Coimbatore', in H.B. Grigg (1880), pp. lx-lxxix.

Washbrook, David (1999), 'India, 1818–1860: The Two Faces of Colonialism', in Andrew Porter, ed., *The Oxford History of the British Empire: The Nineteenth Century,* Oxford: Oxford University Press.

9

Transforming 'Sacred Groves'

YASUSHI UCHIYAMADA

INTRODUCTION

This paper critiques a recent upsurge of nationalist ecological histories of India that valourize Indian 'sacred groves' as an instance of indigenous biodiversity management system. Gadgil and Chandran's 'Sacred Groves' (1992) and Gadgil and Guha's *This Fissured Land* (1992), to name only a few, are exemplary works of this genre (see also Gadgil and Guha 1995; Shiva 1988). What characterizes this body of works is a peculiar combination of an anti-modernist ideology, a post-Enlightenment epistemological framework, and an alternative ecological and political activism with an emphasis on 'indigenous beliefs and practices' which are assumed to be superior to the contrastive 'Western' approaches to environment. This alternative ecological project has three important roots. The first is nationalist thought that extrapolates India's scientific past (see Prakash 1999). The second is an ecological stream of subaltern studies that focuses on peasant resistance to the colonial rule in the Himalayas (e.g. Guha 1989; Gadgil and Guha 1992). The third is a global political and circumstantial context of the Earth Summit held in Rio de Janeiro in 1992. The 1992 conference and the key texts, which happened to be published in that same year, have prepared a fertile ground for a proliferation of ecology that combined the anti-modernist problematic, the post-Enlightenment thematic with resonance with Hindu nationalist movements that shared with this genre the assumptions of 'Hindutva' nation and nature (Sinha, Guruvani and Greenberg 1997: 89-90). What is distinctive of the genre is that it further resonated with *both* the projects of dominant international interventionist institutions, such as UNDP and UNESCO *and* those of prominent critics of the international development regime, such as Escobar (1995). In short, the genre appealed to the national and international interventionist projects of ecology as well as those of anti-development. Why was it possible?

I have engaged in the debate partly because I have been studying 'sacred groves' of south India since 1992, and partly because I was made to engage in discussions with a group of Indian cultural ecologists in a symposium in 1998, which was one of the several extensions of the initial 1992 meeting. In the symposium, I had an opportunity to discuss the issue with a group of anti-modernist cultural ecologists, and with a Muslim scholar, who was deeply concerned about the pro-Hindu connotation of the alternative approach to ecology and ecological history. The dominant mood of such knowledge disseminating symposia, sponsored by interventionist institutions, can be characterized by their tendency to overemphasize the positive ecological effects of religious traditions. Lance Nelson notes, 'the *negative* outcomes of religious teachings that can be used to rationalize environmental neglect are probably greater than the *positive* influence of those that encourage conservation and protection' (Nelson 2000: 5-6, emphases original). The uneasy tension between the anti-modernist representation of national ecological history and the Muslim scholar's anxiety that reverberates in my narrative is a reminder of the productivity of the discourse of religion and ecology. My objective is dual. Firstly, I shall point out a discrepancy between religious norms and actual conduct by drawing on an anthropological *model* of 'sacred grove' (*kaavu*) in Kerala. Secondly, I shall discuss changes in the ways of death and related changes of the sacred geography as well as their implications in the emergence of a new ecological awareness in south India. The historical transformations of the ways of death and the sacred geography in Kerala resonate uncannily with the emergent discourse of ecology, religion and nation. As will become clear towards the end of the paper, the new anti-modernist cultural ecology is not merely imposed from above, but has been increasingly substantiated and co-opted from within.

In the first section, I introduce the readers to the feel of the current state of 'sacred groves' in Kerala. The paradox is that as the notion of 'indigenous beliefs and practices', as a black box without contents, has become the key concept of the genre, the low-status indigenous peoples have lost control of their 'sacred groves'. The second section was originally presented in a politically charged academic context wherein the relations between 'indigenous beliefs and practices' surrounding 'sacred groves' and biological diversity were discussed. In this section, I illuminate the assumptions and premises of cultural ecologists, by contrasting their strategy with an anthropological model of 'sacred grove' I extracted from my fieldwork. The second section is further divided into four subsections. Firstly, I present the image of 'planting the dead' as a key to understanding Malayalee personhood. Secondly, I juxtapose simplified models of 'biodiversity management' and 'death-life reciprocity'. Thirdly, I examine a Malayalee ecologist's exegesis of a proverb 'If grove is polluted, pond dries up'. Finally, I provisionally conclude that a *kaavu* can be reduced to a single tree without compromising its ritual functions. In the third section, I historicize my own argument by focusing on the changing ways of death of Malayalees, which are linked to the transformation of the sacred geography of Kerala as a whole. I conclude that Hinduization of *kaavus*, changes in the ways of death and life, and the transformation of the sacred geography after all coincide and co-opt with the emerging Malayalee placiality: a new sense of place associated with unprecedented spatial mobility and a new ecological awareness. The assertions of Hindu cultural ecologists are, in the final analysis, part of a wider process of making post-colonial India 'ancient', scientific, authentic and national.

A PROLEGOMENON—'KURAVA GROVE' SANS KURAVA

In July 2000, I stayed in a hotel in Ochira—a pilgrimage destination along the coastal national highway—well known for its *aalttara* (banyan pedestal). Although Ochira *aalttara* has a gate with towers typical to newer pan-Indian Hindu temples, there are no architectural structures in the yard. Instead, there are three walled-in banyan trees in the centre and a walled-in grove on the side, officiated over by low-caste ritual specialists. At the far back to the west, there is an unwalled and jungle-like grove of 'auto-ecological' or 'autochthonous' type, which is not only unattended, but seemed to be inaccessible to ordinary persons.[1] Ochira is not a 'temple' as it is often mistakenly referred to, but an *aalttara* with sacred trees and groves, more tamed ones nearer to the national highway and an autochthonous one at the far end.[2]

Although I had lived in a neighbouring village I call 'Nagarajanadu' in 1992-3, and had returned to the area several times, I did not know about this newly-opened hotel by a new bypass. The hotel was owned by a local Izhava, who had worked in the Persian Gulf for 19 years until 1998.[3] As a successful Gulf migrant worker, he had rebuilt his house as well as family temple, and opened the hotel. During my trip to Kerala in 2000, I visited several temples and groves of the Kuravas—the most looked down upon untouchable caste in the area formerly known as central Travancore—in various localities in the region. Until then I had usually stayed in Nagarajanadu. But this time I had a reason to stay in Ochira.

Back in May 1992, while I was still new in the field, the headman of one of the seven Kurava sub-clans in Nagarajanadu told me that the founding ancestor of his kin group came from a place near Ochira. At the south side of Nagarajanadu and its neighbouring Christian junction of 'Pallimood', there was a large cluster of Kurava settlements. Some of the Kurava sub-clans came from other places after having been driven out from their ancestral lands more than a century ago. This Kurava territory was not free from a similar process either. Syrian Christians have been encroaching garden lands of Kuravas, while Nayars and Izhavas have been encroaching upon both ancestral shrines of Kuravas and their agricultural land. Since I realized that the process of the 'double encroachment' of Kurava territories and shrines could not be properly understood without locating the phenomenon in a wider and historical process of modernity in Kerala with reference to placiality, I have been visiting 'knots' where Kurava networks and forces of modernity seemed to be mutually articulating. The following is an edited version of the origin myth of the Kurava sub-clan.

A long time ago, our ancestor lived in a place near Ochira. He left the place and came to Valiya Palli (Big Church) in Pallimood.[4] There he prayed to the god (St. Stephen) and asked to give him a place to live. The god told him to go to the forest, because there were already 101 *rakshasas* (demons) living with him in the church. The Tarakans[5] told our ancestor to go to the forest. So our ancestor came to the forest where there were tigers. In the forest there was a big *ilaññi* tree.[6] Our forefather climbed on the top of the *ilaññi* tree and lived there for four and a half years. At the south-west corner of the forest, there was a Kurava old man who was the *uuraali* (shaman) of the Kurava forest, without whose permission, nobody was allowed to live in the place. Our forefather climbed down the *ilaññi* tree and went to see the *uuraali*. He had 101 *swaruupams* ('one's own natural image' in the form of wooden figurines) with him. The *uuraali* also had similar *swaruupams* but they were not many. So the *uuraali* was less powerful. The *uuraali* asked our forefather to give him the *swaruupams*. He gave his *swaruupams* to the *uuraali*. The *uuraali* buried these 101 *swaruupams* in his garden covering them with a big *uruli* (bell metal vessel) to prevent them from escaping. After burying them, the *uuraali* allowed our forefather to live in the forest. He cleared one and a half acres of the forest and we have been living here since then.

This is a story of how alienated Kuravas established 'blood relations' with the host clan and consubstantial relatedness with the place, after surrendering his 101 *swaruupams* which were buried in the garden of the shaman.

I will present a quick exegesis of the exchange of the 101 *swaruupams* with a piece of land before I proceed. The Kurava from near Ochira, who brought with him the objectified fertility of his former forest in the form of 101 *swaruupams*, surrendered the figurines in exchange for a piece of land in the forest near Nagarajanadu. The shaman who received these *swaruupams* locked them up in a brass vase and buried them in the forest. The objectified fertility belonging to the forest near Ochira, brought by the stranger, was tied to the forest of the host. As a result, the power of the shaman as well as that of his forest was increased. The way the *swaruupams* worked is somewhat similar to that of the Maori 'fertility stones' (*mauri*). The

Maori priests buried the essence of the forest (*mauri*) in the forest both as 'a representation of the productivity of the forest (*ex ante*) and a cause of the forest being fertile (*ex post*). Because *ex ante* fertility can be represented—i.e. objectified in an index—it comes under the control of those who control the index, the priests' (Gell 1998: 107).

When the Kurava lost his ancestral land near Ochira, he left the place and travelled with the objectified fertility of the forest (prototype) in the form of fetish figurines (index), which were both a representation of the fertility of his lost forest (*ex ante*), which were detached from the prototype and were transformed into a means of increasing fertility of potentially any forest (*ex post*). The figurines were, then, handed over to the shaman who buried them in the forest near Nagarajanadu. An aspect of the process can be summarized in a simplified form as: the fertility of the alienated forest near Ochira (*ex ante*)—containing the fertility of the forest in movable *swaruupams* (*ex post* and *ex ante*)—the increased fertility of the forest near Nagarajanadu (*ex ante*).

This funeral-like exchange involves a combination of fluid and distributed nature of autochthonous identity (*ex ante* A—*ex post-ex ante* A'—*ex ante* B) and the alienation of Kuravas from their forest-like former territories (the emergence of Kurava sacred forests without Kuravas) which has been taking place in a wider web of special and placial processes in Kerala during the nineteenth and twentieth centuries, of which the ascendance of Syrian Christians and the decline of the Nayars (Jeffrey 1994), the opening of export-oriented plantations in the Western Ghats by European planters (Baak 1997), the land reforms (Uchiyamada 1995), the strategized social mobility (Osella and Osella 2000) and the shifting balance of mountains and the ocean (this paper), to name only but a few, constitute its part.

During the trip in 2000, I saw hundreds of *swaruupams*, for the first time, in several Kurava ancestral 'palaces' and on pedestals in their lineage groves.[7] Yet I was still unable to locate the place from where the forefather of the Kurava sub-clan came to Nagarajanadu, after losing his ancestral land in his native place. One day I learned that there was a new Kali temple called Kurakkaavu, which literally means 'Kurava's *kaavu*' which was located 5 km to the north-east of Ochira. I was told that a local temple trust, which had been established by the Nayars and the Izhavas, had constructed this temple in 1993. Kuravas were conspicuously absent from the Kurava's *kaavu*. This was a familiar pattern. By this time, I was already familiar with several instances wherein ancestral 'palaces' and lineage groves of Kuravas had been encroached, possessed, and transformed into Hinduized temples by Nayars and Izhavas.[8]

In the vicinity of Kurakaavu, there was only one Kurava family whose house was located about a ½ km to the south. Kuññukuññu, a Kurava old woman in her eighties, told me that she had been the *uuraali* of the *kaavu*. The Kurakaavu was a *kaavu* owned by three Kurava lineages. But Kuravas had gradually left the place as their land had been encroached by Syrian Christians, Nayars and Izhavas. Now Kuravas are barred from approaching the Kurakkaavu. The Nayars and Izhavas were intimidating the Kurava family. Under threat of her grandson's death, the Kurava family do not approach Kurakkaavu.

Today, there is a walled shallow shrub—which does not contain any sacred or fearful auto-ecological trees important for ancestors and deities—at a corner of Kurakkaavu. At the centre of the shrub is a young cashew-nut tree, which seemed to be five or six years old, as if to ridicule the trimmed and disgraced *kaavu*. The iron gate of the walled shrub is locked. A sign written on the wall reads, *vettila parattunna sthalam* (the place to throw betel leaf), which seems to mean: 'Do not enter. Throw your offerings from the road.' In the Kurakkaavu temple yard, there is a shrine of Kiratan, a demi-god associated with 'savages' of forested mountains and with Shiva (see below). Kiratan is a 'terrible' mountain demi-god who is now enshrined in a concrete chamber. This indexes both the connection and separation of Kiratan from the *kaavu* of the 'savages'. More importantly, Kiratan in the new Kurakkaavu temple is an index that implies the presence of the forest of *malaya* (the Western Ghats) and its inhabitants in Kurakkaavu, the significance of which the local Nayars and Izhavas try to repress by religious and violent means. The deity, however, seemed to have been in the process of transformation from an 'uncivilized' mountain demi-god of hill people in *malaya* to a 'civilized' Shiva—the high god of Hinduism associated with a distant, and hence more abstract, mountain Kailas in *himalaya* (iced *malaya* or the Himalayas)—worshipped by the 'cultured' people of the plains.

Many untouchables and tribals have been driven out from their lineage groves in the plains and forests in the hills. Encroachers from the plains, students of environmental science, NGOs, Hindutva activists and tourists are now entering forested mountains for various reasons and purposes. Although the former and the latter do not share a similar intensity of the loss of consubstantial relatedness with place mediated by everyday agricultural and funerary practices, and its implications, both of them are caught up in the moment of ecologization of nature, and a related moment of its commodification with a nationalist twist of Hinduizing non-Hindu deities of the hills. Thus, the deregulation of Indian economy, via the BJP-led government intervention, is taking place side by side with the regulation (or streamlining) of minor deities along the meta-narrative of the Vedic order of things. Today, we regularly hear readings of *Ramayana* and *Mahabharata*, the prime politico-poetic narratives of pan-Indian Hinduism, reverberating from loudspeakers tied to *aatmaavu* (soul) trees in various ancestral shrines and groves of tribals in the plains and the hills. This repetitive and disciplinary performance of offering *Ramayana*, the great epic of the idealized king from Ayodhya, is at the heart of the Hinduization of the Malayalee landscape, and is part of a related process of the making of the post-colonial Hindu national state inscribed in the latter. This is not unique to Hindu India. There are historical precedents wherein forests are invested with the images of authentic past.

CHANGES IN MEANING: *TIIRTHA* AND *KAAVU*

On 24 September 1998, at a conference hall in UNESCO, we heard an ecological exegesis of the Hindu notion of *tiirtha yaatra*, which was translated as 'the journey to the watershed'. I must say here that there is a huge slippage: a slippage that forecloses the mimetic (as opposed to representational) possibilities opened up by the poetics of analogies and contacts, a slippage that creates a new discursive space for problem solving. Following Diana Eck (1981) I understand a *tiirtha* (or *tiirtham* in Malayalam) as a 'crossing place' where one crosses a river from this side to the far shore, a crossing place that connects the world of the living and that of divinities. There are *tiirthas* all over the Indian subcontinent in various forms and shapes. Not only certain well-known pilgrimage destinations beside sacred rivers, but also ponds, rocks, mountain peaks, forests, and even single trees can be *tiirthas*. If peoples of the subcontinent have been practising 'the journey to the watershed' since the Vedic period, implying that they are natural conservationists, I must stress that they have been making journeys to all sorts of crossing places, including *kaavus* where there are paths connecting the world of the living and that of ancestors, to deal with anxieties relating to life and death, which arise from the fundamental problem of the living, viz., mortality and fertility (Gold 1988).

In this paper I am telling you a series of stories. Some are related. Some are discordant. The perspective that connects these stories is *analogy* (see Lévi-Strauss 1966: 35; Strathern 1992: 84) and mimetic *slippage*, following (or analogizing) the strategy of Sandhyabhasha, the esoteric language of Kerala.[9] Collectively, these stories are assumed to form an analogy (and hopefully more direct mimesis) of the narrative and corporeal world of *kaavu*, conventionally translated into English as 'sacred grove', which I think is a misnomer. Kerala in south India is known for its profuse and green vegetation. It has also been known as the land of magic. The richness in green and magic is one of the peculiarities of the Kerala landscape, which is covered with networks of *kaavus*. What follows is an account of the location of *kaavus* in the Malayalee social world. What about biodiversity? I will touch on what I call 'biodiversity by default' later in this paper. Let me start with a description of what a *kaavu* 'looks' like.

A *kaavu* is a grove consisting of several sacred and fearsome trees,[10] demi-goddesses and demi-gods, ancestors, artefacts (such as conch shells and oil lamps used in rituals), embodied and emplaced ritual actions, and narratives of superhuman powers (*shakti*) and fearful faults (*dosham*) narrated in its vicinity. Size and age of *kaavus* vary. There are big, small, old and new *kaavus*. Some are rich in biodiversity, while some *kaavus* have only a few trees. Divinities in *kaavus* also vary but there usually are ancestors, ghosts, demi-goddesses, demi-gods, and the divine snake Naga in them. Malayalees say that there are both life-force (*shakti*) and fault (*dosham*) in *kaavus*—liminal locales connecting the social and the superhuman, enabling the transformation of life into place and death into life.

IMAGE ONE: PLANTING THE DEAD

Let me present one image from south India as an introduction to the world from which the familiar binary distinction of society and nature in general, and our attitudes toward biodiversity in particular, can be questioned in a unique way.[11] This is a sacred topography of south India wherein there are certain places where the social—which is inherently porous—is permeated with the natural and the supernatural (or rather superhuman). The purpose of presenting this image is not to exoticize south Indian society. I am presenting this image as a heuristic aid or satirical rhetoric to look at our own society-nature relationships in a different way; in a less contemplative and a more tactile mode of knowing (cf. Taussig 1993; Gell 1998).

'Hindus'[12] in Kerala plant various seeds and rhizomes in cremation as well as burial pits during funerals. Middle-caste Nayars, for instance, cremate the deceased at the south side of the house, which is usually part of a garden where tapioca, yam, taro and coconut are planted. In other words, the deceased is cremated, not as in north India, in a separate cremation ground, but in agricultural land. After cremation, the bones are picked up, washed and put into an earthen pot, which is then temporarily buried under the 'house jack-fruit tree' until it is dug out a year later and brought to a 'crossing place' on the coast for immersion in the Arabian Sea. In an ideal case, the deceased is believed to depart from this world to the abode of ancestors from a 'crossing place'. At this point the ghost (*pretam*) is transformed into a liberated ancestor (*pitr*). This is an ideal type of Nayar funerary rite. In reality, however, many poorer Nayars buried, rather than cremated, the deceased until recently.[13]

Let me now return to the cremation pit. After the bones are picked up the pit is filled with soil. A coconut will be planted on the spot which corresponds to the navel of the deceased; a rhizome of banana at the place of the head; wheat, paddy, nine kinds of pulses, mustard-seed, and turmeric are planted over the soil. In the case of low-caste and poorer people, connections between the dead, place and edible plants are more direct, for the deceased is buried rather than cremated and the seeds and rhizomes—which vary from caste to caste—are sown directly over the body (Uchiyamada 1998). The soul of the deceased is then moved from the burial ground to a lineage *kaavu* near its former house.

What strikes me is the fractal image of grains, edible seeds, pulses, tubers, fruits, and spices growing out directly from the body of the deceased in the garden, as if they were exuviae of the deceased. As I have discussed elsewhere, the lower the caste and status, the stronger is the people's attachment to place via what I call endo-cannibalism (Uchiyamada 2000). The dead body is a 'seed', as it were, planted in the garden where people's everyday food grows. This is not a mere metaphor, but a metonym of person-locality consubstantiality. To cut a long story short, ancestors of the lowest—especially those of former untouchables—are believed to stay in, or more precisely move in and out of, their lineage *kaavus*, from where they continue to intervene in the everyday life of their descendants. This very phenomenon may be seen from an elitist, middle-class and nationalist Hindu reformist viewpoint (Chatterjee 1986) as that related to the low-caste, 'uncultured' and 'superstitious' practice of worshipping the dead that haunts the domain of the living.

'BIODIVERSITY MANAGEMENT' *VS.* 'DEATH-LIFE RECIPROCITY'

You may now guess that the image of planting the deceased as a 'seed', from which various grains, pulses, tubers, fruits, and spices grow is an indigenous allegory of biodiversity management. This is not the case. The story is instead, firstly, one of reciprocal flows that unite the ancestors, the living and locality (Bloch 1986; de Coppet 1985), and secondly, of the fetishization of the 'indigenous beliefs and practices' as both a representation of archaic biodiversity management (*ex ante*) and its manipulable cause (*ex post*) by the 'Hindu' cultural ecologists, who are ideologically anti-modernist and methodically modernist. Here lies the inherent antinomy: they use the magic of 'indigenous beliefs and practices' in the spirit of utilitarianism to attain the double objective of establishing an alternative and nationalist biodiversity management system, and, by extension, an alternative nationalist modernity complete with a façade of authenticity.

I shall introduce a pair of contrasting and simplified images, one is an analogy of the world of biodiversity management, and the other is an analogy of dead-life reciprocity which is located in particular place, mediated by plants, groves and ancestors. I would like to draw attention to the absence of the distinction of agricultural land and burial ground in the Malayalee social world. There is continuity, rather than separation, of agricultural practices and funerary rites wherein plants, place, ancestors and descendants mutually permeate. The practice of biodiversity management involves the opposite, which is predicated on the act of separating these loosely connected and mutually permeating fractal persons and beings into individual-centred and asymmetric categories imbued with the modern regime of knowledge (*savoir*) and management.

Figure 1 is an analogy of a post-Enlightenment and society-centred society-nature relations, which is paradoxically shared (at the level of 'thematic' but not at the level of 'problematic') by the 'Hindu' cultural ecologists (e.g. Gadgil and Guha 1992; Gadgil and Chandran 1992; Mitra and Pahl 1994), whose alternative ecology constitutes part of a wider 'problematic' of alternative modernity of Indian nationalist thinking, as well as is informed by the latter. 'They' (or 'we'?) are fundamentally bourgeois-rationalist and simultaneously anti-modernist and nationalist. This is a Cartesian model consisting of a series of binary oppositions, viz., nature-society, nature-supernature, visible-invisible, and object-subject. The protagonists of this dualistic world is a modern autonomous *subject*, who gives little heed to its second meaning, i.e. the one who is subjugated to democracy or the modern regime of power (Cruikshank 1999), who is, as an 'autonomous' agent (its first meaning), in an insulated and privileged position to predate and protect—and therefore engage himself (including she) in the management of—the objectified nature, which is now represented as 'natural resources', sanitized from both the social and the supernatural (Descola 1996; Pálsson 1996).

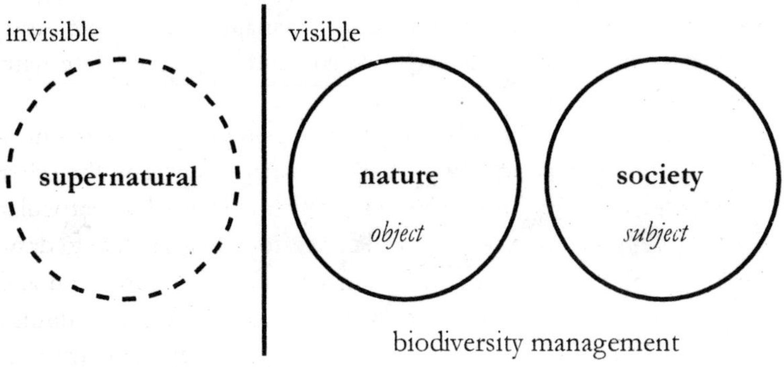

Fig. 1: A simplified biodiversity management model.

The domain of supernature, which permeates that of the living in non-Western societies (Gow 1995; Torren 1995; Dwyer 1996), and Hollywood horror movies in the West (Nuckolls 1999), is invisible to the modern subject's enlightened, contemplative and non-tactile eyes (Taussig 1991), and therefore, remains beyond the reach of modern management thoughts and practices. Nevertheless, a group of ecologists of alternative kind argue that the supernatural is in fact *useful* for managing biodiversity. These anti-modernist 'Hindu' cultural ecologists, who are at the same time bourgeois-rationalist, *re-present* 'sacred groves' as an instance of 'indigenous' or 'traditional' biodiversity management systems (Gadgil and Chandran 1992; Mitra and Pahl 1994).[14] There is a conflation of 'sacred groves'—the existence of which is inseparable from particular exchange relationships and from the ways of life, death and the making of personhood, which is fundamentally non-modern—*and* the 'Hindu' biodiversity management—which uses such embeddedness as a useful fulcrum for achieving the modernist and nationalist objectives. Nevertheless the application of this fulcrum is assumed to be ontologically freed from this embeddedness. Moreover, 'they' (or 'we') show little of this embeddedness, which is instead casually black-boxed and applied as a movable and manipulable magical index. In this model I am attempting to indicate that the project of 'Hindu' (or similarly 'indigenous') biodiversity management is fundamentally modernist and utilitarian in orientation, despite their anti-modernist political outlook.[15]

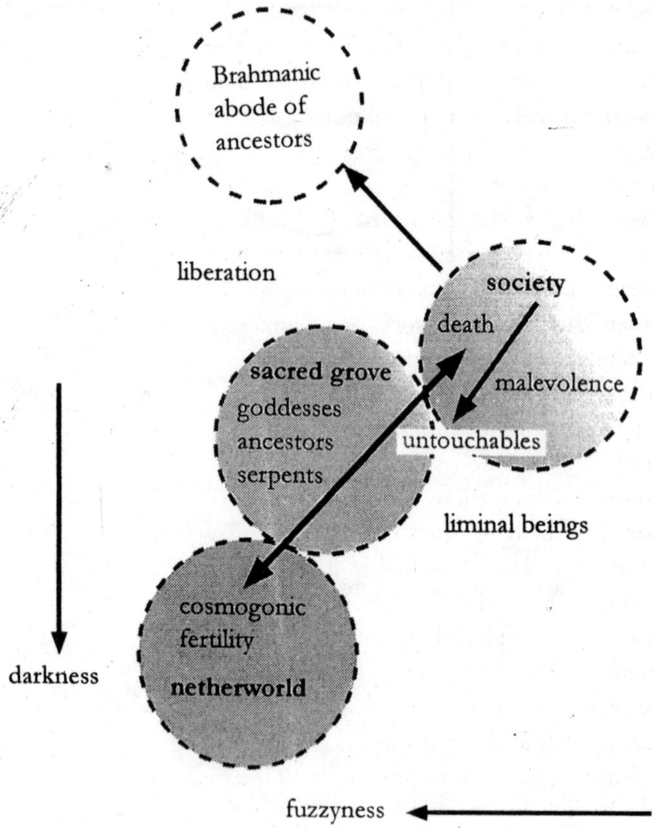

Fig. 2: The location of *kaavu* in Malayalee social world.

Figure 2 is a simplified model of life-death reciprocal exchange centred on 'sacred groves', the underlying assumption of which is endo-cannibalism and consubstantiality of fractal person and place mediated by equally fractal ancestors, edible plants and groves. In this model, which draws on local exegeses, *kaavus* of south India are depicted as (a) depositories of malevolence and negative qualities; (b) locales of super-human life-force which grows jungle-like vegetation as its manifestation; (c) openings to the netherworld and cosmogonic fertility; and (d) fuzzy and dark liminal places where hierarchy, structure, and binary oppositions such as nature/supernature, men/women, living-kind/non-living-kind, plant/people, pure/impure and so on are all dissolved into a chaotic process of becoming.

In this second model, I am presenting *kaavu* as a peculiar tempo-spatial place connecting the world of the living and the netherworld. It is a corporeal metonym, rather than a symbol, of the cosmogonic fertility of the netherworld. Here, society, which is regulated by the dharmic (moral) order, is separated from the 'sacred grove', which is the depository of highly destructive and highly fertile life-force. Yet this separation is partial. The reason is inherent in the very nature of society. Death, sin, pollution of various kinds, such as excrement and menstrual blood, all sorts of malevolence and negative qualities have to be constantly removed from the dharmic social order to maintain its purity and auspiciousness. The hierarchical social order needs *kaavus* and forests at the margins as the dumping ground for unwanted substances and negative qualities as well as the source of its fertility.

Conventionally, *kaavu* is translated into English as 'sacred grove'. Yet the affix 'sacred' is highly misleading. I shall, therefore, add one more affix and call it 'goodbad' (or alternatively 'gboαoαd' to indicats the complete blencling of oppositres) 'sacred grove'. Or alternatively I shall just call it *kaavu*. A *kaavu* is a sacred and fearsome place, which is also a dangerous and powerful place haunted by jealous, greedy and capricious ghosts, demons, ancestors, demi-gods and demi-goddesses who intervene in the lives of the living. These divine beings cause misfortunes and epidemics. They also cure illnesses and protect people if properly propitiated.

It may be assumed more appropriate to call *kaavu* 'bad sacred' grove, following the lead of Srinivas (1952), who followed Durkheim's discovery of evil in the sacred (Das 1977: 114-31) and made a distinction of 'good sacred' and 'bad sacred'. From a modern and reformist brahmanical point of view, many *kaavus*, especially those which are related to low castes, may appear as 'bad sacred' places. Precisely because these are 'bad sacred' places in the eyes of high caste people today, *kaavus* have to be separated from the dominant social order. Nevertheless, viewed from the lowest and the highest ends of the hierarchy, the good-bad distinction may not look so clear-cut.[16]

In ancient Tamil texts, negative qualities were passed to untouchables and were then dumped in the forest (Hart 1975). In Kerala, it was untouchables who received food gifts (*anna daanam*) containing the sins and malevolence removed from the house of their higher-caste masters and mistresses. In short, there was a one-way transfer of sin, fault, and malevolence from the centre to the margins of the social order and to the dark forests and groves.[17] On the other hand, powerful life-force (*shakti*), which is capricious and destructive but at the same time the source of fertility—agricultural, animal and human—had to be brought from the forest and groves to the centre of the hierarchized social order. The well-being of people was, thus, predicated on the existence of the good-bad 'sacred groves' as the depository of negative qualities as well as the narrow paths that connect the social and the cosmogonic fertility in the netherworld (see Shulman 1980).

'IF GROVE IS POLLUTED, POND DRIES UP'

Now let us examine the world of the good-bad 'sacred grove' (hereafter *kaavu*) from a different angle. 'If *kaavu* is polluted, pond dries up (*kaavu tiindiyaal kulam vattum*)' is said to be an old Malayalee proverb. In what follows, I present two exegeses of the proverb: one is by a Malayalee ecologist; the other by Raghu, a son of a local carpenter and my former research assistant. The ecologist's exegesis appeared in an article in a local magazine in 1992. The author argues that a pond in a *kaavu* never dries up even during severe droughts, because trees in the *kaavu* increase its absorption capacity of water, at the same time its canopy prevents evaporation of water from the soil. But if a *kaavu* is 'cleared' (*kaavu teliccaal*), the land's water absorption capacity is decreased and the pond will dry up as a result (Mankattil 1992).

I was not satisfied with this scientific interpretation, because the Malayalee ecologist had replaced 'if *kaavu* is polluted' (*kaavu tiindiyaal*) with 'if *kaavu* is cleared' (*kaavu teliccaal*). Polluting a *kaavu* is one thing and clearing it another. The former is a religious notion, while the latter is not necessarily so.[18] I have attempted various interpretations of the proverb. For instance, I interpreted 'pond' (*kulam*) as a metaphor for paddy field, and as a corollary, a metaphor for people's well-being. Yet this was not satisfactory. Raghu suggested that I replace *kulam* (pond) with *kulam* (clan).[19] His interpretation seemed to me to make more sense. 'If *kaavu* is polluted, pond/clan dries up.' This exegesis was in line with my conviction that the life-force, which carefully brought from a *kaavu* as a path connecting the world of the living and the netherworld, is crucial for agricultural and human (female) fertility. To associate 'pond' (*kulam*) and 'clan' (*kulam*) may appear arbitrary, or it may appear as a slippage. Nevertheless there are many precedents. Vedic sages are known to have attached importance to similarities of words and sounds (O'Flaherty 1976: 170). Ayurvedic medical practitioners of

Fig. 3: A dried pond and a *kaavu* of Kuravas, Pavumbakaavu, July 2000. The Kurava ancestress was removed from this *kaavu* to a temple run by Nayars and Izhavas. This *kaavu* lost its power when the goddess was removed. The pond was dry during the monsoons of 2000.

Kerala associate *himalaya*, the mountains rich in medicinal plants, with their mountains *malaya* (*malayam* in Malayalam), or the Western Ghats in Kerala, to explain *malaya's* richness in medicinal plants (Zimmermann 1982: 70). In this case, *malaya* is a consubstantial and fractal part of *himalaya*.[20]

A *KAAVU* AS A METONYM OF THE FOREST

The question is, then, whether cutting down trees in *kaavu* involves polluting it. The short answer is that it is not always so. Contemporary Kerala, where *kaavus* have been cleared at an unprecedented pace, especially during the past three decades or so, after the land reforms, is profuse with stories about people who suffered the consequences of cutting down trees in *kaavus*. People's fear of capricious divinities who haunt *kaavus* is surely a deterrent from clearing them. Yet this does not prevent people from attempting to cut them down. In fact, there are ritual specialists, such as low caste Pulluvans, who are known for their ability to cut down trees without causing misfortunes. Pulluvans are the people who can propitiate divine serpents, which are the principal owners and residents of many *kaavus*. Yet even Pulluvans are often unable to cut down all trees in *kaavus*. There are a number of sacred and fearsome trees, such as *paala* (known to colonial British as 'milk pine' or 'devil tree') and palmyra palm which often escape felling, because people fear their associations with superhuman (and 'good-bad') life-forces and events.

People are familiar with such stories as: 'When the Christian landlord ordered to cut down the *paala* tree, the labourer who attempted to cut it down died'. 'A Christian landlord bought land from a Nayar landlord. There was a *kaavu* of former slaves on that land. As he was supervising the cutting down of trees in the *kaavu*, a chip of wood hit his eye and he died from the injury.' 'A Nayar man inherited a plot of rubber plantation in which there was a Muurtti *kaavu*. (Muurtti, a terrible form of Shiva, is the god of untouchable Parayas.) The man trimmed the *kaavu*, cut the soil by digging, and expanded his rubber plantation. He got a job in the Gulf where he died from an accident. This is the misfortune caused by Muurtti.'

If certain trees and *kaavus* are known to have extraordinary power, even Pulluvans will not attempt to touch them.

Although there are many instances where trees and *kaavu*s escape being felled, many *kaavus* have disappeared from the rapidly urbanizing landscape altogether, or have been recently trimmed down. Unlike imagined 'hunter-gatherers' who live in the timeless ethnographic present in rain forests in Papua New Guinea or in the Amazon, the everyday life of Malayalees—production, reproduction, circulation, consumption, sharing, exchange, and so on—takes place not in the forest but in multiple locales including the ancestral house, agricultural land, local market, urban centres and even workplaces in the Persian Gulf.

The contradiction between the 'disembedding' forces of modernity, which have been experienced by many Malayalees as land reforms, a massive labour migration to oil-rich Persian Gulf countries, rapid transformation of paddy fields into housing lots, land disputes between siblings, on the one hand, and people's strong attachment to their ancestral lands, on the other, resulted in clearing and trimming of lineage *kaavus* as well as an upsurge of mysterious sufferings known as the 'misfortunes of land' (*vastunde dooshan*) all over Kerala. My first point is, then, precisely because *kaavus* are metonyms of *the* forest in Malaya and are paths to the netherworld, their size (and hence, their biodiversity) can be reduced without compromising their religious functions. Even one tree, with a jungle-like appearance, can be a *kaavu*.[21] Does the *kaavu*, the metonym of cosmogonic fertility, then, have anything to do with biodiversity? The answer is fuzzy.

In a village where I lived in 1992-3, there was a famous Nagaraja (Snake-king) temple, surrounded by a mature and thick *kaavu*. People in the area did not dare to enter this *kaavu*. The reason is that the *kaavu* was the abode of the divine snake Naga—the divinity of the Nagas or the first inhabitants of Kerala after the Creation—responsible for the fertility of the land and women. The Nagaraja temple, surrounded by several Naga *kaavus*, is a narrow opening connecting the abode of the living and primeval fertility. Childless women visit the temple so as to become fertile with the help of the divine snake, the divinity which can move between the netherworld and the world of the living by descending and ascending through the holes in anthills.

My second point is that unlike many other *kaavus* (most of which are relatively new lineage *kaavus*), which have been cut down or trimmed as a result of the process of 'disembedding' modernity, the life-force of this famous snake *kaavu* has been increasing as a result of the very same process. Why was this possible? Before clearing a *kaavu*, divinities inhabiting the *kaavu* were invoked into metal and wooden objects and were either dumped in a new abode or were dispersed from 'crossing places' by the sea.[22] In this process, many smaller *kaavus* were either trimmed or cleared. At the same time, *kaavus* that received divinities of all kinds have become extremely powerful as a result of the process of 'disembedding' modernity that re-embeds. Because they are believed to be more powerful than ever, people do not touch these *kaavus*. The richness of biodiversity in these *kaavus* has been preserved. But this is not the intended consequence. It is biodiversity by default.

What I have presented here is the location of so-called 'sacred groves' in a non-dualistic universe where the natural, the social and the superhuman permeate each other. This is a non-spiritual and non-transcendental religious plane merging with the porous life world. 'Sacred groves' are liminal and non-structural narrow paths that connect the social and the superhuman, that enable reciprocal exchange between the living and the dead, that make the distinction between the living and the dead blurred and mutually participatory, as in the case of spirit possession. All distinctions, binary or hierarchical, are merged and mixed in this fuzzy and chaotic milieu of distributed intersubjectivity. This liminal locale enables the transformation of life into place, and death into life. In short, the liminal locale of *kaavus* expresses non-diversity rather than diversity, which presupposes taxonomic practices. My third point is, therefore, that *kaavus* are exemplary symbols and metonyms of fuzzy *non-diversity*, the locale of *becoming*. Yet the same *kaavus* appear as the exemplary instances of biodiversity management in the eyes (that lack the tactile faculty) of some ecologists. What worries me is the use of government legislation to restore or protect 'sacred groves', for the sake of biodiversity management primarily for the benefit of outsiders.

We are now entering dangerous waters where various actors play out essentialized cultural identities in the political level for different reasons and purposes. Let me reintroduce the us/them divide into the picture to make my point clear. My fourth and final point is, then, that our misconception of uses to which 'sacred groves' are put by those who engage in reciprocal exchange relationships with superhuman forces in the groves may lead to the subjugation of 'their' priority (connecting death, life and place) to that of 'ours' (managing objectified nature for sustainable consumption). Official interventions to protect the biodiversity of 'sacred groves' may yet again deprive former untouchables and tribals of their *kaavus* just as happened during and after the land reforms.

SHIFTING BALANCE OF *MALAYAALAM*

The original version of the above section was a paper I presented at a symposium entitled '"Natural" Sacred Sites—Cultural Diversity and Biological Diversity' held in the autumn of 1998 in Paris. On the first day of the symposium, I heard an Indian ecologist's representation of *tiirtha yaatra* as 'the journey to the watershed'. The exegesis echoed the spirit of the resurgent traditionalist discourse of ecology and Indian civilization. After returning to a cramped hotel room, I rewrote my paper in order to respond to, what I had conceived as, 'Hindu' nationalists' appropriation of religious pilgrimage, to serve the double objectives of establishing the alternative biodiversity management system based on the wisdom of imagined 'Hindu' tradition, and a related and deflected assertion of making the post-colonial Indian state 'Hindu'. On the surface of things at least, these cultural ecologists were presenting a non-Western, or more precisely a 'Hindu', biodiversity management tradition, which is potentially superior, in terms of spirituality and instrumental efficacy, to that of the immoral West, the origin myth of whose ecological history begins with the tales of the Garden of Eden—the harmonious relations of nature and society—and the Fall.

The anxiety I experienced during the opening day of the symposium was not caused by the proposal of an alternative approach to biodiversity management based on a non-Western tradition. In retrospect, I can think about two reasons that caused the uncanny feeling. The first is the casual mating of black-boxed 'indigenous beliefs and practices' with the modern natural resource management objective complete with a façade of traditional 'Hindu' wisdom. The ecologists who presented this alternative formula were less interested in the historically and culturally specific contents of the black box, but were explicitly interested in the practical and positive (and implicitly ideological) effects of the tool. The second is a related issue of the use of a blanket notion of 'Hindu' to represent the polyphony and polysemy of 'sacred groves' and 'sacred forests' in the Indian subcontinent. The assertion of 'Hindu' tradition sounded politically correct once removed from the violent process of the making of the post-colonial national state in the subcontinent, and transplanted in the international context of the 'biological diversity and cultural diversity' symposia sponsored by a supra-nation-state organization such as UNESCO.[23]

This very recognition and inclusion of the 'Hindu' tradition, at the international arena, let alone the allocation of research funds to the specialists of Hinduism and ecology, seemed to have a potential of creating cultural diversity without and exacerbating communal tensions within, by creating ecologically sensitive 'Hindus' and, by implication, ecologically insensitive non-Hindus as invading 'aliens' in India (see Comaroff and Comaroff 2000). Predictably enough, the sentiment of minorities was never articulated in public throughout the conference. Once transferred from the international ecological field to the national political field, such an ambiguous and communally charged 'religion and ecology' project, which deploys powerful signs such as *tiirtha yaatra*, seemed to be convertible into a poetico-political tool to mobilize and divide peoples of the subcontinent—the land of which is now associated with the unitary 'Hindu' Mother Goddess—to create a 'Hindu' post-colonial national state by demarcating non-Hindu aliens to be excluded and, at the same time, enrolling and Hinduizing part of untouchables and tribals, and hence, creating internal fissions within these communities.

In 1992-3, I studied land reforms and religious resistance of untouchables in Kerala (Uchiyamada 1995; 2000). I returned to Kerala in 1996, 1997, 1999 and 2000, during which times, I visited various *tiirthams* located in the mountains, in the plains and in the coastal areas in an attempt to locate Nagarajanadu in a wider sacred geography of Kerala (Uchiyamada 1999a; 1999b). What struck me most, during these revisits, was the rapid changes of the Malayalee landscape: more precisely, the shifting balance of Malayalee sacred geography.[24] In 1992, Nagarajanadu was still a slight hill surrounded by a waterlogged *punja* which regularly flooded at the outset of the south-west monsoon in early June. Then, the margins of Nagarajanadu were low-lying and a soggy place, where untouchables used to live (although the landscape had been changing radically since the early-nineteenth century). These marginal low-lying lands had been reclaimed and were turned into coconut gardens, and then into housing lots. By 1999, the *punja* had receded far away from the northern and southern borders of the village. The paddy fields that used to separate Nagarajanadu from its neighbouring Pallimood to the west had completely disappeared. Thus, the margins of the village, which were once dangerous zones only suitable for snakes and untouchables, where capricious spirits and demons haunted, have disappeared, and there emerged rows of new concrete villas of Gulf migrants.

In 1992, Nayar women in their fifties were the first generation of women who married out from their natal *kudumbams* (family/house) and were living virilocally in their husbands' *kudumbams*. In general, Nayar men in their fifties and sixties, the first generation of Nayar men who remained in their natal *kudumbams*, had good knowledge of their father's—rather than their mother's brother's—*taravads* (matrilineal descent corporation). Nayars of their parents' generations, who were in their seventies and eighties, were the people who had lived their lives in the declining matrilineal descent system. Many old Pulayas, Parayas and Kuravas in their seventies and eighties were knowledgeable informants who narrated their direct experience and stories of the violent treatment of untouchables by Syrian Christian and Nayar landlords. These old people were the most knowledgeable informants, from whom I learnt a great deal about the relationships between person and place. They not merely told me many 'old stories', but more importantly, they were the competent performers—and hence upholders—of older practices embedded and emplaced in the specific placiality of the house and the wider sacred geography. In the nature of things, however, most of these aged informants have passed away during the past decade. Many important qualifier signs, such as *kaavus* and ancestral shrines, too, have disappeared or have been transformed into less 'superstitious', more respectable and more Hinduized forms as these old people have passed away.

Figure 4 represents Keshavan Pillai's house in Thiruvananthapuram in 1992 and 1995. This model is based on the information provided to me by his granddaughter Meena, who lived with Keshavan. When Keshavan died at the age of 93 in 1992, there was a *kaavu* and a shrine of Kiratan—a terrible form of Shiva associated with 'savages' of forested mountains—in the garden located to the west of the house. In the *kaavu* there were fearsome trees such as *paala* (associated with evil spirits and known as the 'devil tree' of India), *pana* (associated with the beautiful and bloodthirsty demi-goddess Yakshi), and *kaaññiram* (associated with the spirit of the dead). In the opening of the *kaavu* were three stone images of divine snakes. The house of Keshavan, located at the east of the garden, was surrounded with a porous hedge of shrubs and cacti with many openings through which people could trespass. There were no walls that separated a place of the living and a place of the *kaavu* either, enabling the members of Keshavan's family, neighbours, ancestors and deities to move back and forth through the garden.

In the shrine of Kiratan, there was a mirror in the centre, a scythe on the right, and a stick on the left. In the early 1980s, Keshavan's grandchildren (son's children) were told that if they opened the chamber of Kiratan at night—which they never attempted—the mirror, the scythe, and the stick would not be there, because Kiratan was wandering the garden, protecting the house. A beautiful and dangerous Yakshi sat on the *pana* tree. A demi-god giant Madan and his sister Maruta, who is an elusive *maya* (illusion), were in the Kiratan's shrine; they were neither represented as idols nor provided with pedestals to sit upon. There were coconut trees, bananas, pineapples, yam and taro in the garden.

Throughout the 1980s, the shrine of Kiratan had lost its importance. A few years after the death of Keshavan, his son, a scientist working for the state space agency, cut down the *kaavu*,

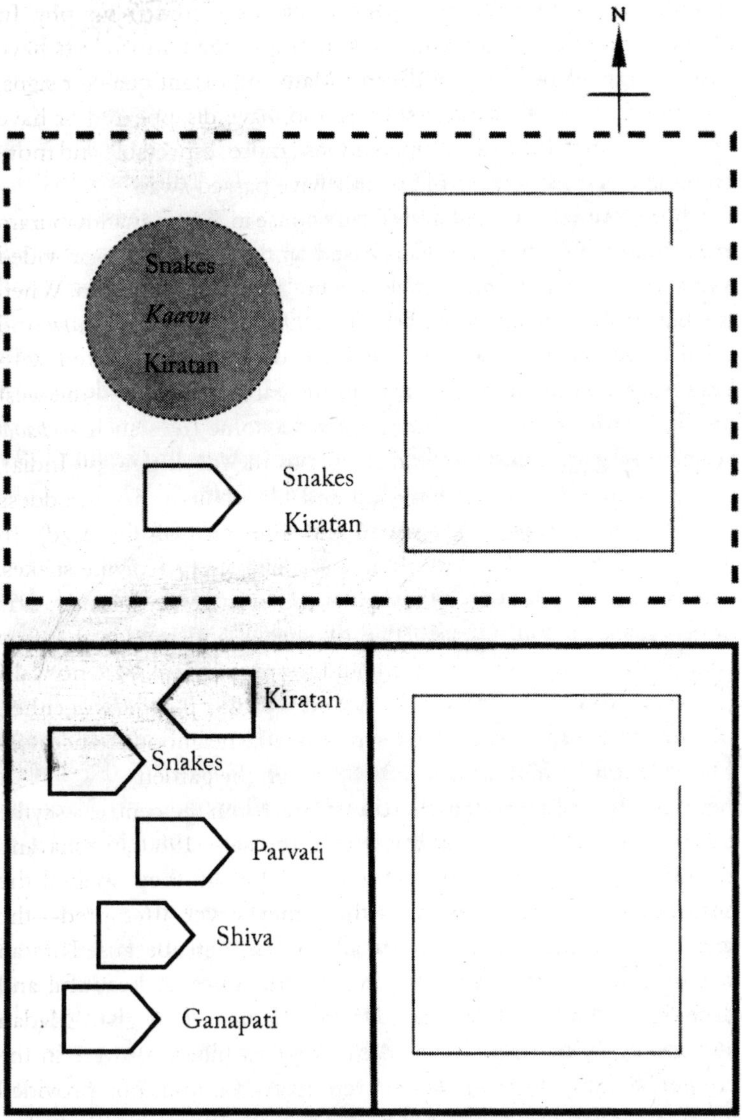

Fig. 4: Keshavan Pillai's house in 1992 and 1995

demolished the chamber of Kiratan, and constructed new shrines of Shiva, his consort Parvati, and his son Ganapati, after consulting an astrologer. A pedestal for the three stone images of divine snakes was raised where the *kaavu* was. A small shrine of Kiratan facing to the west, rather than to the more conventional east, suggesting the crude and terrible nature of the demi-god, was constructed at the north-eastern edge of the garden in which the deity's mirror, scythe and stick were dumped. At the same time, the hedge was uprooted, a new non-porous concrete wall was erected around the house, and the place of the living and the place of the divine were separated with a concrete wall. Permeability and fluidity that once existed between the house and the neighbourhood, between the domain of the living and the forest, between ancestors and descendants, between agricultural garden and the abode of divinities were lost around 1995. The place was 'losing its ground', in Casey's terms (1993).

Before his death, Keshavan told his son to take his bones to Varkkala, a popular Vaishnavite *tiirtham* referred to as *paapanaasham* (destroying sins) located at the coast of the Arabian Sea, 41 days after the cremation. He also told his son not to leave any of his remaining bones in the garden. As I have discussed elsewhere (Uchiyamada 1995; 1998; 2000), Nayars take only half of the bones of the deceased to the coast one year after the cremation, and bury the other half in the garden of the *kudumbam*. Keshavan, nevertheless, told his scientist son to take all his bones to Varkkala, because he thought, according to his granddaughter Meena, that nobody would light an oil lamp every evening to propitiate his soul after his death. The endo-cannibalistic practices of what I call 'planting the dead', cultivating and eating plants that grow in the garden, and defecating in the garden, resulted in establishing consubstantiality between the fractal soil of the garden and the distributed bodily substance of household members. This placial and corporeal relatedness created through daily exchange was no longer reproduced when Keshavan died in 1992. By 1995, the structure of Keshavan's *kudumbam* resembled the model of diversity management (Fig. 1) rather than that of non-diversity (Fig. 2).

Kerala, the land once full of *kaavus* in the plains and deep forests in the mountains, was known as the land of magic (see Gopal

Panikkar 1900). Today *kaavus* have been disappearing, and forests in the Western Ghats have been transformed into plantations. In Malayalam, Kerala is known as *malayaalam*, the land between *mala* (mountains) and *aari* (the ocean).[25] Both mountains and the ocean have played important roles in the sacred geography of *malayaalam*. While ancestors of untouchables departed from their former abodes in the plains to mountains or its metonymic *kaavus*, the bones of high-status and high-caste people were taken to special *tiirthams* known as *paapanaasham*, located by the ocean, from where the souls of the deceased were released from the cycle of life and death, and were drifted for the Brahmanic abode of ancestors. Within the living memory of my informants, Nayars often waited two or three years or even longer before bones of a few deceased were accumulated in the garden of a *taravad*. According to a Nayar informant, in those days, when people travelled by bullock cart, it was extremely time-consuming to take the bones of the deceased to a *paapanaasham*. Ordinary Nayars buried the deceased rather than cremating them, and hence, their ancestors remained in their lineage *kaavus*. Even when the deceased were cremated, it was not unusual to wait for a few years or longer until there were enough bones to be taken to the ocean. Quite often, the bones were never dug out and were never taken to *tiirthams* by the sea. Hence, the gardens of Nayar *taravads* were full of their ancestors and those of their former 'soil slaves' (see Gough 1959).

At the turn of the new century—with the improvement of highways and easier access to hired vehicles and buses, with the promotion of Varkkara and other *paapanaashams* by the state tourist corporation, with the Hinduization of the ways of death and life through consumption of new images, with the mass mobilization of people in the plains and in the mountains by Hindutva activists, and with the growing anxieties that haunted the mind of Keshavan and other old people, viz., the educated younger generation do not propitiate ancestors properly—it has become more 'trendy and convenient' (according to Meena) for many Malayalees to take the bones to *paapanaashams* 41 days after the cremation. Some people have even begun to take the bones only 16 days after the cremation. Moreover, *paapanaashams* are on the increase. The gravity of the sacred geography of *malayaalam*, the land between *mala* and *aari*, has been shifting towards the latter.

In *malayaalam*—a narrow strip of land that lies between the Western Ghats and the Arabian Sea, known as Kerala—the life and death of Malayalees and the sacred geography of mountains and the ocean are mutually implicated. Many *kaavus*, which were associated with ancestors, capricious goddesses and terrible demi-gods related to Shiva, have been either cut down or transformed into Hinduized temples. On the coast, new *paapanaashams*, which are related to Vishnu, have become popular pilgrimage and tourist destinations. A loosely connected 'web' of tourism development, national highways, video coaches, taxis, regular readings of high-Hindu *Ramayana* and *Gita* in the groves of tribals in the plains and mountains, and overall changes that are taking place in the ways of death and life seem to be related to the effects of reducing permeability, fluidity and exchange between fractal persons, locales, vegetations, and ancestors.

Ancestors are removed from the land/soil and made to disappear from Vaishnavite *tiirthams* on the coast after being cleansed of their sins. It seems to me that this changing balance between mountains and the ocean is somehow connected with the processes of commodification and Hinduization of Indian forests, and hence, it is paving the way to naturalize the 'Hindu' cultural ecologists' translation of 'sacred groves' as an old and authentic technique of biodiversity management. Yet the irony is that precisely when ancestral 'sacred groves' are either cut down or transformed into Hinduized shrines and disappearing from the life world of the Malayalees, the imagined 'Indian sacred groves' are emerging in the discourse of religion and ecology.

In the Western Ghats, plantations, the policy of the government to grant title-deeds to encroachers, eco-tourism development, biodiversity management, and so on, are seducing the people of the plains. On the coast, ever-increasing numbers of ancestors are leaving this world from *paapanaashams*. In the plains, successful Gulf returnees are Hinduizing their lineage temples. People (including myself) are tempted to join organized pilgrimages going to multiple sacred sites—in the hills, in the plains, in the coast, connected with highways—in video-coaches. Moreover, former low caste shrines in *kaavus* have been relocated to more convenient sites along the road. The 'Hindu' cultural ecologists are not one-sidedly imposing the hegemonic view about natural resources management. Malayalees themselves, who are transforming their ways of death, are cleansing their gardens and mountains by emptying places once full of ancestors, by so doing making the journeys to watersheds possible. The Malayalee landscape is increasingly charged with an excess of biodiversity: the poetics of new deities embracing the anti-modern 'problematic' and the modern 'thematic' of the post-colonial national state.

Keshavan's grandchildren, Meena and Manu, joined an environmentalist group and made several journeys to forests in the Western Ghats—camping in the hills, studying the environment, meeting with hill tribals, enjoying bird-watching—after the death of their grandfather. The shifting balance of mountains and the ocean, associated with changing ways of death of Malayalees, is enabling a new ecological awareness and a new type of pilgrimage to the forested mountains. The image of dangerous forests haunted by demonic Rakshasas no longer prevents the Nayars from venturing into forested hills (Uchiyamada 2002). Journeys to watersheds are, thus, naturalized by the changes that have been taking place in the backyard gardens of Malayalee homes as well as in the wider sacred geography. The reciprocal exchange relationships with place mediated by plants and ancestors were terminated, and the image alone is projected onto the forested mountains in the Western Ghats and the Himalayas in the distance.

The image of cyclical flows of substance, which is antithetical to the image of linear progress of Western civilization, is at the heart of the controversy. Let me quote a passage from Sinha et al.: 'One of the reasons that the new traditionalist depiction of Indian cultivation has seemed plausible may have to do with this invocation of "cycles" and "flows". These terms are important in ecological analysis, but by themselves have little to say about resource stocks and their regeneration' (1997: 74). The image of 'cycles' and 'flows' dissociated from empirical materiality is projected onto the imagined Indian 'sacred forests' (see Shiva 1988). This image is, then, contrasted against the Spenglerian image of destructive and totalizing Western technicity (see Jünger 2000).

The nagging question that has been driving my enquiry is Martin Heidegger's problematique of authenticity, nature and being, which he addressed in the context of National Socialism in his 1935 Freiburg lecture entitled 'Introduction to Metaphysics'. Heidegger's preferred method is poetry, especially that of Friedrich Hölderlin, that enables the fittest to leap, to overcome nothingness and to arrive at the Being of beings (Heidegger 2000). For Heidegger and his contemporaries such as Ernst Jünger, who inspired the former, secret and sacred forests are the realm of poetry resisting the totalizing and destructive forces of technology and civilization. The Bavarian forest, imbued with poems, was imagined as the site of the German spirit, as the genuine heir of ancient Greek, invested with the manifestation that will free the nation from the destructive forces. Yet for this purpose poems had to be poetized, or a-historicized and purified by foreclosing poetry's relations with the otherness of the Other, in a distinctively Heideggerian manner (Fóti 1992). The poetic sublime that connects the landscape of province with ancient Greece paradoxically totalizes. Let me take a liberty to quote a passage about Jünger from Pierre Bourdieu's *Political Ontology of Martin Heidegger*:

> . . . the remedy to which Jünger turns is a *return*, and we understand why this vision of the social world is resumed in a philosophy of temporality which opposes linear, forward-moving, and 'progressive' time (leading towards the ultimate 'catastrophe' of the technical world), in the name of a cyclical time (which 'turns back' the clock) that is the perfect symbol of the *conservative revolution*, of the *Restoration*, as a denial of revolution. (Bourdieu 1988: 20)

It is against the background of Heideggerian problematique of the sublime that I critique the national ecological history of India that essentializes and totalizes. This tendency coincides with a new sacred geography of India that totalizes a polycentric landscape (Eck 1999). The imagined 'Indian sacred grove' is a powerful, seductive and ambiguous symbol with historical precedents. The genre exists as an antithesis to Western civilization, and hence, has to be dissociated from non-dualistic everyday practices of permeability and becoming, and has to be sublimated into the harmony of authentic past and nature.[26] Its force comes from both within and without. Does not the latent possibility of the restoration arrive, carried on the back of the religion and ecology projects *and* on the back of the transformed ways of death of Malayalees?

POSTSCRIPT

In April 1993, I read a paper entitled 'A Plundered Emerald Island' by B. Prathapan in an English daily. The paper was about how the ancestral grove of Oorali tribals in the Western Ghats has been polluted by civilized people coming from the plains. It was a local journalist's reportage of the effects of 'journeys to watersheds' which had become popular by the early 1990s. As Malayalees have lost their permeability and fluidity in their environment, they seemed to have acquired a new spatial mobility and even a new ecological awareness.

> Once upon a time ... there lived a huge, huge fish in a pond. The pond was amidst a green, green grove atop a mammoth rock. The rock was on the bank of the Periyar river and stood above all the waters and all the lands. The fish was so huge that its tail lay in Meenalakayam in the periyar, a few km away, while its body remained underground. It was a sacred one and the grove was the sanctum sanctorum. There was a 'Great Truth' about the fish which could perform miracles to protect the tribe.

But one day, fishermen from the plains came to the pond in the grove, caught the fish, hauling it down the river, and presented it to their king in the plains. Before the encroachment of the forest, the lineage deity of the grove was, thus, removed. Then the new divinities, such as the Hindu goddess Durga and the Holy Cross appeared in the grove. The grove without tutelary deity was easy to enter. The pond dried up when the new pilgrims from the plains entered the grove. The grove was then destroyed when people from the plains, including the members of environmental NGOs, vandalized trees in the grove. This is after all a story of double-bind modernity: a parable of our own predicament and inability.[27]

The pond has dried up because 'impure' people have entered the place. . . . There used to be a time when nobody would enter the premises without the proper 'vrith' [writ?]. And women never dared to think of going up the slope. But now it's different, says Thevi, the daughter-in-law of the Mooppan. "They come in hordes, the tourists. Men, women and all . . . with packed lunch and bottled drinks. They ate and drank and spread the refuse around . . . break the bottles on the rock." . . . A cross appeared inside the grove a couple of years back, followed soon after by . . . another group which allegedly found that the area had the presence of goddess Durga. Systematic destruction of the grove also started with visitors cutting down trees and setting fire to the leafy litter on the floor and grassy patches on the slope. . . . Visitors just chop off small trees while an organization called Friend's Forestry Club of Pattekudy has joined vandals in carving its name on the tree trunks and rock surface. However, tribals, in spite of all the evils, prefer development of tourism in the area as it . . . is the only guarantee against a few cornering all for themselves and excluding a whole lot of others.

NOTES

1. See n. 21 below.
2. But, it may as well transform itself into a Hindu temple with sacred trees and groves in the future, as this seemed to be the trend. A local pundit, who was supervising various activities taking place under a platformed *aal* (banyan) tree devoted to Shiva, one early morning, said to me, 'Ochira is not a temple *yet*'.
3. A section of the building was still under construction, but some other parts had already been decaying. The building, the growth of which was overtaken by the growth of vegetation, reminded me of a different sense of time opened up by an aniconic *kaavu*, which precedes and follows the life-span of an iconic stone structure (see Uchiyamada 1998; 1999b).
4. The 'Big Church' or St. Stephen's Orthodox Church was constructed in 1835 by a powerful Syrian Orthodox merchant and the landlords were Tarakans who used Kuravas as construction workers.
5. The Syrian Orthodox landlord of Pallimood, the patron of the chapel, and the natal family of the priest.
6. *Ilaññi* is associated with a demi-god Murti (or Muhuurththi) and the soul of the dead.

7. See Uchiyamada (2002) for more details.
8. Furthermore, I learnt that the new owners of one of these Hinduized Kurava shrines removed a powerful Kurava deity from a Kurava lineage grove in an isolated place and relocated the goddess to a newly-constructed shrine beside an asphalted road for the convenience of non-Kurava devotees, who are Hindus, Christians, and Muslims, coming by buses, vehicles and auto-rickshaws.
9. I benefited from talking to Caroline Osella who brought Sandhyabhasha to my attention.
10. Trees I have managed to identify in *kaavus* include *aatmaavu* or 'soul' (*aal* or banyan tree and *maavu* or mango tree twisted and merged into one), *marootti* (*hydnocarpus pentandra,* Gaertn.), *aaññili* (wild jack tree or *artocarpus hirsuta,* Lam.), *kaaññiram* (vomit-nut tree or *strychnos nux vomica,* L.), *ilaññi* (*mimusops elengi,* L.), *tetti* (*ixora coccinea,* L.), chembakam (champak or *michelia champaca,* L.), *paala* (devil tree or *alstonia scholaris,* L.), and *pana* (palmyra palm or *borassus flabellifer,* L.). The form and name of each tree in the *kaavu* evoke many 'old stories' which may be referred to as 'ghost stories' or 'origin myths'.
11. I suspect that plants, trees and groves (as well as their fractal nature and reciprocal exchange relationships between them) do not constitute an important part of the life world of those who are involved in the business of biodiversity management, including anthropologists, both protagonists and antagonists, including myself. What I am attempting here is to present a model of the ways of death as well as life of the Malayalees that is permeated with plants, trees, groves and hills so as to question the contradiction inherent in the use of 'their' religious beliefs and practices to achieve 'our' own management objectives. This us-them divide does not necessarily lie between the Occident and the Orient, nor between elites and subalterns. The divide cuts across Occident-Orient and elite-subaltern distinction. More importantly, the balance of this us-them divide is shifting toward 'us'. This is an analogy.
12. I have a reservation in using the blanket label of 'Hindus' to refer to various non-Christian and non-Muslim 'communities' for two reasons. Firstly, the communal category of 'Hindus' artificially fixes fluid identities. Secondly, I have witnessed the process of Hinduizing ancestral cults of untouchables and tribals in Kerala. The Hinduizing process seemed to be causing inter-communal conflicts along religious and caste lines. Moreover, this same process seemed to be responsible for some intra-communal frictions amongst Untouchables and Tribal

communities. See David Ludden, ed. (1996) *Making India Hindu* (the title of the same book outside India is *Contesting the Nation*) and Kancha Ilaiah (1996) *Why I am not a Hindu.*

13. Moreover, the bones, which were buried under the 'house jack-tree' temporarily, were often left there for a few years or longer. Quite often the bones were never dug out at all.
14. I am indebted to Laura Rival's comment on my ethnography of *kaavu* (1998: 14) and for making me think about different perspectives and positioning of my informants, modern (but self-consciously anti-modern) environmentalists, and myself, on 'sacred groves'.
15. I found the notions of 'problematic' and 'thematic' deployed in Partha Chatterjee's *Nationalist Thought and the Colonial World* (1986) useful in explaining the fundamental contradiction underlying the ideologically anti-modernist but epistemologically modernist thinking of Hindu cultural ecologists such as Madhav Gadgil and Ramachandra Guha. Chatterjee argues that the 'problematic' in nationalist thought is a reverse of Orientalism. Yet its 'thematic' or epistemological framework is adopted from post-Enlightenment Europe. Chatterjee notes: 'Nationalist thought, in agreeing to become "modern", accepts the claims to universality of this "modern" framework of knowledge. Yet it also asserts the autonomous identity of a national culture. It, thus, simultaneously rejects and accepts the dominance, both epistemic and moral, of alien culture' (1986: 11). The 'thematic' in nationalist thought refers to uncritically adopted post-Enlightenment universal framework of objective scientific consciousness. The autonomous 'problematic' in nationalist thought or its ideological claims, such as spiritual superiority of the East (Chatterjee 1986; 1993), or the assertion that ancient India invented scientific and rational thinking which is not different from that of the modern West (Prakash 1999), is argued and legitimized within the epistemological framework of the universal 'thematic'.
16. Das (1977: 91-131) argues that left hand—right hand, and death—life distinctions are central to the Hindu cognitive structure. Although her discussion is helpful for overcoming the Durkheimian distinction of 'good sacred' and 'bad sacred', her model cannot effectively explain the nature of *kaavu* (which is placial, corporeal, distributed and non-textual), because she draws heavily on Brahmanical textual tradition.
17. There is another kind of technique used to remove unwanted qualities from the house of the high caste. A tray containing betel leaves, areca nuts, tobacco leaves and lime paste (*vetta daanam*), to which negative qualities are transferred, is placed at a crossroads as a free gift. The

principle of 'the gift of betel' placed at a crossroad is *dispersal* of the negative qualities, rather than transferring them to the depositories.

18. In retrospect, during my first field in 1992-3, I was looking for anthropological explanations, and by so doing paying little attention to hybridized local explanations which were engaging dialectically with wider processes of global capitalism, their local manifestations, and accompanying neo-liberal discourses of modernity.
19. A Malayalee alphabet *l* used in 'pond' (*kulam*) and that used in 'clan' (*kulam*) are different (see Uchiyamada 1995: 126).
20. For many Malayalees, Himalaya may simply mean 'snowed mountains' (*him* = 'snow' + *mala* = 'mountains') or Malaya covered with snow in the far north, whereas Malaya has familiar mountains to the East in the Western Ghats not far away from where they live.
21. Savyasaachi who worked amongst Kuiankas, hunter-gatherers who live in the forested hills of Orissa, divides the sacred geography of Kuianka territory into three concentric circles. In the centre there is *joku*, the sacred hills covered with 'auto-ecological forests', which is the abode of deities, and people are not allowed to enter these 'auto-ecological forests'. The outer circle is *wango*, the base of hills where there are Kuianka settlements. Between *joku* and *wango* there is an intermediary *soru*, which Kuianka use for shifting cultivation. In *soru* there are some 'auto-ecological trees' which 'initiate the process of recovery of lost forest' after the forest is set on fire (1999: 148). These 'auto-ecological trees' on the hill slopes are the metonyms of the 'auto-ecological forest' in the higher part of the mountains. Savyasaachi notes: 'The place appropriate for shifting cultivation must have auto-ecological trees' (ibid.).
22. There is a parallel between these two methods of relocating divinities and the two methods of removing negative qualities from the house. The cultural logic of the former and the 'gift of food' (*anna daanam*) given to Parayas is *concentration* in depositories. The method of the latter and the 'gift of betel' (*vetta daanam*) left at crossroads is *dispersal*.
23. Across the Atlantic in the same year, the Forum on Religion and Ecology at Harvard University was holding a series of 'Religions and Ecology' symposia, wherein Hinduism was included as one of the ten religions selected by the Forum.
24. The pace of change in Malayalee landscapes have been accelerated since the land reforms in the late-1960s and since the Gulf boom which began in the mid-1970s, and therefore, what I have witnessed is, of course, tiny fragments of a long-term transformation of rural Kerala.

25. The notion of *malayaalam* is polysemous which seems to echo with *mala* (mountains), *malaya* (the Western Ghats), *malayaarma* (Malayalam), *alayaari* (sea), *alaya* (wandering), and *aari* (the ocean). I am grateful to Meena Nair who explained to me the meaning of *malayaalam* as the place between *mala* and *aari*.
26. I am concerned here about a casual application of Heidegger's works on poems and language to anthropological studies of environment without historicizing his peculiar way of interpreting Hölderlin. Tim Ingold (2000), for instance, unproblematically conflates Heidegger with Bateson and Merleau-Ponty, by so doing he unwittingly reproduces Heidegger's silence about the death of remembering (see Fóti 1992).
27. I am primarily concerned with the predicament of Japanese national modernity that has been caught up with its own 'success' and is unable to distinguish what Jack Murray calls a reified 'phantom objectivity', which it has created, from 'the real thing' (1991). See Uchiyamada (2003) for the discussion of the predicament of the bureaucracy-led Japanese national modernity.

REFERENCES

Baak, P.E. (1997), *Plantation, Production and Political Power,* Delhi: Oxford University Press.

Bloch, M. (1986), *From Blessing to Violence,* Cambridge: Cambridge University Press.

Bourdieu, P. (1988), *The Political Ontology of Martin Heidegger,* London: Polity Press.

Casey, E. (1993), *Getting Back into Place: Toward a Renewed Understanding of the Place World,* Bloomington: Indiana University Press.

Chatterjee, P. (1986), *Nationalist Thought and the Colonial World,* London: Zed Books.

———(1993), *The Nation and its Fragments,* Princeton: University of Princeton Press.

Comaroff, J. and J.L. Comaroff (2000), 'Naturing the Nation', *HAGAR International Social Science Review,* vol. 1, no. 1, pp. 7-40.

Cruikshank, B. (1999), *The Will to Empower,* Ithaca: Cornell University Press.

Das, V. (1977), *Structure and Cognition,* Delhi: Oxford University Press.

de Coppet, D. (1985), 'Land Owns People', in R.H. Barnes et al. (eds.), *Contexts and Levels,* Oxford: JASO, pp. 78-90.

Descola, P. (1996), *Constructing Natures*, in P. Descola et al. (eds.), *Nature and Society*, London: Routledge, pp. 82-102.

Dwyer, P.D. (1996), 'The Invention of Nature', in R. Ellen et al. (eds.), *Redefining Nature*, Oxford: Berg, pp. 157-86.

Eck, D.L. (1981), 'India's Tirthas', *History of Religions*, vol. 20, no. 4, pp. 323-44.

Eck, D.L. (1999), 'The Imagined Landscape', in V. Das et al. (eds.), *Tradition, Pluralism and Identity*, Delhi: Sage Publications, pp. 23-46.

Escobar, A. (1995), *Encountering Development*, Princeton: Princeton University Press.

Fóti, V. (1992), *Heidegger and the Poets*, Atlantic Highlands: Humanities Press.

Gadgil, M. and M.D.S. Chandran (1992), 'Sacred Groves', in G. Sen (ed.), *Indigenous Vision*, Delhi: Sage, pp. 183-7.

Gadgil, M. and R. Guha (1992), *This Fissured Land*, Delhi: Oxford University Press.

———(1995), *Ecology and Equity*, London: Routledge.

Gell, A. (1998), *Art and Agency: An Anthropological Theory*, Oxford: Clarendon Press.

Gold, A.G. (1988), *Fruitful Journeys*, Berkeley: University of California Press.

Gopal Panikar, T.K. (1900), *Malabar and its Folk*, Madras: G.A. Natesan.

Gough, E.K. (1959), 'Cults of the Dead Among the Nayars', in M. Singer (ed.), *Traditional India*, Austin: University of Texas Press, pp. 240-72.

Gow, P. (1995), 'Land, People, and Paper in Western Amazonia', in E. Hirsch et al. (eds.), *The Anthropology of Landscape*, Oxford: Clarendon, pp. 43-62.

Guha, R. (1989), *The Unquiet Woods*, Delhi: Oxford University Press.

Hart, G.L. (1975), *The Poems of Ancient Tamil*, Berkeley: University of California Press.

Heidegger, M. (2000), *Introduction to Metaphysics*, New Haven: Yale University Press.

Ilaiah, K. (1996), *Why I Am Not a Hindu*, Calcutta: Samya.

Ingold, T. (2000), *The Perception of the Environment*, London: Routledge.

Jeffrey, R. (1994), *The Decline of Nair Dominance*, Delhi: Manohar.

Jünger, E. (2000), *The Glass Bees*, New York: New York Review of Books.

Lévi-Strauss, C. (1966), *The Savage Mind*, Chicago: University of Chicago Press.

Ludden, D. (1996), *Contesting Nationalism,* Philadelphia: University of Pennsylvania Press.

Mankattil, S. (1992), 'Kaavum Kulavum Kaattaarum' ('Kaavu, Pond, and Forest-stream'), *Kalaakaumudi* 874, p. 11 (in Malayaalam).

Mitra, A. and S. Pahl (1994), 'The Spirit of the Sanctuary', *Down to Earth* 31, pp. 21-36.

Murray, J. (1991), *The Landscape of Alienation,* Stanford: Stanford University Press.

Nelson, L.E. (2000), 'Introduction', in L.E. Nelson (ed.), *Purifying the Earthly Body of God,* Albany: State University of New York Press, pp. 1-10.

Nuckolls, J. (1999), 'The Concept of Self in South India and the United States', *Journal of Social Science,* 40, pp. 77-90.

O'Flaherty, W.D. (1976), *The Origins of Evil in Hindu Mythology,* Berkeley: University of California Press.

Osella, F. and C. Osella (2000), *Social Mobility in Kerala: Modernity and Identity in Conflict,* London: Pluto Press.

Pálsson, G. (1996), 'Human-environment Relations', in P. Descola et al. (eds.), *Nature and Society,* London: Routledge, pp. 63-81.

Prakash, G. (1999), *Another Reason,* Princeton: University of Princeton Press.

Prathapan, B. (1993), 'A Plundered Emerald Island', *The Indian Express,* April (Thiruvananthapuram).

Rival, L. (1998), 'Trees, from Symbols of Life and Regeneration to Political Artefacts', in L. Rival (ed.), *Social Life of Trees,* Oxford: Berg, pp. 1-36.

Savyasaachi (1999), 'Sapangada', in R. Jeffrey et al. (eds.), *A New Moral Economy for India's Forests?,* Delhi: Sage, pp. 130-50.

Shiva, V. (1988), *Staying Alive,* London: Zed Books.

Shulman, D. (1980), *Tamil Temple Myth,* Princeton: Princeton University Press.

Sinha, S., S. Gururani and B. Greenberg (1997), 'The 'New Traditionalist' Discourse of Indian Environmentalism', *The Journal of Peasant Studies,* vol. 24, no. 3, pp. 65-99.

Srinivas, M.N. (1952), *Religion and Society Among the Coorgs of South India,* Oxford: Clarendon.

Strathern, M. (1992), 'Parts and Wholes', in A. Kuper (ed.), *Conceptualizing Society,* London: Routledge, pp. 75-104.

Taussig, M. (1991), 'Tactility and Distraction', *Cultural Anthropology,* 6 (2), 147-53.

———(1993), *Mimesis and Alterity: A Particular History of the Senses*, New York: Routledge.

Torren, C. (1995), 'Seeing the Ancestral Sites', in E. Hirsch et al. (eds.), *The Anthropology of Landscape*, Oxford: Clarendon, pp. 163-83.

Uchiyamada, Y. (1995), 'Sacred Grove (kaavu)', unpublished Ph.D. thesis submitted to the London School of Economics, The University of London.

———(1998), 'The Grove is Our Temple', in L. Rival (ed.), *The Social Life of Trees*, Oxford: Berg, pp. 177-96.

———(1999a), 'Soil, Self, Resistance', in J. Assayag and G. Tarabout (eds.), *La Possession en Asie du Sud, Purushartha*, 21, Paris: EHESS, pp. 289-311.

———(1999b), 'Two Beautiful Untouchable Women', in S. Day et al. (eds.), *Lilies of the Field*, Boulder: Westview, pp. 96-116.

———(2000), 'Passions in the Landscape', *South Asia Research*, vol. 20, no. 1, pp. 63-84.

———(2002), 'Projecting Textual Identities on the Forest of Kuravas in Kerala', in M. Carrin and C. Jaffrelot (eds.), *Tribus et Basses Castes, Purushartha*, 23, Paris: EHESS, pp. 111-29.

———(2003), 'Development Remembered: Two Case Histories', *The Japanese Journal of Ethnology*, vol. 67, no. 4, pp. 450-77 (in Japanese).

Zimmermann, F. (1982), *The Jungle and the Aroma of Meats*, Berkeley: University of California Press.